Greening Industrialisation in Sub-Saharan Africa

T0271692

This book explores the concept of greening industrialisation and issues and considerations surrounding it through the lens of Sub-Saharan Africa.

The book critically examines the concept of greening industrialisation and describes the progress and data challenges of monitoring the Sustainable Development Goals confronting African countries. The chapters summarise the policy and programme literature focused on eight policy regimes essential for greening industrialisation and identify opportunities for greening industrial policies. The authors lay out a research agenda that would inform, enable, and support greening industrialisation in Sub-Saharan Africa and provide an overview of green industrial plans that include climate strategies, energy efficiency strategies, and green industry assessments.

This book will be of great interest to students, scholars, policy-makers, and planners in the fields of Sub-Saharan African development and African environmentalism.

Ralph A. Luken is a Sustainable Development Advisor on environmental issues, having worked for United Nations Industrial Development Organization (UNIDO) from 1990 to 2002 as a Senior Office in the Environment Department. Previously he worked for the US Environmental Protection Agency and consulted for the United Nations Environment Programme, the International Atomic Energy Agency, the US Agency for International Development and the World Bank. He holds a PhD in Environmental Economics from the University of Michigan.

Edward Clarence-Smith is a Senior Green Industry Expert, having worked for the United Nations Industrial Development Organization (UNIDO) from 1998–2016 as Senior Officer in the Environmental Department. Previously, he worked in an environmental consulting firm; the Natural Resources Defense Council; the OECD's Environment Department; and the US Environmental Protection Agency.

Routledge Contemporary Africa Series

Press Silence in Postcolonial Zimbabwe
News Whiteouts, Journalism and Power
Zvenyika E. Mugari

Urban Planning in Rapidly Growing Cities
Developing Addis Ababa
Mintesnot G. Woldeamanuel

Regional Development Poles and the Transformation of African Economies
Benaiah Yongo-Bure

Nature, Environment and Activism in Nigerian Literature
Sule E. Egya

Corporate Social Responsibility and Law in Africa
Theories, Issues and Practices
Nojeem A. Amodu

Greening Industrialisation in Sub-Saharan Africa
Ralph A. Luken and Edward Clarence-Smith

Health and Care in Old Age in Africa
Edited by Pranitha Maharaj

Rethinking African Agriculture
How Non-Agrarian Factors Shape Peasant Livelihoods
Edited by Goran Hyden, Kazuhiko Sugimura and Tadasu Tsuruta

For more information about this series, please visit: www.routledge.com/Routledge-Contemporary-Africa/book-series/RCAFR

Greening Industrialisation in Sub-Saharan Africa

Ralph A. Luken and
Edward Clarence-Smith

Routledge
Taylor & Francis Group

LONDON AND NEW YORK

First published 2020
by Routledge
4 Park Square, Milton Park, Abingdon, Oxon OX14 4RN
605 Third Avenue, New York, NY 10017

First issued in paperback 2023

Routledge is an imprint of the Taylor & Francis Group, an informa business

British Library Cataloguing-in-Publication Data
A catalogue record for this book is available from the British Library

Library of Congress Cataloging-in-Publication Data
A catalog record for this book has been requested

ISBN: 978–1–03–257089–1 (pbk)
ISBN: 978–0–367–40829–9 (hbk)
ISBN: 978–1–003–00471–4 (ebk)

DOI: 10.4324/9781003004714

Typeset in Bembo
by Apex CoVantage, LLC

Publisher's Note
The publisher has gone to great lengths to ensure the quality of this reprint but points out that some imperfections in the original copies may be apparent.

Contents

List of figures   vi
List of tables   vii
List of boxes   viii
Acknowledgements   ix
List of acronyms   x

1   Introduction and overview   1

2   Defining green industrialisation   4

3   Policies and programmes for greening industry   16

4   Policies and programmes for greening services   79

5   Green industry indicators   112

6   Green industry assessments   132

7   Green industrialisation research   151

Annex 1: composite indexes   160
Annex 2: economic and technology policies   171
Index   177

Figures

2.1	Relative and absolute decoupling	11
2.2	Green industrialisation: greening industries and greening services	12
6.1	SGIP overview	133
A.1.1	Scatter plot of the SDG9per and SDGpro of 16 countries	167
A.1.2	Policy and strategy options for accelerating green industrialisation	168

Tables

3.1	Pollution control instruments	17
3.2	Effluent standards (NEQS) and guidelines (EHS)	18
3.3	Emission standards (NEQS) and guidelines (EHS)	18
3.4	Top drivers, barriers, and enablers	36
3.5	Support policies that have been used in Sub-Saharan Africa	55
3.6	SSA countries with one or more facilities to manage hazardous waste streams	70
4.1	Market size and growth for EGS sector, by region (2011)	81
5.1	SDGs impacted by industrial development	113
5.2	MVA and employment in the SSA countries, 2000–2018	117
5.3	Growth of MVA and energy consumption, energy intensity, and CO_2 intensity in SSA countries, 2000–2016	125
A.1.1	Rankings of the SSA countries according to four different global sustainable development indexes	162
A.1.2	SDG9 targets and indicators related to industrialisation	166
A.1.3	SDG9 performance and progress rank for 16 SSA countries	167

Boxes

3.1   Policy instruments relevant to driving RECP   29
3.2   Case studies of RECP projects   39
3.3   Ethiopia's Climate Resilient Green Economy (CRGE)   42
3.4   South Africa's Energy Efficiency Strategy   44

Acknowledgements

The authors wish to acknowledge the funding support which they received from the Institute of African Leadership for Sustainable Development (UONGOZI Institute), based in Dar es Salaam, United Republic of Tanzania. It was this funding which allowed the research behind this book to be undertaken.

Acronyms

AfDB	African Development Bank
APEC	Asia-Pacific Economic Cooperation
CETP	Common Effluent Treatment Plant
CIP	Competitive Industrial Performance
CO_2	Carbon Dioxide
CO_2eq	Carbon Dioxide Equivalent
CP	Cleaner Production
EGS	Environmental Goods and Services
EHS	Environmental Health and Safety
EIP	Eco-industrial Park
ESCO	Energy Service Company
EU	European Union
GDP	Gross Domestic Product
GEF	Global Environment Facility
GHG	Greenhouse Gas
GIP	Green Industrial Performance
GTZ	Gesellschaft für Technische Zusammenarbeit (Corporation for Technical Cooperation)
ICT	Information and Communications Technology
IEA	International Energy Agency
ILO	International Labour Organization
IMF	International Monetary Fund
IRENA	International Renewable Energy Agency
ISO	International Organization for Standardization
LDC	Least Developed Country
MSDS	Material Safety Data Sheet
MVA	Manufacturing Value-Added
NCPC	National Cleaner Production Centre
NEQS	National Environmental Quality Standards
PAGE	Partnership for Action on Green Economy

R&D	Research and Development
RECP	Resource Efficient and Cleaner Production
SAICM	Strategic Approach to International Chemicals Management
SDG	Sustainable Development Goal
SGIP	Strategic Green Industrial Policy
SME	Small and Medium-sized Enterprise
SSA	Sub-Saharan Africa
STEM	Science, Technology, Engineering, and Mathematics
SWOT	Strengths, Weaknesses, Opportunities, and Threats
UN	United Nations
UNCTAD	United Nations Commission on Trade and Development
UNDP	United Nations Development Programme
UNECA	United Nations Economic Commission for Africa
UNEP	United Nations Environment Programme
UNIDO	United Nations Industrial Development Organization
USD	United States Dollars
WEEE	Waste Electrical and Electronic Equipment

1 Introduction and overview

The community of nations, through the Sustainable Development Goals (SDGs) which they adopted in New York in September 2017, recognised that eradicating poverty in all its forms and dimensions, including extreme poverty, was the greatest global challenge and an indispensable requirement for sustainable development. They committed themselves to achieving sustainable development in its three dimensions – economic, social, and environmental – in a balanced and integrated manner. They envisaged, among other things, "a world in which every country enjoys sustained, inclusive and sustainable economic growth and decent work for all. A world in which consumption and production patterns and use of all natural resources . . . are sustainable". They committed "to making fundamental changes in the way that our societies produce and consume goods and services. Governments, international organisations, the business sector, and other non-state actors and individuals must contribute to changing unsustainable consumption and production patterns". They wished to see a strengthening in "the mobilisation, from all sources, of financial and technical assistance to strengthen developing countries' . . . capacities to move towards more sustainable patterns of consumption and production" (UN, 2015).

This book is a modest contribution towards that aim, with a particular focus on supporting policy-makers in the countries in Sub-Saharan Africa (SSA) wishing to accelerate the shift to sustainable patterns of production and consumption through green industrialisation.

Analysis of the data which has been collected to monitor the implementation of the SDGs shows that SSA countries are globally lagging in the pursuit of green industrialisation. To a great extent, this can be put down to the fact that the governments of these countries do not have the necessary policy frameworks in place to promote green industrialisation. At one level, they are failing to fully implement the policies, programmes, and instruments which they already have in place, and at another level they are lagging behind in adopting new and possibly more effective policies, programmes, and instruments which have been adopted with some success by countries in other regions of the world.

This book, then, has been written as a reference tool for policy-makers and planners in SSA countries intent on formulating policies and programmes that are supportive of green industrialisation in their countries. In particular, the book aims to provide a workable definition for green industrialisation, seeing it as composed of two main dimensions: greening industry and greening services, and identifying common policies, programmes, and instruments for greening industries and greening services. The book also lays out for policy-makers and planners (as well as students of SSA development and environment) a research agenda that would inform, enable, and support green industrialisation in SSA countries. As background, it provides an analysis of green industrialisation in the SSA region, focusing on implications (past, present, and future) for policy.

In Chapter 2, various definitions of green industrialisation are first given. The chapter also includes definitions that have been given to several other closely related terms – green economy, green growth, and green jobs – because this could help for a better understanding of policies and support programmes which are needed for green industrialisation. The chapter ends by giving a definition of green industrialisation which is used in this book. An important part of that definition is recognising that green industrialisation has two main dimensions to it: greening industry and greening services. Both need to be promoted to bring about green industrialisation, and while the term 'green industrialisation' is new, many of the activities covered by it were the subject of policy-making before the term itself existed.

Chapter 3 then summarises the policy and support programme literature covering green industry, separated into four complementary and to some extent overlapping regimes: pollution control, resource efficient and cleaner production, energy management, and chemical and waste management.

Chapter 4 goes on to summarise the policy and support programme literature covering green services, also separated into four regimes: environmental services, eco-industrial parks, eco-design, and materials recycling.

Chapter 5 reviews the quality of international databases for assessing the progress of green industrialisation in SSA countries between 2000 and 2018. The review includes all the industry-related SDG targets and indicators. It questions the feasibility of meeting conventional economic, employment, and energy targets and proposes setting additional and more realistic targets based on past country experience.

Chapter 6 describes one process for developing strategic green industrialisation policies at the national level and summarises the findings/ implications identified in three green industry assessments undertaken by the United Nations Industrial Development Organization (UNIDO) in three SSA countries (Ghana, Nigeria, and Senegal).

Chapter 7, the final chapter, identifies areas for further research about policies and support programmes needed to accelerate green industrialisation in SSA countries and about options for monitoring progress in meeting industry-relevant SDG targets.

Annex 1 is an overview with selected references of several recently published sustainable development indexes along with two newly constructed indexes for this book, which document in varying ways that SSA countries are globally lagging in pursuit of green industrialisation. They justify the need for additional research on effective policies and programmes to accelerate green industrialisation in SSA countries.

Annex 2 is a brief overview with selected references of how economic policies, broadly defined, and technology and innovation policies can accelerate green industrialisation.

Reference

UN (2015). *Transforming Our World: The 2030 Agenda for Sustainable Development*. Resolution adopted by the General Assembly on 25 September 2015. A/RES/70/1. 21 October. United Nations. New York. Retrieved from: www.un.org/ga/search/ view_doc.asp?symbol=A/RES/70/1&Lang=E. Last accessed: 14.08.2019.

2 Defining green industrialisation

2.1. Introduction

Green industrialisation is closely related to several other terms: green economy, green growth, and green jobs. The chapter will include definitions that have been given to these terms too, because this could help for a better understanding of green industrialisation. The chapter will start with definitions given to green growth and green economy, and then proceed to definitions of green industrialisation (and the synonymous term green industry) set within the context of green economy. It will also introduce definitions of green jobs. Lastly, we will propose a definition of green industrialisation that will be used in this book.

Virtually all the definitions come from international organisations. There is only limited academic or grey literature on the topic.

2.2. Green economy, green growth

The terms 'green economy' and 'green growth' are closely related. The definitions of several organisations are considered here.

The United Nations Environment Programme (UNEP) defines a green economy as one which is "low-carbon, resource-efficient, and socially inclusive", or to put it another way, a green economy is "one that results in improved human well-being and social equity while significantly reducing environmental risks and ecological scarcities" (UNEP, 2011).

With respect to the term 'green growth', the Organisation for Economic Cooperation and Development (OECD) states that "green growth means fostering economic growth and development while ensuring that natural assets continue to provide resources and environmental services on which our well-being relies". Whereas green growth is a subset of the concept of sustainable development entailing an operational policy agenda that can help achieve measurable progress at the interface between economy and environment, green economy stems from "a growing recognition that achieving sustainability rests almost entirely on getting the economy right" (OECD, 2011) (see also OECD, 2012, for a discussion of the specific concerns of developing countries with the term 'green growth').

The World Bank (World Bank, 2012) defines green growth as

> growth that is efficient in its use of natural resources, clean in that it minimises pollution and environmental impacts, and resilient in that it accounts for natural hazards and the role of environmental management and natural capital in preventing physical disasters. And this growth needs to be inclusive. Inclusive green growth is not a new paradigm. Rather, it aims to operationalise sustainable development by reconciling developing countries' urgent need for rapid growth and poverty alleviation with the need to avoid irreversible and costly environmental damage. As such, efforts to foster green growth must focus on what is required in the next five to 10 years to sustain robust growth, while avoiding locking economies into unsustainable patterns, preventing irreversible environmental damage, and reducing the potential for regret.

The United Nations Economic Commission for Africa (UNECA) described greening as a shift towards more resource-conserving activity, in which production and consumption patterns use fewer resources and create less waste over their life cycle. Typically, greening involves a combination of decoupling (maintaining production while using lower input, especially water and carbon-based energy), avoiding environmentally harmful impacts (including effluent spillage and noxious gas emissions), and supporting a diverse and sustainable biosphere (UNECA, 2016).

For its part, the United Nations Commission on Trade and Development (UNCTAD) states that achieving sustainable development in Africa requires deliberate, concerted, and proactive measures to promote structural transformation and the relative decoupling of natural resource use and environmental impact from the growth process. Sustainable structural transformation is structural transformation with such decoupling (UNCTAD, 2012).

In a joint paper, four international organisations – the African Development Bank (AfDB), the Organisation for Economic Cooperation and Development (OECD), the United Nations, and the World Bank – define inclusive green growth as growth that not only helps to green economies but also helps move towards sustainable development by ensuring environmental sustainability contributes to, or at least does not come at the expense of, social progress (AfDB/OECD/UN/World Bank, 2013).

See also Avis (2018) for a discussion of the various definitions and understandings of the term 'inclusive green growth' in the context of policymaking in developing countries.

In summary, a green economy is one that promotes structural transformation, which leads to the relative decoupling of natural resource use and environmental impact from the growth process through an efficient use of natural resources and minimisation of pollution and environmental impacts. This structural transformation is resilient in that it accounts for natural hazards and the role of environmental management and natural capital in preventing physical disasters, and ensures that natural assets continue to provide resources and environmental services on which our well-being relies. A green economy also ensures that environmental sustainability contributes to, or at least does not come at the expense of, improved human well-being and social equity.

2.3. Definitions of green industrialisation

Various definitions of green industrialisation and the equivalent term 'green industry' have been proposed by several organisations:

UNIDO defines green industrialisation as a process of creating an industrial system that does not require the ever-growing use of natural resources and pollution for growth and economic expansion. The process has two parts to it:

1 *Greening of existing industry*: Enable and support all industries, regardless of their sector, size, or location, to green their operations, processes, and products by using resources more efficiently; transforming industrial energy systems towards greater sustainability by expanding renewable energy sources; phasing out toxic substances; and improving occupational health and safety at the industrial level.
2 *Creating green enterprises*: Establish new, and expand existing, green enterprises that deliver environmental goods and services. Green enterprises form a rapidly expanding and diverse sector that covers all types of services and technologies which help to reduce negative environmental impacts and resource consumption. This includes material recovery, recycling, waste treatment and management, as well as the provision of environmental and energy consulting and services, such as energy service companies and companies that provide monitoring, measuring, and analysis services.

Like the green economy concept, green industrialisation is seen as an important practical pathway towards achieving sustainable development.

While the thrust of green economy is achieving improved human well-being and social equity while simultaneously diminishing environmental risks and reducing ecological scarcities, green industrialisation transforms manufacturing and allied industry sectors by introducing a more efficient/productive/responsible use of raw materials so that they contribute more effectively to sustainable industrial development. It is about doing more, and better, with less. Green industrialisation is thereby the sector process for the realisation of green economy, and ultimately, sustainable development (UNIDO, 2010, 2011).

UNECA describes greening industrialisation as a process that ensures that the structural transformation process reduces resource inputs and increases efficiency in the production process; cuts back on harmful waste emissions, such as chemical effluents and poisonous gases; strengthens infrastructure to reduce environmental impacts (such as pollution and extreme weather events); and maintains or improves the natural resource base, including providing associated environmental goods and services (UNECA, 2016).

UNEP, in the manufacturing chapter of its Green Economy Report, stated that

> Green manufacturing differs from conventional manufacturing in that it aims to reduce the amount of natural resources needed to produce finished goods through more energy- and materials-efficient manufacturing processes that also reduce the negative externalities associated with waste and pollution. This includes more efficient transport and logistics, which can also account for a significant percent of the total environmental impact of manufactured products.

A supply-side strategy involves redesign and improving the efficiency of processes and technologies employed in the major materials-intensive sub-sectors of the manufacturing sector (ferrous metals, aluminium, cement, plastics, etc.). On the other hand, if a green economy means improving not only productivity but also efficiency by a factor of four or more, a demand-side strategy is also required. A demand-side strategy involves changing the composition of demand, both from within industry and from final consumption. This requires modifying output, i.e., to use final goods embodying materials and energy much more efficiently and/or to design products that require less material in their manufacturing. For instance, the need for primary iron and steel from energy-intensive integrated steel plants can be reduced by using less steel downstream in the economy (i.e., in construction, automobile manufacturing, and so on). Design for dismantling is a key step in advancing reuse and recycling of, for example, metals contained in the end-product.

The four supply-side and two demand-side approaches consist mainly of the following components:

- Re-designing products and/or business models so that the same functionality can be delivered with fundamentally less use of materials and energy. This also requires extending the effective lifetime of complex products and improving quality, by incorporating repair and re-manufacturing into a closed-cycle system;
- Introducing new, cleaner technologies and improving the efficiency of existing processes to leapfrog and establish new modes of production that have a fundamentally higher material and energy efficiency. To start with, major savings potential in manufacturing lies in improving the resource efficiency of existing processes;
- Substituting green inputs for brown inputs wherever possible. For example, introducing biomass as a source of chemical feedstocks, emphasising process integration, and upgrading process auxiliaries such as lighting, boilers, electric motors, compressors, and pumps. Practicing good housekeeping and employ professional management;
- Re-manufacturing is also becoming increasingly significant, particularly in areas such as motor-vehicle components, aircraft parts, compressors, electrical and data communications equipment, office furniture, vending machines, photocopiers, and laser toner cartridges (UNEP, 2011);
- Drawing on the principles of industrial ecology, closed-cycle manufacturing is a particularly ambitious approach to supply-side innovation. This concept refers to an ideal manufacturing system that maximises the useful life of products and minimises the waste and loss of valuable and scarce metals; and
- Redesigning systems, especially the transportation system and urban infrastructure downstream, to utilise less resource-intensive inputs. The first target must be to reduce the need for and use of automotive vehicles requiring liquid fuels in comparison to rail-based mass transportation, bus rapid transit, and bicycles.

2.4. Definitions of green industrial policy for promoting green industrialisation

Hallegatte *et al.* (2012) define green industrial policies as policies aiming to green the productive structure of the economy by targeting specific industries or firms. They include industry-specific research and development subsidies, capital subsidies, and tax-breaks; feed-in tariffs; and import protection. They do not include policies targeting demand (such as consumer mandates), which can be met by imports without changing local production.

Hallegatte *et al.* (2013) state that greening growth requires prices to be adequate (in that they reflect environmental externalities) and effective (in that they trigger the needed response). Achieving such a goal will often require a combination of environmental and industrial policies – what we call green industrial policies. We define green industrial policies as industrial policies with an environmental goal, or more precisely, as sector-targeted policies that affect the economic production structure with the aim of generating environmental benefits.

Pegels (2014) and Lütkenhorst *et al.* (2014) define industrial policy as the pursuit by governments of industrial innovation and structural change in ways that enhance competitiveness and the creation of green jobs while fully internalising environmental costs and using resources sustainability. This calls for deliberate government action aimed at incentivising and directing private investment capital into the green markets of the future.

2.5. Green jobs

According to the ILO, green jobs are decent jobs that contribute to preserve or restore the environment, whether they are in traditional sectors such as manufacturing and construction, or in new, emerging green sectors such as renewable energy and energy efficiency (UNEP/ILO/IOE/ITUC, 2008). Green jobs help to improve energy and raw materials efficiency; limit greenhouse gas emissions; minimise waste and pollution; protect and restore ecosystems; and support adaptation to the effects of climate change. At the enterprise level, green jobs can produce goods or provide services that benefit the environment – for example, green buildings or clean transportation. However, these green outputs (products and services) are not always based on green production processes and technologies. Therefore, green jobs can also be distinguished by their contribution to more environmentally friendly processes. For example, green jobs can reduce water consumption or improve recycling systems. Yet, green jobs defined through production processes do not necessarily produce environmental goods or services (ILO, 2016).

The US Bureau of Labor Statistics classifies green jobs as "jobs in business that produce goods or services that benefit the environment or conserve natural resources" or "jobs in which workers' duties involve making their establishments' production processes more environmentally friendly or use fewer natural resources". The Bureau categorises green jobs into the following sectors: water conservation, sustainable forestry, biofuels, geothermal energy, environmental remediation, sustainability, energy auditors, recycling, electric vehicles, solar power, and wind energy. These sectors include jobs which seek to use or develop renewable forms of energy (i.e., wind, hydropower, geothermal, landfill gas, and municipal solid waste) as well as increase their efficiency. Under the green job's domain, education, training, and public awareness are also included. These jobs seek to enforce regulations, support education, and increase public influence for the benefit of the environment (Bureau of Labor Statistics, 2013).

The Agency for Workplace Innovation (2009) reports on selected definitions of green industries and green jobs in the US by the federal government, state governments, and various organisations. The Agency does not present a consolidated definition.

In their assessment of the impact of green jobs in South Africa, Borel-Saladin and Turok (2013) identified the potential sources of green employment and grouped 26 green segments into four categories – energy generation (wind, solar, hydro, and bio-fuels), energy and resource efficiency, emissions and pollution control, and natural resource management. They applied a relatively strict definition of green jobs as those jobs whose activities benefit the environment.

Using data on the US, Consoli *et al.* (2016) compare green and non-green occupations to detect differences in terms of skill content and of human capital. Their empirical profiling reveals that green jobs use more intensively high-level cognitive and interpersonal skills compared to non-green jobs. Green occupations also exhibit higher levels of standard dimensions of human capital such as formal education, work experience, and on-the-job training. While preliminary, this exploratory exercise seeks to call attention to an underdeveloped theme, namely the labour market implications associated with the transition towards green growth.

Bowen *et al.* (2018) propose estimating green skills. They estimate the share of jobs in the US that would benefit from a transition to the green economy and present different measures for the ease with which workers are likely to be able to move from non-green to green jobs. Using US data (no such data are available for SSA countries), they find that 19.4% of US workers are part of the green economy in a broad sense, although most green employment is indirectly rather than directly green. Their estimate is significantly different from the estimate by the US's Bureau of Labor Statistics (2013), which found that in 2011, the number of green jobs constituted 2.6% of total employment (2.3% of private sector jobs and 4.2% of public sector jobs). The difference between the two estimates is that Bowen *et al.* focuses on green skills needed across several sectors rather that green jobs or occupations. Their research needs careful study before undertaking an effort to estimate existing and needed green skills in SSA countries.

2.6. Green industrialisation defined for this book

Central to an understanding of green industrialisation is the concept of decoupling. Decoupling is used to describe an improvement in the use of materials, energy, and water inputs with respect to product outputs and/or a reduction in pollutant releases (non-product output). Decoupling can occur at the level of an individual company, an industry, or a country (Figure 2.1). Green industrialisation must be bringing about decoupling. Absolute decoupling, which implies a constant or absolute reduction in inputs, is rare. Relative decoupling, which is a more realistic target, implies for industry positive growth rates in inputs, and perhaps pollutant discharge, but at rates lower than the growth rate for industrial output.

To bring about decoupling, green industrialisation works along two main dimensions. In the first dimension, industries green themselves. What the term 'green' means in this context has been given concrete descriptions.

- It is about reducing the environmental impacts of industrial processes, which enterprises can do by using resources more efficiently, phasing out the toxic substances they use, introducing new, cleaner technologies, substituting fossil fuels with renewable energy sources, improving occupational health and safety, and reducing pollutant discharges and waste disposal to move towards compliance with environmental norms.
- It is about reducing the environmental impacts of the products which industry manufactures, which enterprises can do by re-designing their products and/or business models to use less materials and energy, to

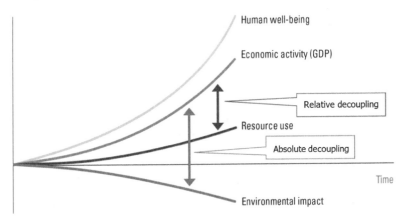

Figure 2.1 Relative and absolute decoupling

Source: UNEP, 2011

extend effective life times (especially of complex products), and to incorporate closed-loop, circular systems – repair, re-manufacturing, recycling at the end of life – while ensuring the same functionality can be delivered.

- It is about inserting industry – very much an urban phenomenon – into the urban fabric in a sustainable way, through proper urban planning procedures, setting up industrial districts in urban areas with sufficient buffer zones, etc.
- It is about reducing the environmental impacts along the supply chain, in particular in the logistics and transport systems which move products around.
- Finally, it is about making industry resilient to the effects of climate change and disasters.

The second dimension of green industrialisation is the establishment of greening services: the creation and/or expansion of existing enterprises so they can deliver the environmental goods and services that the rest of industry, primarily small and medium-sized enterprises (SMEs), requires to green itself. This covers a very diverse set of industrial activities, including at a minimum the manufacture of renewable energy equipment, material recovery and recycling, waste treatment and management, the manufacture of pollution control equipment, provision of environmental and energy consulting and services, and provision of monitoring,

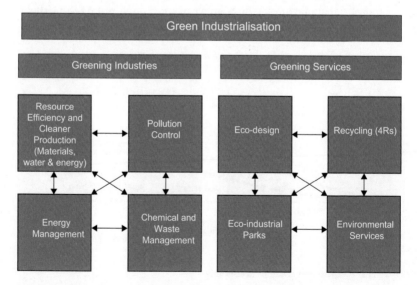

Figure 2.2 Green industrialisation: greening industries and greening services

measuring, and analysis services, as well as service activities such as finance and insurance.[1]

These two dimensions of green industrialisation can in turn be separated into several complementary and to some extent overlapping regimes (Figure 2.2). Greening industry is made up of four such regimes: pollution control for abating conventional pollutants released from plants into the environment; resource efficiency and cleaner production measures implemented within plants; energy management for energy efficiency and use of renewable energy to reduce GHG emissions; and chemical and waste management inside and outside of a plant but for which companies are responsible. For their part, greening services can be divided into another four regimes: the supply of environmental goods and services, the establishment and operation of eco-industrial parks, the adoption of eco-design, and the recycling of waste products and materials.

Overall, green industrialisation must be contributing to a green economy; one, that is, which is achieving improved human well-being and social equity while simultaneously diminishing environmental risks and reducing ecological scarcities (Hoffman, 2015). At a practical level, many of the greening services are also required by the rest of the economy to green itself.

Note

1 UNECA also distinguishes between greening industry and greening services. "Greening of industry can be achieved through three routes: transitioning out of brown industries; greening existing industries by increasing resource productivity, cutting pollution, and managing chemicals more safely; and creating new green enterprise, such as producing green capital goods, generating renewable energy, and providing environmental advisory services" (UNECA, 2016, p. 69).

References

AfDB/OECD/UN/World Bank (2013). *A Toolkit of Policy Options to Support Inclusive Green Growth*. Revised version (July 2013) of the Original Submission to the G20 Development Working Group by the African Development Bank, the Organisation for Economic Cooperation and Development, the United Nations and the World Bank. Retrieved from: www.undp.org/content/undp/en/home/librarypage/environment-energy/toolkit-inclusive-green-growth.html. Last accessed: 15.08.2019.

Agency for Workplace Innovation (2009). *Selected Definitions of Green Industries and Green Jobs*. Retrieved from: www.floridajobs.org/library/pubs/green/green_definitions.pdf. Last accessed: 15.08.2019.

Avis, W. (2018). *Inclusive and Green Growth in Developing Countries*. Helpdesk Report, K4D. 22 March. Retrieved from: https://assets.publishing.service.gov.uk/media/5af9702340f0b622dd7aa2c8/Inclusive_green_growth_in_developing_countries.pdf. Last accessed: 03.09.2019.

Borel-Saladin, J., Turok, I. (2013). The impact of green economy jobs in South Africa. *South African Journal of Science*, 109:9/10:1–4.

Bowen, A., Kuralbayeva, K., Tipoe, E. (2018). Characterising green employment: The impacts of 'greening' on workforce composition. *Energy Economics*, 72:263–275. ISSN 0140-9883.

Bureau of Labor Statistics (2013). *Green Goods and Services News Release*. 19 March. US Department of Labor. Washington, DC. Retrieved from: www.bls.gov/news. release/ggqcew.htm. Last accessed: 15.08.2019.

Consoli, D., Marin, G., Marchuzzi, F., Vona, F. (2016). Do green jobs differ from non-green jobs in terms of skills and human capital? *Research Policy*, 45:5:1046–1060.

Hallegatte, S., Heal, G., Fay, M., Treguer, D. (2012). *From Growth to Green Growth: A Framework*. Working Paper 17841. February. National Bureau of Economic Research. Cambridge, MA. Retrieved from: www.nber.org/papers/w17841.pdf. Last accessed: 15.08.2019.

Hallegatte, S., Fay, M., Vogt-Schilb, A. (2013). *Green Industrial Policies: When and How*. Policy Research Working Paper 6677. October. The World Bank. Washington, DC. Retrieved from: http://documents.worldbank.org/curated/en/994641468156896 733/pdf/WPS6677.pdf. Last accessed: 15.08.2019.

Hoffman, U. (2015). *Can Green Growth Really Work and What Are the True (Socio-) Economics of Climate Change?* UNCTAD Discussion paper 222. July. United Nations Conference on Trade and Development. Geneva. Retrieved from: https://unctad. org/en/PublicationsLibrary/osgdp2015d4_en.pdf. Last accessed: 13.08.2019.

ILO (2016). *Green Jobs: Progress Report 2014–2015*. International Labour Organization. Geneva. Retrieved from: www.ilo.org/wcmsp5/groups/public/-ed_emp/-emp_ent/documents/publication/wcms_502730.pdf. Last accessed: 15.08.2019.

Lütkenhorst, W., Altenburg, T., Pegels, A., Vidican, G. (2014). *Green Industrial Policy: Managing Transformation under Uncertainty*. Discussion Paper 28/2014. German Development Institute. Bonn. Retrieved from: www.die-gdi.de/uploads/media/DP_28.2014.pdf. Last accessed: 13.08.2019.

OECD (2011). *Towards Green Growth: A Summary for Policy Makers*. May. Organisation for Economic Cooperation and Development. Paris. Retrieved from: www. oecd.org/greengrowth/48012345.pdf. Last accessed: 13.08.2019.

OECD (2012). *Green Growth and Developing Countries a Summary for Policy Makers*. June. Organisation for Economic Cooperation and Development. Paris. Retrieved from: www.oecd.org/dac/50526354.pdf. Last accessed: 03.09.2019.

Pegels, A., ed. (2014). *Green Industrial Policy in Emerging Countries*. Routledge. London.

UNCTAD (2012). *Economic Development in Africa, Report 2012: Structural Transformation and Sustainable Development in Africa*. United Nations Commission on Trade and Development. Geneva. Retrieved from: https://unctad.org/en/Publications Library/aldcafrica2012_embargo_en.pdf. Last accessed: 13.08.2019.

UNECA (2016). *Economic Report on Africa 2016: Greening Africa's Industrialisation*. March. United Nations Economic Commission for Africa. Addis Ababa. Retrieved from: www.un.org/en/africa/osaa/pdf/pubs/2016era-uneca.pdf. Last accessed: 13.08. 2019.

UNEP (2011). *Decoupling Natural Resource Use and Environmental Impacts from Economic Growth: A Report of the Working Group on Decoupling to the International Resource*

Panel. Fischer-Kowalski, M., Swilling, M., von Weizsäcker, E.U., Ren, Y., Mori-guchi, Y., Crane, W., Krausmann, F., Eisenmenger, N., Giljum, S., Hennicke, P., Romero Lankao, P., Siriban Manalang, A., Sewerin, S. United Nations Environ-ment Programme. Nairobi. Retrieved from: www.resourcepanel.org/reports/decoupling-natural-resource-use-and-environmental-impacts-economic-growth. Last accessed: 13.08.2019.

UNEP/ILO/IOE/ITUC (2008). *Green Jobs: Towards Decent Work in a Sustainable, Low-Carbon World.* September. United Nations Environment Programme, Inter-national Labour Organization, International Organisation of Employers, Inter-national Trade Union Confederation. Retrieved from: www.ilo.org/wcmsp5/groups/public/-ed_emp/-emp_ent/documents/publication/wcms_158727.pdf. Last accessed: 13.08.2019.

UNIDO (2010). *A Greener Footprint for Industry: Opportunities and Challenges of Sustainable Industrial Development.* United Nations Industrial Development Organization. Vienna. Retrieved from: www.greengrowthknowledge.org/sites/default/files/downloads/resource/Greener_Footprint_Industry_UNIDO.pdf. Last accessed: 13.08.2019.

UNIDO (2011). *UNIDO Green Industry: Policies for Supporting Green Industry.* May. United Nations Industrial Development Organization. Vienna. Retrieved from: www.unido.org/sites/default/files/2011-05/web_policies_green_industry_0.pdf. Last accessed: 13.08.2019.

World Bank (2012). *Inclusive Green Growth: The Pathway to Sustainable Development.* The World Bank. Washington, D.C. Retrieved from: http://siteresources.worldbank.org/EXTSDNET/Resources/Inclusive_Green_Growth_May_2012.pdf. Last accessed: 13.08.2019.

3   Policies and programmes for greening industry

3.1. Introduction

Recognising that many of the topics covered by the term 'green industrialisation' were the subject of policy-making before the term itself existed, this chapter and the next summarise the policy and support programme literature focused on the specific regimes of green industrialisation described in Chapter 2 and shown in Figure 2.2. This chapter covers the policy and support programmes which promote and support the four greening industry regimes: pollution control for abating conventional pollutants released from plants into the environment; resource efficiency and cleaner production measures implemented within plants; energy management for energy efficiency and use of renewable energy to reduce GHG emissions; and chemical and waste management inside and outside of a plant but for which companies are responsible. At the end of each section, there is a summary of reports and studies on policies and support programmes which have either been adopted by SSA countries or have been discussed for possible adoption by these countries.

3.2. Pollution control instruments

Introduction

The justification for pollution control lies in market failures causing environmental externalities, which are only automatically internalised in decision-making in perfectly competitive markets. Unfortunately, such idealised market systems are not fully realisable in practice. Therefore, the objective of pollution is to change market behaviour in ways that are more closely consistent with behaviour when externalities are internalised, using methods that are feasible and cost effective.

The various instruments for industrial pollution control are commonly grouped into one of four direct approaches: (i) command-and-control regulation; (ii) market-based instruments/economic incentives; (iii) voluntary actions; and (iv) transparency and disclosure measures. Most of the instruments that fall into these four direct categories are noted in Table 3.1. In addition to these direct approaches that can alter the behaviour of industrial polluters, governments can indirectly alter their behaviour by planning approaches, such as environmental impact assessment and life cycle assessment, and by integrating environmental considerations into various economic policies including industrial trade and technology policies. For example, industrial policies that aim to influence the scale, sub-sector composition, technological configuration, and location of industrial growth have environmental implications.

Policy instruments

Command-and-control regulation for reducing pollutant discharge

The traditional command-and-control regulatory approach is used in most countries to control pollution. It consists of four activities: standards, licenses, compliance monitoring, and enforcement. The combined purpose of these four activities is to encourage and guide conduct that is favourable to the environment or prohibit conduct that is detrimental.

STANDARDS

Effluent and emission standards (mandatory) or guidelines (advisory) can be concentration based, mass based, or technological. Concentration standards specify the quality of pollutant in the wastewater. Mass-based

Table 3.1 Pollution control instruments

Command-and-control	Economic incentives
Standards	Charges and taxes
Licenses or permits	Grants and subsidies
Compliance monitoring	Fines for non-compliance
Enforcement	Tradable permits
Voluntary actions	*Transparency and disclosure*
Cleaner production programmes	Toxic release inventory
Environmental management systems	Public disclosure
Covenants	Corporate reporting
Product labelling	Corporate environmental performance awards
Corporate social responsibility	

Source: Derived from OECD, 1997

standards fix the quantity of pollutant per unit of production (for example, kg of organic waste per ton of production). These need to vary with the place of discharge (inland waters, sewerage treatment plant, or sea). Technological standards specify the type of equipment that needs to be put in place (e.g., scrubber systems for coal-fired power plants to reduce sulphur dioxide emissions).

Examples of effluent concentration standards and guidelines are listed in Table 3.2. The National Environmental Quality Standards (NEQS) are those for Ghana; the Environmental, Health, and Safety (EHS) guidelines are those recommended by the World Bank. Effluent standards can easily be circumvented by dilution of waste streams unless it is prohibited, nor do they consider the total amount of pollutants discharged.

Examples of emission standards and guidelines are listed in Table 3.3. There are separate guidelines for boilers and process emissions. Note that Ghana has yet to issue standards for process emissions.

Table 3.2 Effluent standards (NEQS) and guidelines (EHS)

Parameter*	Effluent standards and guidelines (mg/l)			
	NEQS			EHS
	Discharge into inland water	Sewage treatment	Discharge into the sea	
BOD	80	250	200	30
COD	150	400	400	160
TSS	200	400	400	50

* BOD: biological oxygen demand; COD: chemical oxygen demand; TSS: total suspended solids

Sources: Ghana, 1999; World Bank, 2007

Table 3.3 Emission standards (NEQS) and guidelines (EHS)

Parameter standard*	Emission standards and guidelines (mg/Nm³)			
	Boiler		Process	
	NEQS	EHS	NEQS	EHS process
PM	300	50–150	–	50
NO_x	400	460		
Chlorine			150	5
Hydrogen sulphide			10	5

* PM: particulate matter; NO_x: oxides of nitrogen; Nm³: m³ normalised to standard temperature and pressure

Sources: Ghana, 1999; World Bank, 2007

The EHS recommends industry-specific parameters for resource and energy consumption and mass-based pollutant discharge as a complement to concentration-based standards. For example, mass-based pollutant limitations are mandated by the US Environmental Protection Agency in order to prevent the achieving of compliance with concentration-based standards by diluting the effluent or emission.

In addition to concentration and mass-based standards, there is a need for ambient air and water quality standards.[1] Ambient quality standards are needed to ensure that the mass of pollutants released, even if in compliance with the existing concentration-based standards does not endanger human health and the environment. If the ambient standards are exceeded as a result of pollutant releases from plants in compliance with standards, then it would be necessary for discharging facilities to further reduce their pollutant releases.

EFFLUENT AND EMISSION LICENSES

Effluent and emissions licenses (also called permits) are industrial facility specific. They specify the concentration and mass of allowable releases and the date that a facility should come into compliance with these limits. They tailor both the concentration and the mass in the discharge to specific circumstances, such as the types of receiving waters (inland water, sewerage treatment plants, the sea, etc.) or the prevailing circumstances in an air shed (current ambient concentration of various pollutants and population exposed). They fix the time period (say five years) for which the license is valid, after which the facility needs to reapply for a new license.

An environmental agency can issue two types of licenses – individual and general licenses. An individual license is specifically tailored to an individual facility. A general license covers multiple facilities within a specific geographical area, such as an industrial estate. Individual or general licenses are often made available for public review at the provincial offices of the environmental agency and at the individual facilities for which they have been issued.

COMPLIANCE MONITORING

Compliance monitoring can be either voluntary or mandatory for a facility. An environmental authority can make industry owners and operators responsible for systematic monitoring and reporting of their environmental performance, saving the authority expense, time, and effort. The frequency of reporting to an environmental agency usually varies with the production level of an enterprise. Larger enterprises are usually required to report their effluents and emissions levels on a monthly basis. Smaller enterprises are usually required to report biannually.

Enforcement is essential for an effective command-and-control approach. Without enforcement, a command-and-control approach will fail. Enforcement requires a body of inspectors who periodically visit industrial facilities and inspect their operations. The periodicity of inspections depends on the size of the facility, the type of operations it is undertaking, whether there has been a history of non-compliance, etc. Monitoring data will be a key piece of data which inspectors will need to have access to, either through their own independent monitoring or through the monitoring required of the enterprise itself. Usually the enforcement process is one of incremental steps. Traditional enforcement sanctions fall into four general categories: informal, administrative, civil, and criminal. A variety of informal responses, such as warning letters and phone calls, fall at one end of the enforcement spectrum, while the federal and provincial environmental agencies can go on to use administrative, civil, and criminal remedies and sanctions.

Market-based instruments/economic incentives

Market-based instruments, or more broadly, economic incentives, have a number of advantages over the traditional command-and-control approach described previously. First, these instruments give sources of pollutants an incentive to reduce pollutant discharge below the permitted amounts when it is relatively inexpensive to do so. That factor, in turn, provides a motivation for sources to become smarter regarding pollution control options and costs. Second, technological improvements and innovation will be stimulated, resulting in greater opportunities to reduce pollutant discharge at low cost. Third, economic incentives are uniquely well suited to many of the pollution problems that countries face today and can be used in specific localities or regions as well as nationally. The more widely dispersed and smaller the sources, the more difficult it is to rely on the traditional command-and-control methods of facility-specific licenses, inspections, and enforcement. Economic instruments harness the forces of the market to give all sources, large and small, the motivation to find the lowest cost means of limiting their polluting activities. In principle, environmental inspections and enforcement become less necessary as sources pursue their own self-interest in reducing pollutant discharges. These features are especially important in countries where the resources to deal with pollution problems are severely limited. Commonly used economic incentives for pollution control are described next.

ENVIRONMENTAL FEES

Environmental fees, charges, and taxes (largely interchangeable in terms of their effects), all of which require that an industrial facility, pay a fee (or charge or tax) for each unit of pollutant it discharges or emits.

POLLUTION TRADING SYSTEMS

Pollution trading systems or so-called 'cap-and-trade' systems, which set a limit on the total amount of pollutant releases into a defined geographical area (the country or a smaller region). Trading allows a particular industrial facility to minimise the cost of achieving pollutant reductions by purchasing pollutant credits earned by or awarded to another source.

GRANTS

Grants, subsidies, and exemptions/reductions in import duties, which are incentives for investing in cleaner technologies which emit less pollution, or pollution control equipment which abates pollution and/or for covering the costs of the operation and maintenance of pollution control equipment.

FINES

Fines for non-compliance with standards, as described previously in the section on command-and-control enforcement, can be inducements to compliance with environmental standards as long as they impose a meaningful economic penalty.

Voluntary instruments

Voluntary instruments include cleaner production, environmental management systems, corporate social responsibility, covenants, product labelling, and industry codes of practice.

CLEANER PRODUCTION

Whereas traditional environmental protection achieved by command-and-control regulation focuses primarily on treatment of wastes and emissions 'at the end of the pipe' (so called because the standards are set at the factory boundaries), cleaner production aims at preventing pollutant generation in the first place by reducing the use of energy, water, and material resources in the production processes themselves. Through this approach, waste and emissions are minimised with the least possible impact on profitability and production capacity. Cleaner production involves rethinking conventional methods to achieve more efficient production processes and to design 'smarter' products.

ENVIRONMENTAL MANAGEMENT SYSTEM (ISO 14000:2015)

An environmental management system (EMS) meeting the requirements of ISO 14001 is a management tool enabling an organisation of any size or type to: (i) identify and control the environmental impact of its activities, products, or services; (ii) continually improve its environmental performance; and (iii) implement a systematic approach to setting environmental objectives and targets, to achieving these, and to demonstrating that they have been achieved. ISO 14001:2015 specifies the requirements for such an EMS. Fulfilling these requirements demands objective evidence that can be audited by an external body to demonstrate that the EMS is operating effectively in conformity to the standard. It is a tool that can generate internal benefits (assurance to management and employees) and external benefits (assurance to external stakeholders, reduced costs of compliance reporting to environmental authorities, and communication and demonstration of conformity to buyers' demands).

According to ISO 14001:2015, cleaner production programmes and EMS have a common objective: to improve the environmental performance of industrial facilities. They also share some common features in their implementation, such as a comprehensive analysis of production processes, reliance on factory teams to identify problems, and the implementation of technical and organisational measures to improve environmental performance. EMS complements cleaner production efforts at the factory level by increasing their sustainability and encouraging factories to go beyond the legal requirements. They also allow firms in some countries to reduce their reporting on compliance with environmental standards to regulatory agencies (ISO, a).

CORPORATE SOCIAL RESPONSIBILITY

Corporate social responsibility (CSR) can best be understood in terms of the changing relationship between business and society. Some people believe it is no longer enough for a company to say that their only concern is to make profits for their shareholders, when they are undertaking operations that can fundamentally affect (both positively and negatively) the lives of communities in countries throughout the world.[2]

The two fundamental building blocks of any CSR programme are improvements in environmental performance and social/human resource management. A UNIDO project documented these benefits for enterprises in four Asian countries in 2001–2002. The positive case for business responsibility has been found to be greater in the environmental area, but addressing social issues was still found to have a major impact on plant level productivity (Luken and Stares, 2005). More recent UNIDO efforts in Vietnam have shown that CSR efforts can positively transform enterprise management.

COVENANTS

Covenants that have been used to reduce pollution are voluntary contracts between the government and industrial sub-sectors that address environmental impacts common to a large number of companies, such as the production of packaging waste. The government typically negotiates with trade associations to meet industry-wide targets, and individual enterprises then sign on to sub-sectoral covenants via letters of declaration. If the covenants are violated or not met, then the government reserves the option to use traditional command-and-control regulation.

The concept of voluntary business-government agreements began in the Netherlands and caught on across Europe in the early 1990s. In the Netherlands, covenants have been negotiated with 18 industrial sub-sectors responsible for most of the nation's industrial pollution, but there are dozens of other covenants that address energy efficiency and other environmental issues. In fact, these contracts have become a key mechanism in the government's environmental strategy to encourage eco-efficiency/cleaner production.

PRODUCT LABELLING[3]

Eco-labels ensure that a product meets rigorous, science-based environmental standards. This gives manufacturers the assurance to back up their claims and purchasers the confidence that certified products are better for human health and the environment. There are several active eco-labelling programmes around the globe. One is the Blue Angel, a German eco-label based on criteria in product design, energy consumption, chemical emissions, noise, recyclable design, and take-back programmes. Another is the Green Seal, a US eco-label promoting the manufacture, purchase, and use of environmentally responsible products and services.

Transparency and disclosure

Information disclosure schemes are provisions, either voluntary or mandatory, for enterprises and public authorities to disclose information relating to the release of pollutants and/or their effect on the environment. These may serve a number of beneficial purposes, including to encourage enterprises to take voluntary action to reduce their discharges to the environment and to encourage better enforcement of existing environmental standards and license conditions. These measures include toxic release inventories, public disclosure programmes, and corporate rewards and reporting.

TOXIC RELEASE INVENTORIES

Toxic release inventories are particularly relevant for pollution control because they require industrial facilities to report annually the quantity of toxic chemicals released to the environment and/or managed through recycling, energy recovery, and treatment. The aim of making this information available to the public in specific communities is to create a strong incentive for companies to improve environmental performance. Thus, the inventories are different than command-and-control regulatory programmes that are designed to achieve better environmental performance by setting standards and specifying how facilities must operate.

There are mandatory toxic pollutant release inventory programmes in North America and Europe. The Toxic Release Inventory of the United States, started in 1985, tracks the management of 650 chemicals and chemical grouping for larger facilities involved in manufacturing, metal mining, electric power generation, chemical manufacturing, and hazardous waste treatment. In 2015, there were approximately 22,000 reporting facilities. The European Pollutant Release and Transfer Register, started in 2000, is a European-wide register of industrial and non-industrial releases into air, water, and land, and off-site transfers of wastewater and waste, including information from point and diffuse sources. As of 2015, the register includes information about more than 33,000 facilities in 33 countries (the 28 member states of the EU, Iceland, Liechtenstein, Norway, Switzerland, and Serbia).

PUBLIC DISCLOSURE

Public disclosure programmes are different from toxic/pollutant release inventory programmes in several significant ways. First, and most important, they constitute an effort to relate, however approximately, pollutant release to environmental degradation. Second, the government does the rating whereas companies participating in the member US Toxic Release Inventory or its equivalent report pollutant releases to the government. The programmes are similar, though, in that there is public disclosure of the ratings.

Indonesia was the first developing country to launch a public disclosure programme. Given the weak enforcement of its command-and-control environmental regulatory programme, BAPEDAL, the Indonesian Environmental Impact Management Agency, with support from the World Bank, initiated the Programme for Pollution Control, Evaluation and Rating in 1995. BAPEDAL used colour-coded ratings of the seriousness of pollutant discharge and public disclosure of the ratings to create incentives for plants to improve environmental performance. The objectives of the programme were to promote compliance with existing regulations and reward plants whose performance exceeded regulatory standards.

The only known public disclosure programme in SSA countries is Ghana's Environmental Performance Rating and Public Disclosure programme and its successor, AKOBEN.[4] AKOBEN ratings indicate how well companies have met the commitments they made in their environmental impact assessments. It, therefore, complements the EIA process and is now serving as a monitoring and verification programme to ensure that companies follow environmental regulations on a continual basis. As of 2015, about 200 of the 500–600 medium and large firms in Ghana are participating in the programme (PAGE, 2015)

CORPORATE AWARDS AND REPORTING

There are basically two types of awards for recognising responsible environmental performance on the part of industry. One is where industrial associations or environmental protection agencies recognise the environmentally responsible performance of companies, a relatively widespread practice. The other goes beyond recognising responsible behaviour to awarding those organisations that report and disclose environmental, social or full sustainability information.

SSA research and reports

Our search for data on industrial pollution found one overview of air pollution problems resulting from all human activity (UNEP, 2006) and a few journal articles about industry related pollution problems in specific countries (for example, Oketola and Osibanjo, 2011, and Bello *et al.* 2013 for Nigeria and Karikari *et al.*, 2006 for Ghana). This limited information is not enough to characterise the industry-related pollution problem in SSA countries. This conclusion should not be surprising as others have come to the same conclusion given that environmental impacts associated with resource use have diverse environmental impacts and are not documented in a way that can be aggregated quantitatively (UNEP, 2010).

In response to this situation, the World Bank assembled the Industrial Pollution Projection System (IPPS) to estimate a comprehensive profile of the pollutant intensities for the manufacturing sector and subsectors within the manufacturing sector (Hettige *et al.*, 1995). The modelling system was developed in the 1990s based on environmental and economic data for approximately 200,000 facilities in all regions of the US in the late 1980s and subsequently applied in several developing countries including Nigeria (Oketola and Osibanjo, 2011). It can be applied to estimate air emissions, water effluents, and solid waste loadings and incorporates a range of risk factors for human and eco-toxic effects.

3.3. Resource efficient and cleaner production

Introduction

In 1990, the United Nations Environment Programme (UNEP) developed the following definition of cleaner production (CP) that is still commonly used: "the continuous application of an integrated preventive environmental strategy applied to processes, products and services to increase efficiency, and reduce risks to humans and the environment" (UNEP/UNIDO, a).

Several complementary CP techniques or practices are possible, ranging from low or even no cost solutions to high investment, advanced clean technologies. A common classification of these CP techniques or practices in developing countries is:

- Good Housekeeping: appropriate provisions to prevent leaks and spills and to achieve proper, standardised operation, and maintenance procedures and practices;
- Input Material Change: replacement of hazardous or non-renewable inputs by less hazardous or renewable materials or by materials with a longer service lifetime;
- Better Process Control: modification of the working procedures, machine instructions, and process record keeping for operating the processes at higher efficiency and lower rates of waste and emission generation;

- Equipment Modification: modification of the production equipment so as to run the processes at higher efficiency and lower rates of waste and emission generation;
- Technology Change: replacement of the technology, processing sequence, and/or synthesis pathway in order to minimise the rates of waste and emission generation during production;
- On-Site Recovery/Reuse: reuse of the wasted materials in the same process or for another useful application within the enterprise;
- Production of Useful By-Products: transformation of previously discarded wastes into materials that can be reused or recycled for another application outside the company;
- Product Modification: modification of product characteristics in order to minimise the environmental impacts of the product during or after its use (disposal) or to minimise the environmental impacts of its production.

Parallel approaches

There are several other approaches with similar aims, some of which are described next.

Resource efficient and cleaner production (RECP)

This term was introduced in 2010 by UNIDO and UNEP to high-light the strategic opportunities to simultaneously address productivity and environmental and social concerns (UNIDO/UNEP, 2010). RECP builds upon CP and in addresses the three sustainability dimensions individually and synergistically:

- Production Efficiency: optimisation of the productive use of natural resources (materials, energy, and water);
- Environmental Management: minimisation of impacts on environment and nature through reduction of wastes and emissions;
- Human Development: minimisation of risks to people and communities and support for their development.

Green productivity

This is a term used by the Asian Productivity Organization since 1994 to address the challenge of achieving sustainable production. Just like cleaner production, green productivity is a strategy for enhancing productivity and environmental performance for overall socio-economic development.

The concept of green productivity and cleaner production are almost synonymous.

Eco-efficiency

This term was coined by the World Business Council for Sustainable Development in 1992. It is defined as the delivery of competitively priced goods and services that satisfy human needs and ensure quality of life, while progressively reducing ecological impacts and resource intensity throughout the life cycle, to a level at least in line with the earth's estimated carrying capacity. This concept is favoured by many in the industrial sector. The concepts of eco-efficiency and cleaner production are almost synonymous.

Waste minimisation

The concept of waste minimisation was introduced by the US Environmental Protection Agency. In this concept, waste and pollution reduction occurs on-site, at the source through changes of input raw materials and/or technology changes, good operating practices, and product changes. Compared to cleaner production, waste minimisation is, in one sense, broader in that it also includes off-site recycling of waste, but in another sense, it is narrower, since it does not cover product (re)design to minimise all life cycle impacts.

Pollution prevention

The terms 'cleaner production' and 'pollution prevention' are often used interchangeably. The distinction between the two tends to be geographic – pollution prevention is mostly used in North America, while cleaner production is used in other parts of the world. Both concepts focus on a strategy of continuously reducing pollution and environmental impact through source reduction – i.e., eliminating waste within the process rather than at the 'end-of-pipe' (a term initially used to denote any activity undertaken at the end of a wastewater discharge pipe to reduce the pollution, but now covering any activity to control pollution or waste once they have been generated). However, cleaner production includes the aspect of reduction of impacts and risks across the life cycle of a product, and in this sense is a more comprehensive concept than pollution prevention.

Source reduction

This is a term that is quite close to cleaner production – reducing generation of wastes or contaminants at the source, and thereby reducing releases that could pose hazards to the environment and public health. It does not include the concept of on-site reuse of wastes or of product (re) design which are included in cleaner production.

Toxics use reduction

Toxics use reduction is the elimination or avoidance of toxic substances in products or processes to reduce risks to the health of workers, consumers, and the public, and to minimise adverse effects on the environment. Toxics use reduction is a special case of cleaner production since it focuses specifically on the aspect of reducing toxicity and hazards.

Energy efficiency

This is very close to cleaner production, differing only in dealing more narrowly with energy use by companies. Cleaner production covers energy efficiency.

In the rest of this book, we will be using the term RECP.

Policies for promoting RECP interventions

To drive the uptake by industry, governments need to set realistic long-term policy objectives and targets, then apply an appropriate mix of policy instruments and finally measure progress toward meeting their objectives. GTZ proposed that governments use several instruments to create a sound policy framework that supports the uptake of RECP across the entire production system. Within five broad categories of instruments, GTZ proposed that there are 18 policy instruments that were particularly relevant for driving RECP uptake. These are listed in Box 3.1.

Box 3.1 Policy instruments relevant to driving RECP

I. Regulatory instruments

- *Norms and standards*: rules and targets set by public authorities that subsequently are enforced by compliance procedures.
- *Environmental liability*: make the causer of environmental damage pay for remediating the damage he has caused.
- *Environmental control and enforcement*: the public sector inspects companies or projects to assess if they comply with environmental regulation, laws and standards.

II. Economic instruments

- *Environmentalt axes*: taxes collected from businesses that usually have both an environmental and a revenue-raising effect. Commonly called 'eco-taxes'.
- *Fees and user charges*: levied by public authorities for services provided (e.g., effluent or refuse disposal), or for a specific purpose (e.g., funding clean-up or abatement measures).
- *Certificate trading schemes*: governments establish a maximum quantity of emissions to the environment in a region and issue certificates or permits allowing certificate holders to emit pollutants or the use of environmental goods up to the defined maximum. The certificates are tradable.
- *Environmental financing*: environmentally beneficial measures are promoted through financial institutions or independent funds.
- *Green Public Procurement*: usually means that the acquisition of goods or services by the public sector takes environmental elements into account (when considering how to create the best possible value for taxpayers).
- *Subsidies*: financial support from government institutions to private enterprises to promote resource-efficient production and services.

III. Research and educational instruments

- *Research and development* (R&D): support systematic investigatory work carried out to increase the stock of knowledge and the use of such knowledge to drive RECP.
- *Education and training*: use education and training programmes to build capacity on resource efficiency and cleaner production.

IV. Cooperation instruments

- *Technology transfer*: support the process of acquiring clean technologies from foreign parties as well as the necessary knowledge and skills to apply them.
- *Voluntary agreements*: encourage single firms, groups of companies, or industrial sectors to improve their resource efficiency and environmental conduct and performance beyond existing environmental legislation and regulations.

V. Information instruments

- *Eco-labelling*: support the adoption of labels displaying information regarding the environmental performance of a certain product or service, in order to provide information to consumers, procurement officials, and retailers.
- *Sustainability reporting*: support the public disclosure of information by an organisation about its 'non-financial performance' (also termed 'triple bottom line') – its management policies, activities, and the result of activities on economic, environmental, and social issues.
- *Information centres*: support their establishment so that they can provide information on resource efficiency and related topics to SMEs that often lack access to the latest information and do not have the capacity to keep updated on every technological development in the market.
- *Consumer advice services*: offer support in the following three dimensions: precaution (consumer advice services), after-care (liability), and control (laws).
- *Environmental quality targets and associated environmental monitoring*: instruments for the quantitative measurement of performance in the implementation of environmental targets.

Building on these, but using the alternative four-quadrant grouping described in Table 3.1, a description of relevant policy instruments is given next (GTZ/UNEP/Wuppertal, 2006).

Regulatory instruments

It is generally agreed that RECP uptake at the process level cannot be driven directly by regulatory instruments; it is not practical to order enterprises to improve the resource efficiency of their industrial processes.

However, the use of traditional 'command-and-control' instruments is seen as particularly important in giving an indirect, economic incentive to enterprises to adopt RECP options. By reducing the amount and toxicity of wastes and emissions, these options reduce the costs to enterprises of having to comply with the end-of-pipe standards.

While accepting the basic voluntary nature of RECP, some attempts have been made to more directly link RECP with 'command-and-control' instruments. For instance, some countries have linked compliance orders with agreements to undertake CP assessments and implement financially viable options. In brief, enterprises are given compliance orders with longer timelines to come into compliance if they work with a Cleaner Production Centre to find CP options for reaching compliance. A somewhat similar approach has been used in China, which has passed a Cleaner Production Promotion Law (China, a). There, companies with whose environmental performance the government has issues are required to undertake a CP assessment, there being an expectation that the results of these assessments will be implemented.

The situation is somewhat different in the case of green products. Governments can, and have, banned the presence of certain toxic chemicals in products, forcing manufacturers to eliminate those chemicals from their products, possibly replacing them with non- or less toxic chemicals. In effect, governments have used regulation to make products greener. An example of a less direct pressure on companies to green their products is Japan's Top Runner programme, which has been successfully used to promote energy efficiency in certain classes of products. In brief, the government periodically determines which product in a given product class is the most energy efficient. It then makes that level of energy efficiency the standard, with every product in the product class required to meet it. Those companies which voluntarily worked to make their product the most efficient will be rewarded by seeing costs of having to meet the new standard imposed on their competitors – or the elimination of competitors which cannot meet the new standard (Japan, 2015).

Economic instruments

As in the case of regulatory instruments, a number of the possible economic instruments available to policy-makers – environmental taxes, fees, and user charges, certificate trading schemes, fines for non-compliance – are also seen as supporting the uptake of RECP for the same reason: they increase the cost to enterprises of generating waste or pollution and so encourage them to reduce them through RECP. This also includes the removal of subsidies which artificially reduce the cost of virgin materials, non-renewable materials, and toxic and hazardous materials.

Subsidies can also be used to support RECP. One such form of subsidy is environmental financing. This can be used to promote RECP in a number of ways: loans and/or grants can be provided on more favourable terms than those in the prevailing market, to fully or partially finance the purchase of cleaner production technologies, or technologies which allow on-site recycling, or even cleaner production assessments leading to measurable efficiency improvements.

Another form of subsidy is Green Public Procurement. This can be used by the public sector to acquire goods or services which have been (re)designed to create less impacts during their use or (more rarely) have been produced in eco-efficient production processes.

Other forms of subsidies could be used to lower the price of resource efficient devices, items, and services to improve their competitiveness and to enhance their competitiveness.

Voluntary instruments

Given the essentially voluntary nature of RECP, voluntary instruments which support industry's adoption of RECP are where government policies most directly promote the uptake of RECP by enterprises.

Centres of various types have been established with government backing to provide support to companies, primarily SMEs, which are considering or have decided to adopt RECP measures. The services which they offer can run from information dissemination and training to consulting and support on technology transfer. For instance, UNIDO and UNEP have been developing a network of National Cleaner Production Centres (NCPCs) in developing and transition countries since 1994 in partnership with their governments. The activities of these centres in SSA countries are described later. Governments have also been establishing energy efficiency centres, as have several international organisations in partnership with national governments.

Governments can also use their influence or direct responsibility in the sectors of higher education and vocational training to build the necessary technical and other necessary capacities for resource efficiency and cleaner production in the new entrants into the job market.

Funding of research and development (R&D) which is aimed at increasing resource efficiency is another way governments can be involved. This requires systematic investigatory work carried out to increase the stock of knowledge and the use of such knowledge to devise new products and processes.

Linked to supporting R&D is support to technology transfer. Governments have been supporting technology transfer – both incoming transfer and outgoing transfer – for many years and have developed many tools and approaches to do this. Governments can use these same tools and approaches to support enterprises to import low-carbon and resource efficient technologies and products which they need and to export such technologies and products which they produce.

Governments can use the instrument of covenants to draw up voluntary contracts between them and chosen industrial sub-sectors, which aim to encourage members of the latter to improve their resource efficiency and environmental conduct and performance beyond existing environmental legislation and regulations. The companies commit to increasing their resource efficiency by a specified amount for some of the materials they use, while in return the government commits to certain specific forms of support which the enterprises need in order to meet the agreed resource efficiency target. In the Netherlands, covenants have been negotiated with 18 industrial sub-sectors responsible for most of the nation's industrial pollution, but there are dozens of other covenants that address energy efficiency and other environmental issues. In fact, these contracts have become a key mechanism in the government's environmental strategy to encourage eco-efficiency/cleaner production.

Finally, governments can use eco-labelling schemes to encourage companies to (re)design their products to make them greener and lessen their environmental impacts during use or at disposal. For products where green alternatives are known, governments can create labelling criteria which encompass those green traits. Companies which voluntarily redesign their products to meet those criteria can then use the eco-label as part of their promotional campaigns, or these can be used by governments as green specifications in public procurement.

Transparency and disclosure

Through such programmes as eco-labelling, governments can encourage companies to voluntarily adopt labels. Governments can also require labelling on products. In the form of energy efficiency labelling, these can directly support RECP by encouraging consumers to purchase more energy efficient products. Labels which instead are safety driven, such as chemical labelling, can indirectly promote RECP by possibly encouraging consumers to purchase products which do not contain toxic or hazardous components, or by possibly encouraging producers to avoid the negative impacts on their brands of having to put such labels on their products by designing out the toxic/hazardous components.

Toxic release inventories can also exert an indirect but powerful pressure on companies to adopt RECP. The inventories are made public. Companies listed as having had to report can find that this publicity negatively affects their brand or public image and will take active steps to eliminate emissions or wastes and so avoid having to report them in the next inventory, or at a minimum be able to show that they have reduced their emissions and wastes. More general public disclosure of environmental performance by companies, through required sustainability reporting or similar, can have the same effect.

While all these types of reporting can drive companies to RECP to avoid negative publicity, governments can also encourage companies to take up RECP by offering them positive publicity. They can do this, for instance, by setting up an award scheme where the government gives awards to companies which have made significant, measurable progress in RECP uptake.

SSA research and reports

The degree of uptake of RECP in several of the SSA countries has been described only to a limited extent in the literature focused on this topic in SSA countries. The more important drivers, barriers, and enablers found in articles and reports are summarised in Table 3.4. *Drivers* are those actions which push or pressurise firms to adopt RECP options; *barriers* are those aspects about a firm's culture, skills, commitment, etc., which, when firms have decided they want/need to deploy RECP options, make it difficult for them to do so; and *enablers* are those actions which lower these barriers. As defined here, drivers can be either internal or external to firms, and barriers are always internal, while enablers are always external because they are primarily the instruments by which external actors can assist firms overcome their barriers.

The biggest cluster of drivers in the 11 articles and reports just cited concerns material costs: the high costs of inputs and the allied need for cost savings. If the drivers related to maintaining a competitive edge are added under an overall objective of firm profitability, these dominate the drivers. This suggests that in the SSA countries, purely economic market considerations mostly underlie any sensitivity which firms have towards RECP; the pursuit of other, more social goods, such as climate change related energy efficiency or environmental protection more generally, seem to still play a relatively minor role in their decision-making. This further suggests that the governments (but also civil society more generally) are either too weak to bring the relevant pressure to bear or are themselves unaware of the social goods which RECP can deliver to society.

This situation seems to be reflected in the set of barriers identified as important in the articles and reports considered. The strong cluster of barriers relating to the lack of information points to firms still being very much in the 'starting blocks' when it comes to RECP deployment, the gathering of information generally being the first step in a firm's journey towards RECP. The cluster of barriers focusing on the high costs or risk of implementation can also reflect this perceived lack of knowledge, because lack of knowledge tends to magnify the 'downside' of any move away from the status quo. An important cluster related to

Table 3.4 Top drivers, barriers, and enablers

Article/report	Drivers	Barriers	Enablers
Retta (1999) firms in Ethiopia	Awareness (I) Management commitment (I)	Technology configuration inhibits new green investment (I)	
Peart (2002) 26 firms in South Africa	Obtain competitive edge (I) Need for cost savings (I) Expansion (I)		
Siaminwe et al. (2005) 60 firms in Zambia	Enforce environmental regulations (E)	Financial problems (I) Lack of knowledge (I)	Economic incentives (E) Government support and training (E)
Luken and Van Rompaey (2008) 30 key informants Kenya and Zimbabwe	Current regulations (E) High costs of production inputs (E) Product specifications in foreign markets (E)	Lack of technical information (I) High implementation cost (I) Uncertainty about performance (I)	
Luken and Van Rompaey (2008) 19 firms in Kenya and Zimbabwe	Future regulations (E) High cost of production inputs (E) Requirements of owners (I)	High implementation cost (I) Lack of skills (I) Lack of technical information (I)	
Koefoed and Buckley (2008) ten firms in South Africa	Awareness of CP (I) Strong enforcement of environmental regulations (E) Obtain competitive edge (I) Need for cost savings (I)	Lack of information about cost savings (I)	
Masselink (2009) 13 firms in Nigeria	Energy prices (E)	Lack of information (I) Other investment priorities (I)	Suppliers/ consultants (E) Information sharing among firms (E)
Morris et al. (2011) 30 firms in South Africa	Energy costs (E) Electricity costs (E)	Lack of financial resources (I) Lack of information (I) Lack of management skills (I)	Government support (E)

Article/report	Drivers	Barriers	Enablers
Apeaning and Thollander (2013) 30 firms in Ghana	Awareness of cost reduction potential (I) Rising energy prices (E) Energy efficiency requirements of the government (E)	Lack of budget funding (I) Other priorities for investments (I) Lack of available borrowing capital (E)	
Never (2016) 45 SMEs in Uganda	Electricity costs (E)	Short-term thinking (I) Habit/status quo bias (I) Lack of financial resources (I) Lack of first-hand experience with efficient technology (I)	Comparison with others (E)
Luken *et al.* (2018) 47 key informants in SSA countries	Reduce production cost (I) Productivity benefits (I) Product requirements in foreign markets (E)	High cost of implementation (I) Lack of technical information (I)	Government support (E)

Note: Internal (I) to firm and external (E) to firm

Source: Luken *et al.* 2019

the lack of management commitment shows that this is still a problem in SSA countries: company management does not yet see RECP as an important strategy to adopt and consequently the necessary allocation of resources, both human and non-, are not being made. An important cluster of barriers around the theme of lack of investment funds could reflect the chronic lack of capital in SSA countries but could also be a reflection of the lack of management commitment, where those investment funds available internally to a company get shunted to some other use, viewed by management as having a higher priority.

The possible weakness of governments in SSA countries just alluded to could explain why enablers figure weakly in the 11 articles and reports reviewed. As described earlier, governments can play an important role in lowering the barriers in firms to RECP deployment, through various free or subsidised programmes, focusing on information diffusion, skills upgrading, readier access to finance, and other aspects. The fact that this is not mentioned very often as an important element leads one to suspect that the respondents in the various studies simply did not see government as being able or willing to offer these services. In the few instances where this was mentioned as important, only very generic descriptions of government support were given, which suggests that governments have offered few if any of these services and those respondents were not in a position to distinguish in any way between which kinds of government programmes were most needed.

National Cleaner Production Centres supporting RECP interventions in SSA countries

Industrialised countries have committed themselves to provide developing and transition countries access to sustainable production methods, practices, and techniques. This commitment was included in Agenda 21, which was agreed upon during the United Nations Conference on Environment and Development in Rio de Janeiro in 1992. Subsequently, UNIDO and UNEP launched pilot Cleaner Production (CP) projects to demonstrate preventive environmental strategies in selected countries. Upon their successful completion, UNIDO and UNEP jointly launched a programme to establish National Cleaner Production Centres (NCPCs). The first batch of eight NCPCs was established during 1994–1995 (Luken *et al.*, 2016).

As of 2016, the Programme has supported capacity development in 56 NCPCs in developing and transition countries. The regional distribution of the centres is as follows: 11 in Sub-Saharan Africa, 11 in Asia, 19 in Europe, ten in Latin America, and five in the Middle East and North Africa.

In each of these countries, national experts have been trained in plant assessments completed and CP results and experiences disseminated. In addition, an institutional platform for ongoing service delivery and CP promotion was created, typically through a NCPC but in some countries through other mechanisms. The results of a few completed in-plant assessments are described in Box 3.2.

The NCPCs have started to collaborate regionally to capture knowledge, share information and resources, and foster learning. In Africa, NCPCs lead the process of regional institutionalisation of sustainable consumption and production. The NCPCs have been instrumental in the creation of the Africa Roundtable for Sustainable Consumption and Production. The Cleaner Production Centre of Tanzania provides its executive secretariat. The Roundtable developed the African 10 Year Framework Programme on Sustainable Consumption and Production, which was approved by the African Ministerial Council on Environment.

Box 3.2 Case studies of RECP projects

Sector	Company	Size*	Savings (USD/yr)	Resource savings (%)	Pollutants red'n (%)**	Product output (%)
Kenya						
Food and Beverage	Kibos *Sugar and Allied Industries Factory*	–	259,230	• energy use: -24 • material use: 31 • water use: -38	• air emissions: -24 • wastewater: -40 • waste: -14	13
	Kitumbe *Tea Factory*	–	602,990	• water use: -36 • electricity use: -53	–	–
	United Millers Limited *Bakery Division*	220	20,930	• energy use: -3 • material use: 0 • water use: -3	• air emissions: -72 • waste: 4	-3
Textile, Finishing	Ken *Knit Factory*	1,200	1,273,070	• energy use: -5 • materials use: -7 • water use: -30	• wastewater: -30 • waste: -35	13
Chemicals, Petro-chemicals, and Petroleum	Haco Industries	–	548,260	• energy use: -11 • materials use: 5 • water use: 29	• air emissions ($CO_{2eq.}$): -11 • wastewater: -19 • waste: -38	18
Tanzania						
Food and Beverage	Nile Perch Fisheries Ltd	–	703,300	• energy use: 4 • materials use: 8 • water use: -52	• air emissions: 4 • wastewater: -50 • waste: -65	16
	Tanzania Breweries Ltd Mwanza Plant	295	98,750	• energy use: -44 • materials use: -74 • water use: -56	• air emissions: -50 • wastewater: -42 • waste: -39	-2
Textile, Finishing	Musoma Textile Mills Ltd	150	79,300	• energy use: -15 • materials use: 123 • water use: -7	• air emissions: -15 • wastewater: -7 • waste: 15	160

(Continued)

(Continued)

Sector	Company	Size*	Savings (USD/yr)	Resource savings (%)	Pollutants red'n (%)**	Product output (%)
Uganda						
Food and Beverage	Crown Beverages Ltd.	513	513,320	• energy use: 12 • materials use: 11 • water use: 6	• air emissions (CO_{2eq}): 12 • wastewater: 0 • waste: –5	14
Leather, Tanneries	Leather Industries of Uganda	–	583,170	• energy use: –20 • materials use: –27 • water use: –74	• air emissions (CO_{2eq}): –20 • wastewater: –74 • waste: –27	–27
Chemicals, Petro-chemicals, and Petroleum	Sadolin Paints (U) Ltd	320	100,130	• energy use: –22 • materials use: 15 • water use: 3	• air emissions (CO_{2eq}): 6 • wastewater: 25 • waster: 0	16

* No. of employees

** Absolute indicator: a measurement of how much resource use/pollution output has changed in absolute terms. A negative percent indicates a decrease and a positive percent indicates an increase.

Source: RECPnet 2018

This includes activities in four priority areas: energy; water and sanitation; habitat and sustainable urban development; and industrial development.

A recent study (Quartey and Oguntoye, 2020) explored the performance of NCPCs in the SSA countries in promoting corporate sustainability in SMEs. As a qualitative study, interview responses from 32 experts working in NCPCs in four SSA countries were analysed using an inductive thematic approach. The findings suggest that NCPC capacity constraints, regulatory and international pressure, the attitudes of SMEs, the relevance of corporate sustainability to business performance, and the position of the NCPCs in the network of service providers are the key determinants of the NCPCs' performance in promoting corporate sustainability. As far as the NCPCs are concerned, developing their capacities and enhancing their position in the network of service providers are important for improving their effectiveness.

3.4. Energy management: industrial energy efficiency

Whereas the RECP policies and programmes promote complete resource assessment (energy, water, raw materials) with the aim or improving environmental compliance, energy policies and programmes promote energy use assessments with the aim of improving energy productivity and reducing GHG emissions. These assessments fall into two categories. One focuses on improving energy productivity based on energy audits to come into compliance with ISO 50001. The other focuses on supporting the use of modern renewable energy sources as a viable alternative to fossil fuels.

Energy demand

Since 2000, primary energy demand in SSA has increased by half, reaching 570 Mtoe in 2012, although this still accounts for only 4% of the world total. While growth in Sub-Saharan energy demand has outpaced that in the rest of the world, it has lagged economic expansion, as in many SSA countries it was led by sectors with relatively low energy intensity such as tourism and agriculture. The energy intensity of the SSA region economy has decreased by around 2.5% per year since 2000, but is more than double the world average (IEA, 2014).

While data on energy consumption in the manufacturing sector is limited, manufacturing in South Africa and Nigeria are the two largest consumers. South Africa and Nigeria are the only countries with a significant petrochemical industry, while other notable energy-intensive large manufacturing activities include aluminium smelting in Mozambique and the automotive and iron and steel sectors in South Africa.

Energy demand for cement production is growing particularly in Nigeria. Despite ambitions for manufacturing, to date most economic activity and growth is focused in non-energy-intensive sectors, such as agriculture, tourism, and textiles (IEA, 2014).

Energy efficiency potential

The industrial sector is responsible for one third of global primary energy use and two fifths of global energy-related carbon dioxide (CO_2) emissions. There is significant potential to reduce the amount of energy used to manufacture most commodities. The technical reduction potential ranges from about 10% to 40% for the five energy-intensive industrial sub-sectors in SSA countries. The financial savings potential is smaller, but also significant.

Policies and programmes to promote industrial energy efficiency

A wide range of National Energy Plans and more specifically National Energy Efficiency Strategies or Plans have been formulated for many developing countries, primarily in Asia. More recently, these plans have morphed into Green Economy and Climate Resilience Plans. These plans are essential for increasing the adoption of energy-efficient practices by overcoming informational, institutional, policy, regulatory, and market-related barriers. They also provide enabling environments for industrial enterprises to more easily implement energy-efficient technologies, practices, and measures. SSA initiatives along these lines are the Ethiopian Climate-Resilient Green Economy Strategy and the South African Energy Efficiency Strategy, both of which are summarised in Boxes 3.3 and 3.4, respectively.

Box 3.3   Ethiopia's Climate Resilient Green Economy (CRGE)

The document lays out a strategy for reducing GHG emissions across all sectors of the economy (Ethiopia, 2011). With respect to the industrial sector, the strategy focuses on 12 individual plants that make up the major part of Ethiopia's industrial activities (and hence account for most of the industrial GHG emissions).

Given the comparatively small share of organised industrial activity in the economy, the 4 Mt CO_2 emitted by industry account for only 3% of GHG emissions. At nearly 2 Mt CO_2 (50% of the industry total), cement is the single largest industrial source of emissions, followed by plants in the mining (32%) and the textile and leather (17%) sectors. Emissions from plants in the steel, other types of engineering, the chemicals sector (including fertiliser), pulp and paper sector, and food processing together account for only around 2% of industrial GHG emissions.

Among the industrial sectors, cement will be one of the fastest growing, causing the vast majority of future GHG emissions from the industrial sector. Output was slated to increase tenfold from 2.7 Mt in 2010 to 27 Mt in 2015. Some cement factories use outdated technology that is not only energy inefficient but also causes high emissions from the production process. The CRGE programme identified a series of initiatives that could help to increase the competitiveness of the cement industry by reducing production costs while at the same time yielding significant environmental and health benefits.

The government also planned take action to put the other industrial sectors on a sustainable economic development path. The textile, leather, and fertiliser industries are important parts of the envisaged economic development model. The government aims to promote – among other initiatives – energy efficiency and the use of alternative fuels in these subsectors.

Of the identified industry abatement potential, around 70% is concentrated in the cement industry. The main lever, clinker substitution, would increase the share of additives in cement, particularly pumice (5 Mt CO_{2eq} of abatement). Upgrading to more energy efficient technologies and waste heat recovery could reduce up to 6 Mt CO_2 emissions in 2030, while the use of biomass (mainly agro-residues) will help to reduce GHG emissions by 4 Mt CO_{2eq}. All the other industrial sectors that were analysed (e.g., chemicals, fertilisers, textiles, leather, paper and pulp) account for an abatement potential of around 6 Mt CO_2 emissions in 2030. The strategy estimated that the cement industry initiatives, for which the cost had been evaluated, would require a total of around USD 6.2 billion by 2030. Of this total, about USD 4.9 billion is capital expenditure and USD 1.3 billion is operating expenditure. Around USD 2.1 billion of the total expenditure would already be required by 2015.

For many of the sectors included in the CRGE strategy, data were not readily available or were of poor quality. As a result, the authors of the strategy had to take a pragmatic approach to compiling the baseline data required to support the analytical process, combining domestically available data with international benchmarks, experiences from other countries, expert interviews, and making several assumptions.

In summary, the government has formulated a reasonably well-documented, feasible, and time-bound strategy for reducing GHG emissions from the industrial sector. However, it is not a strategy for greening the industrial sector. It does not address the need for improving the efficiency of all resource inputs (energy, materials, and water) and reducing the discharge of pollutants into the ambient environment. Also, the CRGE appears not to take advantage of all the institutions working to reduce GHG emissions, such as drawing on the services of the Ethiopian National Cleaner Production Centre or the Ethiopia Climate Innovation Centre, nor does it include a specific programme for monitoring progress in reducing GHG emissions.

Box 3.4 South Africa's Energy Efficiency Strategy

The Department of Energy released its first national energy efficiency strategy in 2005. It set a national target for energy efficiency improvement of 15% by 2015 relative to projected consumption. The programme was implemented on a sector-by-sector basis with progress monitored and the targets reviewed after each of three stages. The strategy aimed to achieve the required energy efficiency improvements through the following enabling instruments and interventions: energy efficiency standards; appliance labelling; education, information, and awareness; research and technology development; energy audits; monitoring and targeting and energy management systems.

The target for the industrial sector was a reduction in final energy demand of 15% by 2015. Within the industrial sector the target was focused on the following sectors: iron and steel (1% improvement per year), chemical/petrochemicals (1% improvement per year), mining (reduce total energy demand by 10% by 2015), paper and pulp and printing (2% improvement per year), and cement (2% improvement per year). The strategy thus focused on energy intensive industry with no mention of light industry. While the Department claimed that the industrial sector offered energy savings of around 50% of current consumption in comparison with international best practices, a "savings potential of at least 11% is readily achievable using low-cost to medium-cost technical interventions. Furthermore, an additional 5–15% energy saving would be achievable via proven no-cost and low-cost techniques of energy management and good housekeeping" (de la Rue du Can *et al.*, 2013). Monitoring has shown that the target for industry has indeed been greatly exceeded. As of 2012, industrial energy efficiency had been reduced 34.3% (DOE, 2016).

Ideally, national strategies put forward by UN Energy (a) for promoting industrial energy efficiency described below would include the following policies and programmes.

Industrial energy efficiency target-setting, voluntary agreements, and voluntary actions

Establishing appropriate and ambitious energy efficiency or GHG emissions reduction targets can provide a strong incentive for the adoption of energy-efficient technologies, practices, and measures. More specifically, the process would include the following actions:

- Setting specific energy decoupling targets first for the manufacturing sector and then for several resource intensive sectors within the manufacturing sector. At a later date, targets could be set for decoupling material and water use as these can affect energy use;
- Focusing on the more energy intensive and older plants in each sector;
- Involving sub-sector business associations in setting sector decoupling targets for energy intensity and entering into voluntary agreements to meet agreed upon targets;
- Encouraging, where feasible, the use by enterprises of renewable energy sources;
- Attempting to integrate energy use and environmental compliance targets into long-term comprehensive operating permits for industrial enterprises.

Industrial energy management standards

Once targets have been established and/or a company's management has made a commitment to improve energy efficiency or reduce GHG emissions, it is important to institutionalise the company's energy management within a wider culture and context for sustained improvement. Energy management standards can provide a useful organising framework for accomplishing this in industrial facilities and for sharing experiences.

Adoption of an energy management standard begins with a strong commitment to continual improvement of energy efficiency. A first step is to develop an energy policy – realistic in its goals, environmentally sound, and achievable in a given time frame, phased or otherwise – is top management's official statement of the organisation's commitment to managing energy. The policy is typically developed by a cross-divisional/functional team, established by top management, and formally approved by top management. The team is then authorised to implement the policy as part of the energy management system. Energy performance improvement targets and objectives are established for the company, which are met through the development and implementation of action plans. Implementation relies on procedures, documentation, operational controls, training, and communication. The effectiveness of energy performance improvement efforts and the management system as a whole, as is the case for environmental management systems, are checked through internal audits and periodic management reviews, with corrective actions taken as needed.

Industrial equipment standards

Most motors and boilers used in industry today perform at levels well below those of the high efficiency that are currently available. The adoption of minimum efficiency performance standards has been shown to be the most effective way generally to improve the energy efficiency of motors and boilers in industry over a given period.

System assessment standards

The overall performance of the systems in which components (motors, furnaces, and boilers) are embedded can also be the source of very significant industrial energy inefficiencies. System assessment standards define, based on current expert knowledge and techniques, a common framework for assessing the energy efficiency of industrial systems.

Certification and labelling of energy efficiency performance

A market-based plant certification framework includes three essential building blocks: energy management standards, system assessment standards and measurement, and verification protocols. Two certification programmes that incorporate the three building blocks are the Superior Energy Performance Partnership managed by the US Department of Energy and the Programme for Improving Energy Efficiency in Energy Intensive Industries managed by the Swedish Energy Agency.

Capacity building for energy management and energy efficiency services

Experience in countries with energy management standards or specifications have shown that the appropriate application of energy management standards requires significant training and skills. The implementation of an energy management standard within a company or an industrial facility requires a change in existing institutional approaches and attitudes to the use of energy, a process that may benefit from technical assistance from experts outside the organisation. There is a need to build not only internal capacity within organisations seeking to apply the standard, but also external capacity from knowledgeable experts to help establish an effective implementation structure.

Delivery of industrial energy efficiency products and services

Industrial energy efficiency information programmes aim to make it easier for plant managers to evaluate energy efficient options creating and disseminating relevant technical information through energy efficiency assessment and self-auditing tools, case studies, reports, guidebooks, and benchmarking tools. Industrial energy efficiency products and services can be provided by governments, utilities, consulting engineers, equipment manufacturers or vendors, or by energy service companies (ESCOs).

Demand side management

Energy users do not demand energy at the same time each day nor each season of the year (more heating may be required in winter, cooling in summer, lighting at night, etc.). By managing the 'demand-side', the profile of energy use can be changed. Various demand side management options exist. Sometimes the demand for energy can be shifted, with so-called 'load shifting' measures. Peak demand can be changed by, amongst other things, improving the efficiency of appliances that contribute to peak demand.

Utility programmes

Many utility companies, especially those whose profits have been decoupled from sales and/or who have dedicated funding for energy efficiency through a public benefits charge, have demand-side management programmes for industry.

Energy service companies

ESCOs are entities that provide services to end-users related to the development, installation, and financing of energy efficiency improvements.

They help to overcome informational, technical, and financial barriers by providing skilled personnel and identifying financing options for the facility owners.

Financing mechanisms and incentives for industrial energy efficiency investments

The World Bank, the African Development Bank, and many UN agencies have established energy efficiency financing projects. In addition, several governments have promoted investment in industrial energy efficiency through various financial instruments such as taxes, subsidies, and programmes that improve access to capital. Also, there is the often repeated need to reduce rather than extend energy subsidies. See AfDB (a), EC (a), Afrepren (a) and Gujba et al. (2012) for descriptions of international and national financing programmes for SSA countries.

SSA research and projects

Kenya

The overall objective of this GEF project was to reduce CO_2 emissions through increased energy efficiency in Kenya's SMEs and consequently provide growth of Kenya's industrial sector. The project, which started in January 2001 under the Kenyan Ministry of Trade and Industry through the Kenyan Association of Manufacturers (KAM), aimed to remove barriers to energy efficiency in SMEs. The project evaluation found that the project laid a solid foundation for further energy efficiency activities and removed some of the barriers to increasing energy efficiency in the manufacturing sector The sustainability and replicability of the project lies in the universities being able to attract students for the courses, the capacity and willingness of KAM to support and develop the Centre for Energy Efficiency and Conservation and the Industrial Energy Efficiency Network, and for the ESCO to develop contracts with manufacturing firms (Eco, 2006).

South Africa

ArcelorMittal Saidanha Works in South Africa (an uncompetitive marginal plant in the ArcelorMittal Corporation) introduced with UNIDO funding for an energy management system along with energy systems optimisation measures in line with the international energy management standard ISO 50001. Behaviour change and process innovation have resulted in substantial energy savings, thereby contributing to plant competitiveness. Challenging the status quo, providing clear information to employees about energy efficiency, rewarding achievements, and drawing on social norms to create a focus on energy efficiency are some of the contributors to energy efficiency uptake. As this case demonstrates, behavioural insights can contribute near-term and low-cost opportunities for energy savings (Figueroa, 2015).

Nigeria

Researchers in Nigeria surveyed 13 firms in four sectors to answer the question of why energy efficiency measures, if they pay for themselves, are not being implemented. Pertinent outcomes from the study are: (i) the general level of information in Nigeria on energy efficiency was low; (ii) few companies have adequate awareness and knowledge about implementing energy efficiency projects; (iii) most companies have never carried out an external energy audit to determine areas where efficiency can be enhanced; (iv) most companies need an active policy on identifying and repairing leakages such as air, heat, and steam, through a combination of internal and external energy audits; (v) the relative low price of fuel in Nigeria, combined with the high investment costs for machines, results in long payback periods for investments in energy efficiency; (vi) despite the major problem of energy supply facing the companies, a number of them have no clear information on energy efficiency options; and (vii) finance for investment in energy efficiency is not readily available either from retained earnings or bank loans due mainly to financial crisis (Ogwumike and Aregbeyen, 2012).

Kenya and Nigeria

The challenges to the uptake of renewable energy technologies as well as adoption of energy efficiency measures are well described in a recent survey of renewable energy technology suppliers/marketers and cassava processors in Nigeria and maize processors in Kenya. The sample of firms included 62 cassava processing firms and 22 technology suppliers/markets in Nigeria, and 40 maize processing firms and 41 technology suppliers/marketers in Kenya. Two of the key findings of this survey are:

- The most influential drivers of energy efficient technology adoption are similar in both countries. The key drivers and facilitating factors for the adoption of energy efficiency measures by cassava and maize processors are in-house knowledge about energy management, the availability of technical expertise, and the desire and need to save costs.

- The major factor facilitating the sale of renewable energy technology is the unreliable and sporadic power supply in Nigeria; in Kenya, the volatility of the foreign exchange rate acts as a positive stimulus for technology deployment as changes in the exchange rate affect electricity utility costs.

The findings of the study reveal that the diffusion of energy efficiency and renewable energy technologies in Africa and other developing economies depends, to a large extent, on existing government policies and regulatory conditions. The results also confirm the notion that the market for energy efficiency and renewable technologies in Africa is relatively underdeveloped and that government policies are important because of their capacity for creating an enabling environment for the diffusion of green technologies, especially through the mobilisation of critical resources, encouragement/incentives for private sector involvement, and the facilitation of development cooperation activities (UNIDO/UNU-MERIT/KEEI, 2014).

Factors influencing energy intensity in 19 SSA countries

This study investigates the influence of firm-specific characteristics on energy intensity using a data set of 1,545 firms in 19 Sub-Saharan African countries. It finds that exporting firms, foreign ownership, firm size, and productivity are associated with lower levels of energy intensity. Surprisingly it did not find a significant association with the age of capital equipment, ownership of a generator, or our proxy for an energy management system. Lastly, it finds capital intensity, human capital, and share of fuels in total energy consumption associated with higher levels of energy intensity. The authors recommend conducting regular repeat interviews with firms in the dataset to establish a panel dataset which would allow a causal analysis and improve the possibility of deriving universal policy conclusions for greening of industry (Kaulich *et al.*, 2016).

Strategic frameworks for inclusive green economy with industrial energy efficiency components in SSA countries

- *Ethiopia Climate-Resilient Green Economy Strategy.* The vision of this strategy is to achieve middle-income status by 2025 in a climate-resilient green economy. The country plans continued rapid economic growth, expanding industrialisation and jobs but, by avoiding the conventional development pathway, Ethiopia aims to cut greenhouse gas emissions and shift to sustainable patterns of land, soil, and water management (see Box 3.3 for more information about the strategy) (Ethiopia, 2011).

- *Kenya Green Economy Strategy and Implementation Plan.* The objective of this plan is to guide the transition to a green, low-carbon, and climate-resilient economy. Scenario analysis shows that a green economy pathway delivers higher and more stable growth than business as usual. Building on Kenya Vision 2030 and the constitutional provisions of 2010, the plan promotes infrastructural investment, resilience, and sustainable livelihoods. The priorities and approach were defined through an inclusive, participatory process (Kenya, 2015). In line with the governmental plan, Kenya has implemented sustainable consumption and green production policies, and adopted green strategies under a SWITCH Africa Green project launched in 2014 by the UN Environment Programme (SWITCH Africa Green, a).
- *Mozambique Roadmap for a Green Economy.* Aimed at accelerating sustainable economic, social, and environmental development, the vision for Mozambique is to become an inclusive middle-income country by 2030, based on protection, restoration, and rational use of natural capital and its ecosystem services to guarantee development that is sustainable, inclusive, and efficient within planetary limits (AfDB, 2015).
- *Rwanda Green Growth and Climate Resilience: National Strategy for Climate Change and Low Carbon Development 2011–2050.* The vision of this plan is for Rwanda to be a developed, climate-resilient, low-carbon economy by 2050. Strategic objectives include achieving energy security and a low-carbon energy supply that supports development of green industry and services, and achieving social protection, improved health, and disaster risk reduction that reduces vulnerability to climate change (Rwanda, 2011).
- *South Africa Green Economy Accord.* This partnership was signed by organised labour organisations, community constituents, businesses, and government. It lays out 12 commitments to green the economy, including roll-out of solar water heaters and renewable energy; energy efficiency; biofuels; and waste recycling, reuse, and recovery. Other commitments relate to clean coal initiatives, electrification of poor communities, and reduction of open fire cooking and heating (South Africa, 2011). South Africa is also part of the SWITCH Africa Green Programme and has implemented its sustainable consumption, green production policies, and green national strategies (SWITCH Africa Green, a).

Low-carbon development in Sub-Saharan Africa

The Overseas Development Institute has identified 20 long-term sectoral transitions that can be undertaken to promote low-carbon development in SSA. Their review included six sectors – agriculture, forestry, energy, extractives, construction, and manufacturing – based on their importance to the productive capacity of SSA and their contribution to current and future GHG emissions. As a result of limited industrialisation in SSA, most GHG emissions are not linked to fossil fuels; rather, they are linked to agriculture and wider land use changes. The report stressed the importance of not creating technological, infrastructural, and institutional lock-in to high carbon development pathways, which include energy (electricity), transport, extractives, construction, and manufacturing. Countries need to decide in the short term if they want to avoid lock-in in these sectors.

There are three broad categories of technological options available for reducing GHG emissions from the manufacturing sector. One category encourages the use of energy efficient technologies in heavy manufacturing sector, cement, and iron and steel. In addition, a range of industries, including petro-chemicals, metal, oil refining, pulp and paper, and food processing, can improve their energy efficiency using cogeneration or combined heat and power. A second category requires changing or substituting energy sources. Switching from fossil fuels to biomass is clearly an attractive option not only for light manufacturing such as food, textiles, and wood processing, but also for heavy industry, such as cement, in some cases. Using renewable energy technology can replace back-up generators in some cases, particularly attractive if governments reduce fuel subsidies. A third category shifts the technological basis of the product mix from heavy to light manufacturing industries. Examples include waste-to-energy techniques to convert agricultural residues to fuel products, biodegradable cleaning products, and certified products from sustainable forests and manufacture of equipment for renewable energy.

A low carbon transition for the manufacturing sector implements three policy-driven scenarios. The first scenario increases the use of energy efficiency processes and technologies and clean energy in heavy manufacturing. Potential policy tools for this transition include regulatory tools such as sector-wide technical norms and standards that impose maximum emission limits and mandatory energy audits. A second scenario shifts industrial production to light manufacturing. Potential policy tools are increasing access to financing and supporting manufacturing clusters. A third scenario grows the market for low-carbon products. Potential policy tools are nation-wide energy efficiency standards for low-carbon products and tax incentives for manufacturing these products (ODI, 2015).

3.5. Energy management: renewable energy

In comparison with other regions of the world, industry in Africa is currently more focused on activities that are not energy intensive. These include wood and food processing and textiles production. Industries in Africa rely on a mix of fossil fuel and biomass. About 70% of thermal energy demand comes from coal, oil, and natural gas, whereas 30% is a mixture of biomass and waste products (IRENA, 2015).

Overcoming the insufficiencies and lack of quality in power supplies would greatly help in achieving a transformation of SSA economies. However, it would also imply a tripling of industrial energy demand in these countries from 3.5 EJ to 9.6 EJ by 2030 despite significant efficiency improvement. In 2013, modern renewable energy sources met 8% of industrial energy demand and provided 19% of electricity consumed by the industrial sector. Projections for 2030 estimate that 23% of the industry demand can be met by modern renewable energy technologies and provide 49% of electricity consumption (IRENA, 2015).

Renewable energy potential in the industrial sector

While much of the discussion on the use of renewable energy by industry has focused on its use of electricity produced off-site from renewable energy sources, this section focuses on the on-site use of renewable energy by enterprises, especially SMEs. There is significant renewable energy potential for them in the form of solar heating and cooling and agro- and wood processing residue applications. There is also potential for larger enterprises in the form of hydro and geothermal applications. These applications are briefly described next.

Solar heating and cooling applications

Solar heaters can be used to produce process heat, primarily in low- to medium-temperature ranges. Uses include the drying of goods, heating of water, and steam generation. These are all relevant applications for SSA countries, where, as we have noted, enterprises which process food or wood or produce textiles are common. It is also possible to utilise solar energy for cooling. These installations are particularly useful for the dairy industry, which require cooling for product storage.

Agro- and wood-processing residue

These residues can be used to generate electricity and heat on-site. For instance, sugarcane bagasse is widely used worldwide in this way. As elsewhere in the world, the African sugar industry has made efforts to adjust the efficiency of combustion to utilise as much as possible of the bagasse it generates and so minimise its disposal. In Mauritius and South Africa, the industry is also moving toward selling any excess electricity to the grid. Biomass residues are suitable for a range of industrial applications, providing process heat, as well as heating and cooling of industrial facilities. Food processing is one of the most developed industrial activities in Africa, with typical products including sugar, dairy, baking, beer brewing, fish smoking, tea, coffee, and cocoa, among others. These industries sometimes use traditional methods of production, which are often inefficient. The use of modern renewable energy could modernise processes and provide opportunities to add more value to their products.

Hydropower

In the past, large hydropower plants have often been designed as multi-national projects or with energy-intensive aluminium smelters as planned off-takers, including in Ghana and in Mozambique. Small hydro is suitable for connecting other industrial users to existing grids or for the provision of green electricity for industrial development in remote areas.

Geothermal

Geothermal heat could also be applied directly to industrial processes that require low-temperature heat. These processes dominate a large share of Africa's manufacturing industry, and geothermal heat is a low-cost and secure substitute for fossil fuels for a few countries.

Policies and programmes

To pursue green industrialisation, renewables also need to be further integrated into national and regional energy plans. As African countries move to develop their renewable energy potential, they are pursuing a range of policy instruments. These are mostly embedded in National Energy Plans that can include various targets for how much renewables should contribute to the energy mix. To date, 37 countries (out of 47) have introduced at least one type of renewable energy target for specific technologies or for specific sectors, as well as dedicated off-grid policies for rural electrification and sustainable cooking. Most targets are numerical, taking the form of non-binding, aspirational goals embedded in energy planning tools or at a broad policy level. Devising regional plans for renewable energy deployment and applying regional cooperation and integration can help take advantage of efficiencies and economies of scale by increasing renewable energy supply capacity; managing shared natural resources; and adopting an integrated approach of trans-boundary issues such as trade, regulatory frameworks and policies, regional infrastructure, and other cross-border issues.

Countries have adopted a wide variety of policy mechanisms to promote renewable energy – both regulatory policies and fiscal incentive. As Table 3.5 shows, the prevailing policies in Africa are fiscal incentives, including tax

Table 3.5 Support policies that have been used in Sub-Saharan Africa

	Regulatory policies							Fiscal incentives and public financing				
	Feed-in-tariff (incl. premium payment)	Electric utility quota obligation/RPS	Net metering	Tradable renewable energy certificate	Auctions	Heat obligation/Mandate	Biofuel obligation/Mandate	Capital subsidy, grant or rebate	Investment or production tax credits	Reduction in sales, energy, CO_2 VAT, or other taxes	Production payment	Public investment, loans, or grants
Angola							•					•
Benin											•	
Botswana									•	•		
Burkina Faso				•					•		•	•
Cabo Verde			•	•							•	•
Cameroon											•	
Côte d'Ivoire											•	
Ethiopia							•				•	•
Gambia											•	
Ghana	•	•		•		•	•		•		•	•
Guinea											•	
Kenya	•					•	•				•	•
Lesotho		•		•								•
Madagascar											•	
Malawi							•				•	
Mali							•				•	
Mauritius	•			•					•			
Mozambique							•					•
Niger											•	
Rwanda	•										•	•
Senegal		•			•						•	
South Africa		•	•		•		•		•		•	•
Tanzania	•				*		•				•	
Togo											•	
Uganda	•								•		•	•
Zambia							•		•			
Zimbabwe							•					

* Tanzania announced that it would be launching an auction

Source: Data for SSA countries extracted from IRENA 2015

reductions, public investments, loans, and grants. Tax reductions – the most widespread incentive – require no additional budget allocation (but a budget loss), fewer administrative procedures, and minimal regulatory supervision compared to other support policies. Several SSA countries have overcome many obstacles to adopt feed-in-tariffs, including Ghana, Kenya, and South Africa.

SSA research and projects

Nigerian tea factory

With a population of about 50,000, Kakarla's economic mainstay was the Mambilla Beverages Company. The company produces Highland Tea on its tea plantation that consists of 6,000 farms. But the tea factory itself, the only industry in the area, could only employ 350 to 500 workers. Unemployment remained a major problem in the area. The adult men and women were engaged in primitive farming and husbandry, and a lack of a good power supply meant no new businesses or industries could be established. Running on diesel generators and using wood fuelled boilers for drying, the tea factory was economically drained by the energy costs involved.

In 2013, with the support of the Government of Taraba State and funding from the United Nations High Commissioner for Refugees, the International Centre for Small Hydro Power in China and UNIDO supplied and installed electro-mechanical equipment for a small hydro-power plant with an operating capacity of 400kW. It is owned by Taraba State and managed by the Mambilla Beverages Company, supplying clean electricity to the factory and local communities.

This allowed the tea factory to look at plans to expand its production capacity, a move that is expected to provide more employment opportunities in the area. Moreover, the plant has had a profound environmental impact in the area, leading to a drastic cut in greenhouse gas emissions as the tea factory no longer uses diesel generators. A large forested area has also been preserved since clean power replaced the burning of wood to dry the tea (UNIDO, 2015).

Rwanda

Under the 'Private Sector Participation in Micro-Hydro Development Project in Rwanda', four newly registered Rwandan companies are each constructing a micro-hydro plant (100–500 kW) and building a low-voltage distribution grid. These companies financed their plants in part through their own equity and debt with support from the PSP Hydro project. This support comprised a subsidy of 30–50% of investment costs, technical and business development assistance, project monitoring, and financial controlling. The experiences gained so far have important implications for similar future micro-hydro energy sector development projects: (i) institutional arrangements rather than technical quality determine the success of such projects; (ii) truly sustainable rural electrification through micro-hydro development demands a high level of local participation at all levels and throughout all project phases, not just after plant commissioning; and (iii) real impact and sustainability can be obtained through close collaboration of local private and financial sector firms requiring only limited external funds. In short, micro-hydro projects can and will be taken up by local investors as a business if the conditions are right. Applying these messages could result in an accelerated uptake of viable micro-hydro activities in Rwanda, and in the opinion of the authors elsewhere too (Pigaht and Van der Plas, 2009).

Jobs in renewable energy

According to a recent study (Cantore *et al.*, 2017), a transition towards low carbon power generation in Africa would lead to additional jobs, but with a potential trade-off in terms of electricity generation costs. Energy savings do not always compensate for a higher cost of renewable energy (RE). From a societal perspective, the results of the study are quite robust and indicate that policy actions for a higher penetration of RE and energy efficiency (EE) generate a social dividend in terms of additional employment together with lower costs of generation per additional employee. Higher costs of renewable energy and employment creation may affect this positive prospect. The study adds an additional insight into the debate on the desirability of RE and EE for economic, social, and environmental sustainability in low/middle income countries. The results of this study reveal that if RE becomes competitive with fossil fuels and simultaneously technologies for EE become less expensive, there is a potential for positive impacts on all three pillars of sustainable development. If costs were to decrease slowly, the higher bill for RE and EE could be compensated by reduced impaired health impacts and may make cost-effective contributions to unemployment reduction in terms of societal costs. From a policy perspective, these results suggest justification for a fuller integration of green technologies beyond the traditional boundaries of environmental policy.

3.6. Industrial chemicals management

Introduction

Because of their unique capability of interacting with biological organisms by disrupting their biochemical pathways, chemicals have been the subject of regulatory oversight for many decades. Thus, pharmaceutical chemicals have been the object of regulatory regimes since at least the beginning of the 20th century, as have psychoactive chemicals. Chemicals used in weaponry have been under regulation since their use in the First World War. Radioactive chemicals have been regulated since their use in the Second World War. Pesticides and industrial chemicals have been regulated since the late 1960s when their environmental impacts became apparent.

Certain chemicals can also be a hazard to human health and the environment through their ability to explode or burn easily. Chemicals with explosive or flammable properties have been the object of regulation since the late 19th century. Only 'industrial chemicals' will be considered in this section, recognising that separate regulatory regimes exist everywhere for pharmaceutical and psychoactive chemicals, radioactive substances, and chemicals used in weaponry, while agricultural chemicals also often have their own regulatory regimes. Mirroring these distinctions, the government authorities regulating industrial chemicals are often different from those regulating these other categories of chemicals.

Policies and programmes to manage industrial chemicals

As with other aspects of industrial environmental management, the various instruments for the control of industrial chemicals can be grouped into one of four approaches: (i) command-and-control regulation; (ii) transparency and disclosure measures; (iii) market-based instruments/economic incentives; and (iv) voluntary actions.

Command-and-control regulation

These measures have dominated the menu of instruments in use for the environmental management of industrial chemicals. When evidence of the environmental impacts of industrial chemicals began to appear in the 1960s, the initial government response, in large part following the example of the instruments already used to control chemical products used as pharmaceuticals, was to use command-and-control instruments. Thus, standards were introduced which limited the presence of specific chemicals in the wastewaters or air emissions released from certain industrial sectors (see, e.g., US EPA, a). For further discussion of wastewater and air emissions standards, see Section 3.2 on Pollution Control Instruments. In certain cases, where the risks posed to the environment were considered great enough, national bans or severe restrictions were imposed. This happened in the case of several organochlorine pesticides (dichlorodiphenyltrichloroethane (DDT) and others), polychlorinated biphenyls (PCBs), lead when used in gasoline, and a few other industrial chemicals. Very quickly, it became apparent that many of these chemicals posed a global threat because of their persistence in the environment and/or their ability to migrate long distances. By 1973, the first international control instrument for a specific chemical family was in place, a Decision-Recommendation by the OECD countries to severely restrict the use of PCBs in their countries (OECD, 1987). This has been followed over the decades by a number of UN multilateral conventions whose aim is to eliminate or severely restrict the use of specific chemicals or families of chemicals which pose a global environmental threat: the Montreal Protocol on Substances that Deplete the Ozone Layer (entered into force in 1989) (UN, a), the Stockholm Convention on Persistent Organic Pollutants (entered into force in 2004) (UN, b), and most recently, the Minamata Convention on Mercury (entered into force in August 2017) (UN, c).

It also quickly became apparent that there was little data available on many if not most of the chemicals in commercial use upon which to make a reasoned judgment of the effects of these chemicals on human health and the environment. UNEP has estimated that 150,000–200,000 chemicals are currently traded globally. In addition, new chemicals continuously enter the market; in the US alone, some 700 new chemicals are introduced into the market every year. Worldwide, the chemicals industry produces about 1 billion tonnes of basic organic and inorganic chemicals per year. These are then transformed into the hundreds of thousands of other chemicals produced for the market. Even today, 40 years after the problem was recognised, there is little or no information available on the effects of many commercial chemicals on human health and the environment. UNEP has estimated that only a fraction of the hundreds of thousands of chemicals on the market have ever been thoroughly evaluated to determine their effects on human health and the environment. In 2013, of 2,500 high-production-volume chemicals in EU, only 14% had sufficient data to comply with the basic requirements in the EU's Dangerous Substances Directive; 65% had incomplete data; 21% had no data at all. In another study in the US focusing on 3,000 substances sold above 450 tonnes/year, a comparison of the data available on these substances with the OECD's minimum data set showed that only 7% had all these data, while 43% had no data at all. UNEP concludes that "it is reasonable to assume that even less information is available on lower-volume substances" (UNEP, 2013).

Governments have reacted to this situation in broadly similar ways by placing on companies (to a greater or lesser degree) the burden of collecting and presenting to the authorities data and information on the toxicological and environmental effects of the chemicals which they are planning to manufacture, import, or use (so-called 'new chemicals'), and now more on those chemicals which they already manufacture and/or import and/or use (so-called 'existing chemicals'). On the basis of the information submitted, the authorities can decide to impose controls of greater or lesser severity, and even bans, on these chemicals. While legislation to this effect was first introduced in the then-industrialised countries (see, e.g., US EPA, b; EC, b; CIRS, a; ECCC, a; ADH, a), similar legislation has been introduced over the years, or is in the process of being introduced, in a number of other countries (see, e.g., CIRS, b; CIRS, c; Chemcon Daily, 2012; NLR, 2016). In parallel, the testing of chemicals for their toxicological and eco-toxicological effects has been standardised, primarily through the work of the OECD, whose guidelines are now accepted worldwide (OECD, a). This has greatly aided in the mutual acceptance of data between countries, an important concern given the fact that chemicals are widely traded.

A number of governments have also enacted rules governing the way in which chemicals are managed along the chain from their production to their use (e.g., the manner in which chemicals are stored, design specifications for equipment holding them, etc.), the manner in which spills are to be handled, design specifications for vehicles transporting chemicals, the special licenses or other certifications which drivers of such vehicles are required to have, and the routes which these vehicles are required to take.

The explosivity and flammability of certain classes of chemicals (especially petrochemical products and explosives, but also certain products like ammonium nitrate fertiliser) have meant that governments have had laws in place regulating the processing, storage, and transport of such chemicals since at least the end of the 19th century. Since the Seveso disaster in 1976, the Bhopal disaster in 1984, the Sandoz disaster in 1986, and other such disasters where exposure to toxic chemicals was the main occurrence rather than explosion and fire, governments have also focused on events leading to the massive release of toxic industrial chemicals. Many governments have now enacted legislation whose aim is prevention, preparation, and response: the legislation requires companies to adopt management approaches which prevent industrial disasters, but which also prepare them for any such disasters so as to respond to them correctly (together with the relevant public authorities) should the latter ever occur. The EU's Seveso Directive is perhaps the best known in this category of legislation (EC, c).

Ever since the first multilateral environmental agreements on the control of specific chemicals were adopted (these were mentioned earlier), chemicals have been the subject of numerous global agreements. The latest such case is the SDGs, where a number of targets focus specifically on minimising the impacts of chemicals on human health and the environment (goal 3, target 9; goal 6, target 3; goal 12, target 4). In 2006, the international community adopted the Strategic Approach to International Chemicals Management (SAICM). SAICM is a policy framework and plan of action whose aim is to guide efforts by countries to ensure that by 2020 chemicals will be produced and used in ways that minimise their impacts on human health and the environment (SAICM, a). It is administered by UNEP.

Transparency and disclosure measures

These measures have also seen strong use as instruments for the environmental management of industrial chemicals. In particular, governments have enacted many regulations requiring labelling of chemical products or products containing chemicals, to alert users (from factory workers all the way to end-use consumers) to the potential chemical hazards they are facing from using those products. Labelling is now generally standardised through the Globally Harmonized System of Classification and Labelling of Chemicals administered by the UN Economic Commission for Europe (UNECE) (UN, 2011). In addition, many countries require chemical products or products containing chemicals to be accompanied by Material Safety Data Sheets (MSDSs), the purpose of which is to give more detailed information to workers and others handling these products in the workplace. UNECE also gives detailed guidance on the preparation of MSDSs. Some governments also have regulations requiring companies to report periodically on various aspects of their use of chemicals.

Because international trade in chemicals is so important, and recognising that the governments of developing countries in particular might not be in the position to appreciate the hazardousness or toxicity of chemicals which are being imported into their country, the Rotterdam Convention ('Rotterdam Convention on the Prior Informed Consent Procedure for Certain Hazardous Chemicals and Pesticides in International Trade') was adopted in 1998; it came into force in 2004. The Convention focuses on the international trade of industrial chemicals and pesticides which have been banned or severely restricted. The parties to the Convention have drawn up a list of such chemicals. Governments have the right to decide if they wish to allow the import of these chemicals, or allow it under certain specified conditions, or not allow it at all. In addition, in cases where a country party to the Convention has banned or severely restricted a chemical that is not on the Convention's list, the government has to inform the government of the importing country of that fact; the latter can decide if it wishes to allow the import and if so, under what conditions (UN, d).

Market-based instruments/economic incentives

Economic instruments have had much less weight to date in the menu of instruments used for the environmental management of industrial chemicals. There are some isolated examples of taxes on certain classes of chemicals (e.g., the use in Nordic countries of taxes on pesticides) (IEEP, 2016). Green Public Procurement is also used by some governments in their purchase of chemical-containing products such as cleaning products, to prioritise their purchase of products with less or no toxic chemicals in them (see, e.g., the EU's Green Public Procurement programme (EC, d)).

Voluntary measures

Companies have also used voluntary measures to control the chemicals they use. However, since the approaches they have adopted are not specific to chemicals but are used for general environmental management, readers are referred to Section 3.2 on Pollution Control Instruments for a discussion of these approaches.

SSA research and reports

Despite a number of SSA countries having the basic raw material for a modern chemicals industry – oil, and to a lesser degree, natural gas – there is relatively little production of chemicals in SSA. The one exception is South Africa, where chemicals are responsible for about 25% of the country's manufacturing sales (KPMG, a). This means that the majority of the SSA countries' demand for chemical products is met through import. The potential future growth of the SSA countries suggests that there will be an increasing demand for chemical products in the future.

The status of the control and management of chemicals in Africa was the subject of a report by the UN Economic Commission for Africa (UNECA, 2009). Its conclusions are quoted here verbatim:

> Legislation on chemicals management is still new in most of the countries, and proper coordination of the National Action Plans is lacking in various government departments.
>
> This is further constrained by lack of adequate information to chemical users and poor enforcement.
>
> There are no specific policies on chemicals management to ensure recognition of chemicals management as a national priority, and mainstreaming into national development plans and strategies such as National Strategies for Growth and Reduction of Poverty. Similarly, there is low awareness on the health and environmental effects of chemicals, particularly the long-term effects.
>
> Subsequently, there are limited institutional capacities and capabilities such as poison centres, a reporting system on chemical incidences and a comprehensive inventory of obsolete pesticides and other chemical wastes, to reduce the environmental and health effects of hazardous chemicals and wastes.
>
> There is limited participation of the private sector and civil society in government decision-making with regard to issues of chemicals management.
>
> There is no comprehensive national data on chemicals or adequate monitoring programmes of chemical residues in the environment and human health.
>
> Above all, there is an overlap in the existing legislation, causing conflicting functions and interest, competing priorities in the different sectors, low level of awareness on issues related to chemical management among stakeholders and the general public.
>
> Lastly, funding of chemicals management related programmes and activities is inadequate.

The SAICM process mentioned earlier is in part a process through which African (and other developing) countries can build up the knowledge, awareness, and capacities required to fill the gaps identified by UNECA, and SSA countries are well represented among the countries accessing the technical assistance funds made available through SAICM's Quick Start Programme (QSP). Thirty-five countries from SSA have completed or have ongoing QSP projects (SAICM, 2015). That being said, there is no clear upward trend in chemicals controls in the SSA countries.

As part of the SAICM process, the SAICM Secretariat has prepared a baseline report, which are to be followed by periodic progress reports: three such progress reports, covering the periods 2009–2010 (SAICM, 2012), 2011–2013 (SAICM, 2014), and 2014–2016 (SAICM, 2019), have been prepared to date. The reports are based on voluntary responses by the SAICM stakeholders to a questionnaire, so not all stakeholders have reported. The progress reports do not give the results on individual countries, and the same countries, especially African countries, did not necessarily report in all progress reports, making comparisons difficult. Nevertheless, it is possible to perceive trends on what is happening in SSA countries. It would seem that the situation has not much changed since the report by UNECA was published.

3.7. Hazardous waste management

Introduction

To properly understand the regulatory regimes for hazardous wastes, it is first necessary to consider a core element in all waste regulatory regimes: the categorisation of wastes. Categorisation is important because the level of care required for the management of specific wastes depends on it. At the highest level, many regulatory regimes distinguish between wastes generated by the productive sector (normally termed 'industrial waste') and those generated by households (normally termed 'domestic waste', 'household waste', or 'urban waste'). Industrial wastes are generally held to a higher standard of care than wastes from households, even though the waste streams generated can be quite similar (this is the case for packaging wastes, for instance). Wastes from the commercial sector (shops, the service sector, etc.) can fall into either one of these categories, or can be considered a separate category altogether.

Within these broad categories, most regulatory regimes draw finer distinctions. In particular, an important criterion for determining more precisely the level of regulatory control and oversight required for specific waste streams is their toxicity or hazard, with much stronger regulatory controls being adopted in the case of wastes which are strongly hazardous or toxic. This is particularly important for industrial wastes; the generation of hazardous wastes is common in industry. With respect to such wastes, many regulatory regimes rely on an inventory system to categorise wastes as hazardous or not. Here, certain waste streams which are generated by specific industrial sectors are de facto categorised as hazardous/toxic because of their known impacts on human health and the environment. In addition to this inventory system, some regulatory regimes also categorise wastes as hazardous or not based on the amounts or concentrations of certain specified hazardous or toxic chemicals which they contain; these kinds of categorisations will not be sector-specific as in the case of the inventory system.

Although certain types of household wastes or commercial wastes can also be toxic or hazardous (car batteries are an example), and are subject to stricter regulatory control than normal household wastes or commercial wastes, the vast majority of hazardous wastes are industrial in origin. Therefore, the rest of this section will focus on the instruments used to control hazardous industrial wastes. Where the term 'hazardous waste' is used, it should be understood to relate to hazardous industrial wastes only.

Policy instruments

Very often, industrial wastes are hazardous or toxic because of the chemicals which these wastes contain, which means that there is generally a close relationship between regulatory regimes controlling chemicals and those controlling hazardous wastes. As in the case of industrial chemicals, the various policy instruments for the control of hazardous wastes can be grouped into one of four approaches: (i) command-and-control regulations; (ii) market-based instruments/economic incentives; (iii) voluntary measures; and (iv) transparency and disclosure measures.

Command-and-control regulations

These measures have dominated the menu of instruments in use for the environmental management of hazardous wastes. The purpose of most regulatory regimes has been to ensure that such wastes are managed in a manner which minimises their impacts on human health and the environment. This has primarily meant that regulatory regimes have focused on ensuring (i) that the wastes are sent to companies which have the proper facilities for treating and/or disposing of the wastes, (ii) that the wastes are transported to these companies by companies which have the proper vehicles to do so, and (iii) that a chain of custody exists between the original waste generator and the final recycler, treater, or disposer. Regulators have therefore put in place an authorisation system, requiring that any company wishing to transport, treat, dispose, and in some cases recycle hazardous wastes has to first receive an authorisation from the regulatory authorities permitting it to conduct this type of business. They have also put in place a series of standards on the air emissions, wastewater streams, and wastes generated by treatment and disposal activities, and – especially in the case of landfills – have heavily regulated the design and operations of these activities (in countries with Environmental Impact Assessment [EIA] and planning requirements for industrial activities, waste treatment, and disposal facilities are also almost always subject to these requirements). Finally, regulators have put in place a chain of custody system (often called a manifest system), which tracks a hazardous wastes as they pass down the chain from waste generator to transporter to treater/disposer and can alert regulators if a waste does not reach its planned destination. (It should be noted that many regulatory regimes apply a similar system of authorisation, treatment, and disposal standards and chain of custody arrangements for non-hazardous industrial wastes, and even household wastes, although generally the requirements are not so strict.)

In many regulatory regimes, the reuse or recycling of hazardous wastes is subject to somewhat less strict supervision. The legislators' intent has been to encourage reuse and recycling over other waste management options like treatment and disposal by making them easier and therefore less costly. However, there has always been a tension in regulatory regimes about how much laxer the controls on reuse and recycling should be. While it is true that these methods of waste management should be encouraged over other waste management options, unfortunately 'recycling' and 'reuse' have often be used as a cover for activities where there was little if any recycling or reuse taking place, and recyclers have caused some significant environmental damage by not carrying out their recycling/reuse activities in a manner which properly safeguarded human health and the environment. This regulatory tension particularly affects hazardous wastes such as industrial solvents, which are recyclable but which, if not recycled properly, can cause significant harm to human health and the environment.

Since industrial wastes, both hazardous and non-hazardous, are traded internationally, in some cases for recycling (e.g., steel scrap), and in other cases for treatment and disposal; and since cases came to light where hazardous wastes in particular were essentially being dumped in countries which had neither the facilities to deal with such wastes nor the necessary regulatory oversight, the Basel Convention (full name: Basel Convention on the Control of Transboundary Movements of Hazardous Wastes and their Disposal) was adopted in 1989 and came into force in 1992. The Convention focuses on the international trade in hazardous wastes and certain other types of waste streams ('other wastes'). The parties to the Convention have drawn up a list of hazardous wastes and other wastes. Governments which are party to the Convention have the right to prohibit the import of some or all of these hazardous wastes and other wastes. Furthermore, if countries have categorised wastes as hazardous but these are not on the Convention's list, before the export of these wastes can take place the government of the exporting country must notify the governments of the importing country and countries of transit. The trade can only take place if and when all the governments concerned have given their written consent (Basel Convention, a).

The countries of Africa followed up on the Basel Convention with the Bamako Convention (full name: Bamako Convention on the Ban on the Import into Africa and the Control of Transboundary Movement and Management of Hazardous Wastes within Africa) (UN Environment, a). The Convention was adopted in 1991 and came into force in 1998. Currently, it has 29 signatories and 25 Parties. The African countries felt the need for an additional Convention because the Basel Convention failed to prohibit trade of hazardous waste to developing countries, which was leading to many developed countries exporting their toxic wastes to Africa. The format and language used in the Bamako Convention is similar to that of the Basel Convention, but is much stronger in prohibiting all imports of hazardous waste. Additionally, unlike the Basel Convention, it includes radioactive wastes. The purpose of the Convention is to

- prohibit the import of all hazardous and radioactive wastes into the African continent for any reason;
- minimise and control transboundary movements of hazardous wastes within the African continent;
- prohibit all ocean and inland water dumping or incineration of hazardous wastes;
- ensure that disposal of wastes is conducted in an environmentally sound manner;
- promote cleaner production over the pursuit of a permissible emissions approach based on assimilative capacity assumptions;
- establish the precautionary principle.

Market-based instruments/economic incentives

Economic incentives have primarily played an indirect role in the management of hazardous wastes. The regulatory regimes described previously have resulted in the treatment and disposal of hazardous wastes becoming a significant cost for the waste generators, thus increasing the economic viability of not generating the wastes in the first place. It should be noted, however, that the increase in the costs of managing hazardous wastes in the developed countries has also been the driving force behind the export of hazardous wastes to developing countries – notably in Africa – where regulatory regimes are much laxer or even non-existent.

Research conducted in the 1980s and 1990s, for instance, showed that the average disposal costs for one tonne of hazardous wastes in developed countries ranged between USD 200 and 3,000, while in Africa the range was between USD 2.50 and 50 (Ajibo, 2016). Clearly, such disparities in costs will drive hazardous waste exports, and it was in reaction to this pressure that the Bamako Convention was drawn up, prohibiting the export to Africa of hazardous wastes.

More direct economic incentives exist in some countries, where companies can benefit from grants, subsidies, and exemptions or reductions in import duties for cleaner, less waste-generating technologies. Such incentives encourage them to invest in such technologies.

Voluntary measures

Many of the national laws governing industrial waste state that the priority is to prevent or minimise the generation of waste in the first place. This is echoed in the Basel Convention. However, almost never has prevention or minimisation of waste (or indeed any other form of pollution) been the subject of command-and-control measures prescribing it. One exception is China's Cleaner Production Law, which requires companies to undertake cleaner production (pollution prevention) assessments under certain circumstances (State Council, a). However, the law is not considered to have been terribly successful. The consensus seems to be that companies cannot be forced to be more efficient or reduce their waste and pollution generation. They must instead be encouraged to do so through programmes which support them in their efforts. This has been the driving principle behind the establishment of nearly all cleaner production centres or similar such centres.

Companies have also used their own voluntary measures to control the wastes they generate. However, since the approaches they have used are not specific to wastes but are used for general environmental management, readers are referred to Section 3.2 on Pollution Control Instruments for a discussion of these approaches.

Transparency and disclosure measures

These measures have also been heavily used as instruments for the environmental management of industrial wastes and hazardous industrial wastes in particular. Governments have enacted many regulations requiring labelling of hazardous (and other) industrial wastes to ensure that these wastes are properly managed as they move from the point of generation to the point of recycling, treatment, or disposal.

SSA research and reports

Regulatory programmes for hazardous waste have been tracked to some degree by the Basel Convention Secretariat. Countries are required to report annually through an online electronic questionnaire on the status of their hazardous waste management in relation to the Convention; the latest of these submissions available online is for 2017 (Basel Convention, b). From these individual country reports, the Secretariat has compiled various annual status reports summarising the information received between 1997 and 2011 (Basel Convention, c). From a review of the latest status reports for 2009 to 2011, which include 16 of the SSA countries, one can deduce an important trend with respect to hazardous waste definitions; as we have seen, this is a key starting point in regulatory regimes for hazardous wastes. Many SSA countries seem to have quite generic definitions of what constitutes a hazardous waste, which would be difficult to apply to concrete waste generation situations. Another trend has to do with the existence of authorised (i.e., formal) facilities which are appropriately designed and operated to recycle, treat, or dispose of hazardous wastes. The latest information available online from the Basel Secretariat (from the 2015 to 2017 reports) gives a broad snapshot of the existence of such facilities in the SSA countries. The information is summarised in Table 3.6. Of the 16 SSA countries which have responded during these three reporting years to the question on the existence of such facilities, 14 have said that they have one or more facilities treating waste streams listed as hazardous in the Basel Convention.

The most common are facilities treating and recycling used oils as well as incinerators burning hospital and medical wastes. South Africa dominates the picture, having by far the greatest number of facilities listed as recycling, treating, or disposing of hazardous wastes. Thus, the picture which emerges is one where, with the notable exception of South Africa, the management of hazardous wastes is still in its early stages in the SSA countries. It is important to remember that these data relate to authorised facilities, i.e., facilities in the formal sector. Much waste is processed in the informal sector in SSA countries with little if any health and environmental safeguards; some of these will be hazardous (e.g., waste electrical and electronic equipment [WEEE], lead acid batteries). Finally, there were some anomalous responses. For instance, Equatorial Guinea reported having three specially engineered landfills, more even than South Africa. Text accompanying the response suggests that they are receiving hazardous wastes from elsewhere. The same is true for the response from Burundi, which reports treating certain waste streams such as waste batteries in plants with very large capacities and which

Table 3.6 SSA countries with one or more facilities to manage hazardous waste streams

Country	Hazardous waste stream									
	Used oils	Medical wastes	Lead acid batteries	Paint wastes	Heavy metal wastes	Insecticides	Haz saste disposal	Energy recovery	WEEE	Haz. waste incineration
Burundi				x	x	x				
Congo, Republic of								x		
Equatorial Guinea							x			
Eritrea	x									
Eswatini		x								
Ethiopia		x								
Madagascar	x									
Mauritius	x						x			
Mozambique			x				x			
Nigeria		x								
Rwanda		x	x							x
Senegal	x									
South Africa	x	x	x		x		x		x	
Togo	x	x								x

Source: Data extracted from Basel Convention, b

are in addition reported as receiving imported wastes. This raises some questions about the actual implementation of the Bamako Convention, which, as was noted earlier, prohibits the import of all hazardous wastes into Africa for whatever reason.

Notes

1 In terms of ambient water quality standards, there has been an attempt to relate discharges to ambient conditions with concentration-based NEQS that vary by three water body types. Further categorisation of water body types is needed to reflect water use and consumption patterns (e.g., drinking, bathing, industrial, or agricultural use).

2 There are several definitions of corporate social responsibility from such organisations as the World Business Council for Sustainable Development, the European Commission, and Business for Social Responsibility. The European Commission defines it as "being socially responsible means not only fulfilling legal expectations, but also going beyond compliance and investing more in human capital, the environment and relations with stakeholders" (EC, 2001).

3 Not all product labels are voluntary, such as those mandated by governments for chemicals.

4 The term AKOBEN has its roots in Ghana's tradition of Adinkra symbols. AKOBEN stands for vigilance and wariness. It also signifies alertness and readiness to serve a good cause.

References

ADH (a). *Industrial Chemicals (Notification and Assessment) Regulations 1990.* Australian Department of Health. Retrieved from: www.legislation.gov.au/Details/F2019C0 0351. Last accessed: 26.07.2019.

AfDB (2015). *Transition towards Green Growth in Mozambique: Policy Review and Recommendations for Action.* African Development Bank. Abidjan. Retrieved from: www.afdb.org/fileadmin/uploads/afdb/Documents/Generic-Documents/Transition_ Towards_Green_Growth_in_Mozambique_-_Policy_Review_and_Recommen- dations_for_Action.pdf. Last accessed: 13.08.2019.

AfDB (a). *Sustainable Energy Fund for Africa.* African Development Bank. Abidjan. Retrieved from: www.afdb.org/en/topics-and-sectors/initiatives-partnerships/ sustainable-energy-fund-for-africa/. Last accessed: 13.08.2019.

Afrepren (a). *Energy News.* Energy, Environment and Development Network for Africa Website. Retrieved from: www.afrepren.org/news.htm. Last accessed: 13.08. 2019.

Ajibo, K. (2016). Transboundary hazardous wastes and environmental justice: Implications for economically developing countries. *Environmental Law Review,* 18:4:267–283.

Apeaning, R., Thollander, P. (2013). Barriers to and driving forces for industrial energy efficiency improvements in African industries: A case study of Ghana's largest industrial area. *Journal of Cleaner Production,* 53:204–213.

Basel Convention (a). *Basel Convention Web-Page*. Overview of the Convention, to Be Found at Basel Convention > the Convention > Overview. Retrieved from: www.basel.int/TheConvention/Overview/tabid/1271/Default.aspx. Last accessed: 28.07.2019.

Basel Convention (b). *Basel Convention Web-Page*. Basel Convention National Reports: Year 2017, to Be Found at Basel Convention > Countries > National Reporting > National Reports > BC 2017 Reports. Retrieved from: www.basel.int/Countries/NationalReporting/NationalReports/BC2017Reports/tabid/7749/Default.aspx. Last accessed: 29.07.2019.

Basel Convention (c). *Basel Convention Web-Page*. Status of National Reporting, to Be Found at Basel Convention > Countries > National Reporting > Status & Compilations. Retrieved from: www.basel.int/Countries/NationalReporting/StatusCompilations/tabid/1497/Default.aspx. Last accessed: 28.07.2019.

Bello, O., Inyinbor, A., Dada, A., Oluyori, P. (2013). Impact of Nigerian textile industry on economy and environment: A review. *International Journal of Basic and Applied Sciences*, 13:1:98–106.

Cantore, N., Nussbaumer, P., Wei, M., Kammen, D. (2017). Promoting renewable energy and energy efficiency in Africa: A framework to evaluate employment generation and cost effectiveness. *Environmental Research: Letters*. 12. 035008. Retrieved from: http://iopscience.iop.org/article/10.1088/1748-9326/aa51da/pdf. Last accessed: 13.08.2019.

Chemcon Daily (2012). Mexico's first national chemicals inventory. Retrieved from: https://chemicalwatch.com/downloads/ChemConDaily/12us_chemcon_daily3.pdf. Last accessed: 26.07.2019.

China (a). *Law of the People's Republic of China on Promotion of Cleaner Production (Order of the President No.72)*. State Council. Retrieved from: www.gov.cn/english/laws/2005-10/08/content_75059.htm. Last accessed: 28.07.2019.

CIRS (a). *New Japan Chemical Substances Control Law (CSCL)*. Chemical Inspection and Regulation Service. English summary. Retrieved from: www.cirs-reach.com/Japan_CSCL/New_Japan_Chemical_Substances_Control_Law_CSCL.html. Last accessed: 26.07.2019.

CIRS (b). *Korean Toxic Chemicals Control Act (TCCA)*. English summary. Chemicals Inspection and Regulation Service. Retrieved from: www.cirs-reach.com/KoreaTCCA/Korea_Toxic_Chemicals_Control_Act_TCCA.html. Last accessed: 26.07.2019.

CIRS (c). *New Chemical Substance Notification in China: China REACH*. Chemical Inspection and Regulation Service. English summary. Retrieved from: www.cirs-reach.com/China_Chemical_Regulation/China_REACH_Typical_Notification.pdf. Last accessed: 26.07.2019.

de la Rue du Can, S., Letschert, V., Leventis, G., Covary, T., Xia, P. (2013). *Energy Efficiency Country Study: Republic of South Africa*. LBNL Report 6365E. August. Ernest Orlando Lawrence Berkeley National Laboratory. Retrieved from: https://ies.lbl.gov/sites/all/files/south_africa_country_study_lbnl_report_final_0.pdf. Last accessed: 13.08.2019.

DOE (2016). Post-2015 National Energy Efficiency Strategy. Department of Energy, Republic of South Africa. Draft Version 1.2 (September 2016). Retrieved from:

https://cer.org.za/wp-content/uploads/2017/01/National-Energy-Efficiency-Strategy.pdf. Last accessed: 11.03.2020.

EC (2001). *Green Paper: Promoting a European Framework for Corporate Social Responsibility.* COM (2001) 366 final. European Commission. Brussels. Retrieved from: https://ec.europa.eu/transparency/regdoc/rep/1/2001/EN/1-2001-366-EN-1-0.pdf. Last accessed: 13.08.2019.

EC (a). *Financing Energy Efficiency and Renewable Energy Investments of Private Companies.* Project ID: ITF-57. European Commission. Brussels. Retrieved from: https://ec.europa.eu/europeaid/node/78771. Last accessed: 13.08.2019.

EC (b). *Regulation (EC) No 1907/2006 of the European Parliament and of the Council of 18 December 2006 Concerning the Registration, Evaluation, Authorisation and Restriction of Chemicals (REACH), Establishing a European Chemicals Agency, Amending Directive 1999/45/EC and Repealing Council Regulation (EEC) No 793/93 and Commission Regulation (EC) No 1488/94 as Well as Council Directive 76/769/EEC and Commission Directives 91/155/EEC, 93/67/EEC, 93/105/EC and 2000/21/EC.* European Commission. Retrieved from: https://eur-lex.europa.eu/legal-content/EN/TXT/?uri=CELEX:32006R1907. Last accessed: 26.07.2019.

EC (c). *Directive 2012/18/EU of the European Parliament and of the Council of 4 July 2012 on the Control of Major-Accident Hazards Involving Dangerous Substances, Amending and Subsequently Repealing Council Directive 96/82/EC Text with EEA Relevance.* European Commission. Retrieved from: https://eur-lex.europa.eu/legal-content/EN/TXT/?uri=CELEX:32012L0018. Last accessed: 26.07.2019.

EC (d). *Green Procurement.* European Commission. Retrieved from: http://ec.europa.eu/environment/gpp/index_en.htm. Last accessed: 26.07.2019.

ECCC (a). *Current Regulations: New Substances Notification Regulations (Chemicals and Polymers) (SOR/2005-247).* Environment & Climate Change Canada. Retrieved from: www.ec.gc.ca/lcpe-cepa/eng/regulations/detailReg.cfm?intReg=92. Last accessed: 26.07.2019.

Eco (2006). *Final Evaluation of the UNDP-GEF Project: Removal of Barriers to Energy Efficiency and Conservation in Small and Medium Enterprises in Kenya (KEN/98/G31, KEN/98/031), "GEF-KAM Industrial Energy Efficiency Project".* 10 November. Retrieved from: www.thegef.org/sites/default/files/project_documents/573%2520PIMS%2520874%2520-%2520KENYA%2520TE_0.pdf. Last accessed: 13.08.2019.

Ethiopia (2011). *Climate Resilient Green Economy: Green Economy Strategy.* Federal Democratic Republic of Ethiopia. Addis Ababa. Retrieved from: www.adaptation-undp.org/sites/default/files/downloads/ethiopia_climate_resilient_green_economy_strategy.pdf. Last accessed: 14.08.2019.

Figueroa, A. (2015). Industrial energy efficiency in South Africa: Challenging the status quo with behavioural change and process innovation. *The Human Factor in Energy Efficiency: Lessons from Developing Countries.* DIE (Deutsches Institut für Entwicklungspolitik). Bonn. Retrieved from: www.die-gdi.de/uploads/media/The_Human_Factor_in_Energy_Efficiency_FINAL_LOW_RES.pdf. Last accessed: 13.08.2014.

Ghana (1999). *Environmental Sanitation Policy.* May. Ministry of Local Government and Rural Development, Government of Ghana. Retrieved from: http://extwprlegs1.fao.org/docs/pdf/gha170015.pdf. Last accessed: 13.08.2019.

GTZ/UNEP/Wuppertal (2006). *Policy Instruments for Resource Efficiency: Towards Sustainable Consumption and Production*. August. Deutsche Gesellschaft für Technische Zusammenarbeit GmbH, United Nations Environment Programme/Wuppertal Institute Collaborating Centre on Sustainable Consumption and Production. Retrieved from: www.iclei.org.br/polics/CD/P2_1_Referencias/8_Instrumentos %20de%20Pol%C3%ADtica%20P%C3%BAblica/PDF35_GTZ-CSCP-Policy InstrumentsResourceEfficiency.pdf. Last accessed: 13.08.2019.

Gujba, H., Thorne, S., Mulugetta, Y., Rai, K., Sokona, Y. (2012). Financing low carbon energy access in Africa. *Energy Policy*, 47:1:71–78.

Hettige, A., Martin, P., Singh, M., Wheeler, D. (1995). *The Industrial Pollution Projection System*. Policy Research Working Paper 1431. March. The World Bank. Washington, DC. Retrieved from: http://documents.worldbank.org/curated/en/69088 1468761745598/pdf/multi-page.pdf. Last accessed: 13.08.2019.

IEA (2014). *Africa Energy Outlook: A Focus on Energy Prospects in Sub-Saharan Africa*. International Energy Agency. Paris. Retrieved from: www.iea.org/publications/ freepublications/publication/WEO2014_AfricaEnergyOutlook.pdf. Last accessed: 13.08.2019.

IEEP (2016). *Branth Pedersen, A: Pesticide Tax in Denmark*. Aarhus University-DCE, Institute for European Environmental Policy. December. Retrieved from: https:// ieep.eu/uploads/articles/attachments/504788d7-db01-4dd8-bece-ee7b9e63979e/ DK%20Pesticide%20Tax%20final.pdf?v=63680923242. Last accessed: 26.07.2019.

IRENA (2015). *Africa 2030: Roadmap for a Renewable Energy Future*. October. International Renewable Energy Agency. Bonn. Retrieved from: www.irena.org/ publications/2015/Oct/Africa-2030-Roadmap-for-a-Renewable-Energy-Future. Last accessed: 13.08.2019.

ISO (a). *ISO 14000 Family: Environmental Management: ISO Website*. International Organization for Standardization. Geneva. Retrieved from: www.iso.org/iso-14001-environmental-management.html. Last accessed: 13.08.2019.

Japan (2015). *Top Runner Programme: Developing the World's Best Energy Efficient Appliance and More*. March. Ministry of Economy, Trade and Industry & Agency for Natural Resources and Energy. Retrieved from: www.enecho.meti.go.jp/category/ saving_and_new/saving/data/toprunner2015e.pdf. Last accessed: 13.08.2019.

Karikari, K., Asante, K., Biney, C. (2006). Water quality characteristics at the estuary of Korle Lagoon in Ghana. *West African Journal of Applied Ecology*, 10:73–79.

Kaulich, F., Luken, R., Mhlanga, A., Polzerova, I. (2016). *Energy Intensity and Manufacturing Firm Characteristics in Sub-Saharan African Countries*. Working Paper 16/2016. Department of Energy, United Nations Industrial Development Organization. Vienna. Retrieved from: www.unido.org/sites/default/files/2016-12/ Final_14122016_Energy_intensity_in_SSA__3__0.pdf. Last accessed: 13.08.2019.

Kenya (2015). *Green Economy Strategy and Implementation Plan: Kenya 2016–2030: A Low Carbon, Resource Efficient, Equitable and Inclusive Socio-Economic Transformation*. August. Government of the Republic of Kenya. Nairobi. Retrieved from: www. environment.go.ke/wp-content/uploads/2018/08/GESIP_Final23032017.pdf. Last accessed: 13.08.2019.

Koefoed, K., Buckley, C. (2008). Clean technology transfer: A case study from the South African metal finishing industry, 2000–2005. *Journal of Cleaner Production*, 16SI:S78–S84.

KPMG (a). *KPMG South Africa Blog: African Chemical Industry: A Hidden Opportunity?* Retrieved from: www.sablog.kpmg.co.za/2014/04/african-chemical-industry-hidden-opportunity/. Last accessed: 27.07.2019.

Luken, R., Clarence-Smith, E., Langlois, L., Jung, I. (2019). Drivers, barriers, and enablers for greening industry in Sub-Saharan African countries. *Development Southern Africa*, Vol 36:5:570–584.

Luken, R., Stares, R. (2005). Small business responsibility in developing countries: A threat or an opportunity? *Business Strategy and the Environment*, 14:38–53.

Luken, R., Van Berkel, R., Leuenberger, H., Schwager, P. (2016). A 20-year retrospective of the United Nations Industrial Development Organization and United Nations Environment Programme National Cleaner Production Centres Programme. *Journal of Cleaner Production*, 112:1165–1174.

Luken, R., Van Rompaey, F. (2008). Drivers for and barriers to environmentally sound technology adoption by manufacturing plants in nine developing countries. *Journal of Cleaner Production*, 16S1:S67–S77.

Masselink, D. (2009). *Industrial Energy Efficiency in Nigerian Companies.* Draft background paper prepared for the 2010/2011 UNIDO Industrial Development Report. United Nations Industrial Development Organization. Vienna.

Morris, M., Barnes, J., Morris, J. (2011). *Energy Efficient Production in the Automotive and Clothing/Textiles Industries in South Africa.* Working Paper 04/2011. Development Policy, Statistics and Research Branch, United Nations Industrial Development Organization. Vienna. Retrieved from: https://open.unido.org/api/documents/4814916/download/Energy%20efficient%20production%20in%20the%20automotive%20and%20clothing-textiles%20industries%20in%20South%20Africa. Last accessed: 13.08.2019.

Never, B. (2016). Behave and save? Behaviour, energy efficiency and performance of micro and small enterprises in Uganda. *Energy Research & Social Science*, 15:197–206.

NLR (2016). Brazil proposes chemicals legislation. *National Law Review*, July 19. Retrieved from: www.natlawreview.com/article/brazil-proposes-chemicals-legislation. Last accessed: 26.07.2019.

ODI (2015). *Low-Carbon Development in Sub-Saharan Africa: 20 Cross Sector Transitions.* October. Overseas Development Institute. London. Retrieved from: www.odi.org/sites/odi.org.uk/files/odi-assets/publications-opinion-files/9878.pdf. Last accessed: 13.08.2019.

OECD (1987). *Decision-Recommendation of the Council on Further Measures for the Protection of the Environment by Control of Polychlorinated Biphenyls.* Organisation for Economic Cooperation and Development. Paris. Retrieved from: https://legalinstruments.oecd.org/en/instruments/55. Last accessed: 27.07.2019.

OECD (1997). *Reforming Environmental Regulation in OECD Countries.* ISBN 92641 55139. Organisation for Economic Cooperation and Development. Paris.

OECD (a). *Guidelines for the Testing of Chemicals.* Organisation for Economic Cooperation and Development. Paris. Retrieved from: www.oecd.org/chemicalsafety/testing/oecdguidelinesforthetestingofchemicals.htm. Last accessed: 26.07.2019.

Ogwumike, F., Aregbeyen, O. (2012). Energy use and sustainable development: Evidence from the industrial sector in Nigeria. *Energy, Sustainability and Society*, 2:article 15, 23 July. Retrieved from: https://energsustainsoc.biomedcentral.com/articles/10.1186/2192-0567-2-15. Last accessed: 13.08.2019.

Oketola, A., Osibanjo, O. (2011). Assessment of industrial pollution load in Lagos, Nigeria by Industrial Pollution Projection System (IPPS) versus effluent analysis. In Broniewicz, E. (ed.) *Environmental Management in Practice*, ISBN: 978-953-307-358-3. InTechOpen. Retrieved from: www.intechopen.com/books/environmental-management-in-practice/assessment-of-industrial-pollution-load-in-lagos-nigeria-by-industrial-pollution-projection-system-i. Last accessed: 13.08.2019.

PAGE (2015). *Ghana Green Industry and Trade Assessment*. Copyright © United Nations Industrial Development Organization, 2015, for Partnership for Action on Green Economy. Retrieved from: www.greengrowthknowledge.org/sites/default/files/downloads/resource/GhanaGreenIndustryAndTradeAssessment_PAGE_0.pdf. Last accessed: 13.08.2019.

Peart, M. (2002). A survey of the adoption of cleaner technology by South African firms. *Development Southern Africa*, 19:2.

Pigaht, M., Van der Plas, R.J. (2009). Innovative private micro-hydro power development in Rwanda. *Energy Policy*, 37:4753–4760.

Quartey, S., Oguntoye, O. (2020). Promoting corporate sustainability in small and medium-sized enterprises: Key determinants of intermediary performance in Africa. *Business Strategy and the Environment*, 30:1–13.

RECPnet (2018). *Knowledge Management System*. Retrieved from: www.recpnet.org. Last accessed: 13.08.2019.

Retta, N. (1999). Cleaner industrial production practice in Ethiopia: Problems and prospects. *Journal of Cleaner Production*, 7:409–412.

Rwanda (2011). *Green Growth and Climate Resilience: National Strategy for Climate Change and Low Carbon Development*. October. Republic of Rwanda. Kigali. Retrieved from: https://cdkn.org/wp-content/uploads/2010/12/Rwanda-Green-Growth-Strategy-FINAL1.pdf. Last accessed: 13.08.2019.

SAICM (2012). Progress in implementation of the Strategic Approach to International Chemicals Management for 2009 and 2010. International Conference on Chemicals Management Third session Nairobi, 17–21 September. Retrieved from: www.saicm.org/Portals/12/Documents/reporting/ICCM_3_INF6_first%20progress%20report_Final.pdf. Last accessed: 27.07.2019.

SAICM (2014). Progress in strategic approach implementation for 2011–2013. Open-ended Working Group of the International Conference on Chemicals Management Second Meeting Geneva, Switzerland, 15–17 December 2014. Retrieved from: www.saicm.org/Portals/12/Documents/reporting/k1403579-eowg2-inf4-second-progress-report.pdf. Last accessed: 27.07.2019.

SAICM (2015). Report on the status of projects funded under the Quick Start Programme Trust Fund as of October 2015. Eighteenth Meeting of the Quick Start Programme Trust Fund Implementation Committee, 5 November. SAICM/TF.18/5. Retrieved from: www.saicm.org/Portals/12/Documents/QSP/Status%20QSP%20projects.pdf. Last accessed: 27.07.2019.

SAICM (2019). Progress in strategic approach implementation for 2014–2016. Open-ended Working Group of the International Conference on Chemicals Management Third Meeting Montevideo, Uruguay, 2–4 April. Retrieved from: www.saicm.org/Portals/12/Documents/meetings/OEWG3/inf/OEWG3-INF-4-2014-16-third-Progress-Report-.pdf. Last accessed: 27.07.2019.

SAICM (a). *UN Environment, SAICM Website.* Retrieved from: www.saicm.org/ Home/tabid/5410/language/en-US/Default.aspx. Last accessed: 26.07.2019.

Siaminwe, L., Chinsembu, K., Syakalima, M. (2005). Policy and operational constraints for the implementation of cleaner production in Zambia. *Journal of Cleaner Production*, 13:1037–1047.

South Africa (2011). *Green Economy Accord.* 17 November. Economic Development Department, Republic of South Africa. Pretoria. Retrieved from: www.sagreenfund. org.za/wordpress/wp-content/uploads/2015/04/Green-Economy-Accord.pdf. Last accessed: 13.08.2019.

SWITCH Africa Green (a). *Homepage.* About. Retrieved from: www.switchafricagreen. org/index.php?option=com_content&view=article&id=206&Itemid=1292&lang= en. Last accessed: 13.08.2019.

UN (2011). *Globally Harmonized System of Classification and Labelling of Chemicals (GHS).* 4th Revised edition. United Nations. New York and Geneva. ST/SG/AC. 10/30/Rev.4. Retrieved from: www.unece.org/fileadmin/DAM/trans/danger/ publi/ghs/ghs_rev04/English/ST-SG-AC10-30-Rev4e.pdf. Last accessed: 26.07. 2019.

UN (a). *Montreal Protocol on Substances That Deplete the Ozone Layer.* Retrieved from: https://treaties.un.org/Pages/ViewDetails.aspx?src=TREATY&mtdsg_no= XXVII-2-a&chapter=27&lang=en. Last accessed: 27.07.2019.

UN (b). *Stockholm Convention on Persistent Organic Pollutants.* Retrieved from: https:// treaties.un.org/Pages/ViewDetails.aspx?src=TREATY&mtdsg_no=XXVII- 15&chapter=27&clang=_en. Last accessed: 27.07.2019.

UN (c). *Minamata Convention on Mercury.* Retrieved from: https://treaties.un.org/ Pages/ViewDetails.aspx?src=IND&mtdsg_no=XXVII-17&chapter=27&clang=_ en. Last accessed: 27.07.2019.

UN (d). *Rotterdam Convention on the Prior Informed Consent Procedure for Certain Hazardous Chemicals and Pesticides in International Trade.* Retrieved from: https://treaties.un.org/ pages/ViewDetails.aspx?src=TREATY&mtdsg_no=XXVII-14&chapter=27. Last accessed: 27.07.2019.

UNECA (2009). Wandiga, S.O., Madadi, V., Olum, P.O., Centre for Science and Technology Innovation, University of Nairobi, Kenya [Coordinating Lead Authors]. *Africa Review Report on Chemicals: Main Report.* Prepared for the United Nations Industrial Development Organization. Submitted to the UN Economic Commission for Africa's Sixth Session of the Committee on Food Security and Sustainable Development (CFSSD-6)/Regional Implementation Meeting (RIM) for CSD-18, Addis Ababa, Ethiopia, 27–30 October. E/ECA/CFSSD/6/14. Retrieved from: http://repository.uneca.org/handle/10855/3253. Last accessed: 26.07.2019.

UN Energy (a). *Policies and Measures to Realise Industrial Energy Efficiency and Mitigate Climate Change.* Retrieved from: https://inis.iaea.org/collection/NCLCollectionStore/_ Public/42/081/42081948.pdf. Last accessed: 13.08.2019.

UN Environment (a). *The Bamako Convention.* Retrieved from: www.unenvironment. org/explore-topics/environmental-rights-and-governance/what-we-do/meeting- international-environmental. Last accessed: 28.07.2019.

UNEP (2006). *Report on Atmosphere and Air Pollution.* African Regional Implementation Review for the 14th Session of the Commission on Sustainable Development

(CSD-14). United Nations Environment Programme. Nairobi. Retrieved from: https://sustainabledevelopment.un.org/content/documents/ecaRIM_bp2.pdf. Last accessed: 13.08.2019.

UNEP (2010). *Assessing the Environmental Impacts of Consumption and Production: Priority Products and Minerals.* A Report of the Working Group on the Environmental Impacts of Products and Materials to the International Panel for Sustainable Resource Management. Hertwich, E., van der Voet, E., Suh, S., Tukker, A., Huijbregts, M., Kazmierczyk, P., Lenzen, M., McNeely, J., Moriguchi, Y. United Nations Environment Programme. Nairobi. Retrieved from: www.unep.fr/shared/publications/pdf/DTIx1262xPA-PriorityProductsAndMaterials_Report.pdf. Last accessed: 13.08.2019.

UNEP (2013). *Global Chemicals Outlook: Towards Sound Management of Chemicals.* United Nations Environment Programme. Nairobi, Kenya. Retrieved from: https://sustainabledevelopment.un.org/content/documents/1966Global%20Chemical.pdf. Last accessed: 26.07.2019.

UNEP/UNIDO (a). *Guidance Manual: How to Establish and Operate Cleaner Production Centres.* United Nations Environment Programme and United Nations Industrial Development Organization. Retrieved from: www.unep.fr/shared/publications/pdf/WEBx0072xPA-CPcentre.pdf. Last accessed: 13.08.2019.

UNIDO (2015). *UNIDO-Supported Small Hydro Power Plant in Nigeria's Taraba State.* 13 August. Retrieved from: www.unido.org/news/unido-supported-small-hydro-power-plant-nigerias-taraba-state-inaugurated-local-officials. Last accessed: 13.08. 2019.

UNIDO/UNEP (2010). *Taking Stock and Moving Forward: The UNIDO-UNEP National Cleaner Production Centres.* April. United Nations Industrial Development and United Nations Environment Programme. Vienna. Retrieved from: www.unido.org/sites/default/files/2010-11/Taking%20stock%20and%20moving%20forward-November 2010_0.pdf. Last accessed: 16.08.2019.

UNIDO/UNU-MERIT/KEEI (2014). *Diffusion Strategy of Green Technology and Green Industry in Africa: A Study of Renewable Energy Technology Market and Energy Efficiency Adoption in Maize and Cassava Processing Industries in Kenya and Nigeria.* May. United Nations Industrial Development Organization, United Nations University-Maastricht Economic and Social Research Institute on Innovation and Technology, Korean Energy Economics Institute. Retrieved from: www.unido.org/sites/default/files/2015-10/EE_africa_0.pdf. Last accessed: 13.08.2019.

US EPA (a). Water pollution, battery manufacturing point-source category effluent limitations guidelines, pre-treatment standards and new source performance standards, final rule. *Federal Register,* 51:167, 1986. US Environmental Protection Agency. Retrieved from: www.epa.gov/sites/production/files/2016-11/documents/battery-mfg_final_51-fr-30814_08-28-1986.pdf. Last accessed: 26.07.2019.

US EPA (b). *Summary of the Toxic Substances Control Act.* US Environmental Protection Agency. Retrieved from: www.epa.gov/laws-regulations/summary-toxic-substances-control-act. Last accessed: 27.07.2019.

World Bank (2007). *Environmental, Health, and Safety Guidelines.* 30 April. The World Bank. Washington, DC. Retrieved from: www.ifc.org/wps/wcm/connect/29f5137d-6e17-4660-b1f9-02bf561935e5/Final%2B-%2BGeneral%2BEHS%2BGuidelines.pdf?MOD=AJPERES&CVID=jOWim3p. Last accessed: 13.08.2019.

4 Policies and programmes for greening services

4.1. Introduction

The previous chapter focused on the first dimension of green industrialisation, greening industry. This chapter instead covers the policy and support programmes which promote and support the four greening service regimes: the supply of environmental goods and services, the establishment and operation of eco-industrial parks, the adoption of eco-design, and the recycling of waste products and materials. The first of these is covered in some detail; the others are covered more briefly. At the end of each section, there is a summary of reports and studies on policies and support programmes which have either been adopted by SSA countries or have been discussed for possible adoption by these countries.

4.2. Environmental goods and services

Introduction

Individual enterprises can do much to green themselves by being more efficient, reducing their consumption of materials and energy, phasing out their use of toxic chemicals, minimising the pollution and waste which they release into the environment, and redesigning their products so that they consume less during use and are easier to reuse, recover, and recycle. However, enterprises, and especially SMEs, cannot be expected to manage all their environmental impacts alone. For their efforts to be truly sustainable, they will require the support of third-parties for many things:

- For instance, it is not practical to assume that enterprises can treat and dispose of their wastes in the most environmentally protective manner. This requires that properly designed and operated centralised waste treatment and waste disposal facilities exist, run by third parties, which can take these wastes and manage them in the most environmentally compatible manner. Reputable companies must also exist which can transport these wastes in a manner that is safe and environmentally protective to these centralised waste treatment and disposal facilities.

- If the process wastes which they generate are recyclable, enterprises will need the services of specialised companies which can separate out the recyclable fractions and find buyers for the recycled materials. As economies move towards circular flows, they will also need the services of specialised companies which can repair, remanufacture, refurbish, or recycle their products.
- If enterprises need to treat their wastewaters prior to discharging them, or treat their air emissions before releasing them to the atmosphere, they will need the services of specialised engineering companies which can design and build the necessary wastewater treatment plants or air pollution abatement plants.
- They will require access to specialised laboratories which can accurately measure the concentrations of pollutants in their wastewater and air streams (to assure that they meet the standards) and in their wastes (to support their categorisation).
- They will require access to technology providers who can sell them cleaner process technologies. A special, but very important, case of this is renewable energy technology which companies can use on-site to generate their own energy (electricity or heat).
- They will require access to consulting companies which can give them specialised services in all of the fields related to their sustainability.
- They will require access to product designers who can (re)design their products to make them greener.
- They will require support from governments or public-private partnerships to develop and manage eco-industrial parks.

This section will focus on all but the last two of these broad sets of services.

In many countries, environmental services are part of the environmental goods and services (EGS) sector. While there are discussions about what activities exactly are covered by the term 'environmental goods and services sector' (discussions which will be reviewed later in this section), Table 4.1 gives an indication of the size of this sector by region (Environmental Business Journal, 2012). (Ricardo [2017] provides a more current overview of the global market for low-carbon goods and services. Unfortunately, the report does not show market segmented by region as in Table 4.1, but does show global potential in 2030 and 2050.)

Several things are apparent from this table. The first is that those countries with the longest history of robust environmental policy regimes have

Table 4.1 Market size and growth for EGS sector, by region (2011)

	Market in US$ billion	Market, USD/capita	% growth
US	311.3	998.7	5%
Japan	103.3	806.4	-1%
Western Europe	256.0	737.1	2%
Australia/New Zealand	13.6	501.8	2%
Middle East	17.5	80.9	9%
Latin America	28.5	47.8	5%
Central and Eastern Europe	13.7	34.9	4%
Rest of Asia	78.0	20.1	9%
Africa	10.3	9.8	10%

Source: Data derived from Environmental Business Journal, 2012

the largest markets for EGS (Fankhauser *et al.*, 2013). This point will be returned to later. The second is that the markets for environmental goods and services are quite large in these markets. For instance, comparing the size of the market in the US (in terms of gross output) with the size of the traditional manufacturing sector in 2017, the EGS sector ('waste management and remediation services') was comparable to the 'wood products' and 'non-metallic mineral products' sectors and greater than 'furniture and related products' and 'textile mills and textile products mills' sectors (US Department of Commerce, a). On these counts, Africa is lagging, with the smallest EGS sector (at least in the formal sector of the economy). That being said, the table also shows that the biggest markets are the most mature, with the smallest markets, and notably Africa, growing the fastest and therefore having the greatest potential to add to economic activity.

Note that it is not only industrial enterprises which are the clients of the EGS sector. Very importantly, the sector also caters to municipal authorities for municipal waste management, fleet management, and so on. Environmental consultants offer their services not only to the industry but also to the government and other sectors of the economy. Nevertheless, the industry is an important client for the EGS sector.

Policies and programmes to promote environmental services

'Levelling the playing field'

An important element of efforts by governments to promote the growth of environmental services is to 'level the playing field' for those services; that is to say, to eliminate any barriers to their growth in the current policy regime. In this regard, there are two important issues: ensuring proper regulatory control of pollution releases and waste generation, and elimination of subsidies.

As already noted, Table 4.1 shows that the countries which have had a longer history of robust environmental policies now have the largest markets in EGS. This is a direct consequence of applying the Polluter Pays Principle. By restricting where pollutants and wastes can be released into the environment and in what quantities, and by making polluters pay for managing the pollution and waste which they generate, the regulatory regimes create a demand for specialised services, and it is this demand which feeds the growth of the EGS sector. It is for this reason that one of the main ways in which a government can grow a country's EGS sector is to develop the necessary policy regimes, and just as importantly, to enforce them. It is primarily their existence which makes many environmental goods and services economically viable. Even without promulgating policies which explicitly promote and support the supply of environmental goods and services, just having a robust environmental policy regime and enforcing it will go a long way to creating a vibrant EGS sector.

Note that enterprises in the EGS sector can themselves be covered by environmental policy regimes. This is certainly the case for enterprises involved in the waste management chain. As described in Section 3.7 on Hazardous Waste Management, for a waste management system to work properly, the enterprises offering waste transport, treatment, disposal, and to a lesser degree, recycling services, need to be closely regulated. Centralised wastewater treatment plants, treating effluents from different sources – households, commercial, industrial – are normally required to have licenses and to meet effluent standards as described in Section 3.2 on Pollution Control Instruments. In general, any environmental service where wastes or pollution are handled will be subject to environmental regulatory regimes. For their part, environmental goods – green products, cleaner technologies – will normally be subject to the same safety regulatory requirements and consumer protection requirements to which all goods are subject.

In the same vein, the removal of subsidies which encourage unsustainable behaviour will greatly support the economic viability of the environmental goods and services sector. The most discussed subsidies are without doubt those for fossil fuels, which it has been estimated amount to USD 600 billion a year (IISD, 2013). It is argued that these subsidies artificially depress the price of fossil fuels, making it harder for renewable energy technologies to compete. Other forms of resource extraction also receive subsidies (TAI, 2013). Subsidies for other raw materials exist. For instance, in a number of countries, subsidies for irrigation comprise a significant portion of a country's budgetary expenditure; at the same time, by artificially depressing the cost of water, these subsidies could be encouraging wasteful use of water and may be contributing to the depletion of scarce water supplies (IISD, 2011). Many types of subsidies are used, some of them not being very obvious, which can make their removal complex (IISD, a). Removal of subsidies can also be highly political as those sectors which receive them are often politically powerful, while in some cases, there are issues of social justice. Nevertheless, their removal will greatly help more sustainable behaviour and the growth of the environmental goods and services sector.

It should be noted that some of the sub-sectors of the environmental goods and services sector also receive subsidies. This is notably the case for some renewable energy technologies. This issue will be discussed later.

Developing a national strategy for developing an EGS sector

Before governments start developing programmes to support the development of their EGS sector, they need to set priorities so as to channel the always scarce funds to developing those green services which the country most needs. Governments therefore need to undertake some sort of strategic planning exercise. The types of questions such a planning exercise should endeavour to answer are:

- Where are the country's greatest needs for green services, currently and in the near- to medium-term? Is it wastewater treatment? Is it waste management? Is it support for resource efficiency efforts? Are certain types of needed green products available on the market?
- In what sectors does the country already have the local capacities? Where does it not?
- Where does the country have natural advantages to develop green services? Does it have good sources of renewable energy (solar, wind, biomass)? Does it have good sources of raw materials for green products (e.g., lithium deposits for use in battery manufacture)? On the human resources side, does the country have young people well-educated in the STEM (Science, Technology, Engineering, and Mathematics) disciplines?
- What are global trends? Where could there be regional or global markets that the country could access?

The outputs of such an exercise could be a gap analysis, a strengths, weaknesses, opportunities, and threats (SWOT) analysis, and the development of a strategic action plan to develop the priority environmental services. An example of such an exercise can be found in BMU (2014).

Government programmes to support the development of the EGS sector

Defining the EGS sector

Once a government is clear about the overall direction it wants the EGS sector to develop in, it can start putting in place the programmes to support this development path. But before it can do this, it needs to create a formal definition of what constitutes the EGS sector. This is necessary because a key to any government programmes aimed at supporting the development of the EGS sector is agreement on what goods and services are in the EGS sector and therefore can receive support, and conversely what activities are outside of the sector and should not receive support.

Various governments have elaborated definitions of the EGS sector. For instance, in its data collection handbook on the environmental goods and service sector, Eurostat (2009) considers that the ESG sector

> consists of a heterogeneous set of producers of technologies, goods and services that:
>
> - Measure, control, restore, prevent, treat, minimise, research and sensitise environmental damages to air, water and soil as well as problems related to waste, noise, biodiversity and landscapes. This includes 'cleaner' technologies, goods and services that prevent or minimise pollution.
> - Measure, control, restore, prevent, minimise, research and sensitise resource depletion. This results mainly in resource-efficient technologies, goods and services that minimise the use of natural resources. These technologies and products (i.e., goods and services) must satisfy the end purpose criterion, i.e., they must have an environmental protection or resource management purpose (hereinafter 'environmental purpose') as their prime objective.
>
> These technologies and products (i.e., goods and services) must satisfy the end purpose criterion, i.e., they must have an environmental protection or resource management purpose (hereinafter 'environmental purpose') as their prime objective.

Another definition has been given by the US Department of Commerce in its report *Measuring the Green Economy* (US Department of Commerce, 2010). The report's authors defined green products or service as those whose predominant function serves one or both of the following goals:

- Conserve Energy and Other Natural Resources: This includes products or services that conserve energy to reduce fossil fuel use and promote water, raw material, land, and species and ecosystem conservation; or
- Reduce Pollution: this includes products and services that provide clean energy or prevent, treat, reduce, control or measure environmental damage to air, water and soil. The remediation, abatement, removal, transportation or storage of waste and contaminants also are considered to reduce pollution.

These two definitions are broadly similar, as are others which other governments have elaborated. Governments could use any of these to begin defining their EGS sector. It is important to recall, however, that while there is broad consensus about what constitutes the EGS sector, there are many points of contention when it comes to defining what specific goods and what services should be considered as actually belonging to this sector.

This is particularly challenging in the area of trade (but also national statistics), and has been the subject of much debate since the Doha declaration of 2001, in which ministers called for the liberalisation of trade in environmental goods and services (ITC, 2014). The core problem is that, more than many other sectors, the EGS sector is very heterogeneous, covering very many different types of products and services. In the case of some categories of goods and services, their placement in the EGS sector is relatively straightforward, because they form a relatively homogenous group. This is the case, for instance, for renewable energy technologies and services. Categorisation as belonging to the EGS sector is also relatively straightforward in the case of so-called 'add-on' technologies and services; that is, technologies and services that are added on to other processes and systems – for instance, technologies at 'the end of the pipe' such as wastewater treatment technologies or air pollution abatement technologies or waste treatment technologies. However, where parts of such units are being manufactured in the country (in the case of statistics) or being imported (in the case of trade), issues arise when the parts in question are multipurpose. For instance, pieces of equipment like pumps, centrifuges, and filters can be used in environmental units delivering environmental services, but can equally be used in other types of process units, so how should they be treated? For instance, attempts were made in a West African country to import the individual parts of photovoltaic (PV) units to manufacture them locally. However, the customs authorities refused to waive the tariffs on many of the parts, arguing that they had multiple uses. Complete PV units, on the other hand, could be imported without a tariff being imposed. The result was that local manufacture of PV units became uneconomic (personal communication, October 2016). Even whole units can be questioned. For instance, incinerators can be used to burn hazardous wastes, but they can also be used to burn other materials. In national statistics, this multi-purpose problem extends to companies which can be manufacturing environmental goods and services but also other types of goods and services (e.g., pumps manufactured for wastewater treatment plants and pumps manufactured for other purposes). To which sector should such companies be assigned?

Cleaner technologies pose another sort of challenge since, by their very definition, their level of cleanliness is relative. Today, a technology may be cleaner than alternative competing technologies, but tomorrow it may no longer be as a still cleaner technology is marketed. So while today it could be useful for a government to reduce the tariff to encourage its importation, tomorrow it would not. The challenges are even greater when the environmental services are so-called integrated approaches. For instance, many modern production units have embedded in them technologies whose purpose is to render the overall unit cleaner or to abate a pollution or waste stream generated in the unit. In the case of such a unit being imported into a country with a lower tariff for 'clean technologies', how should the tariff to be applied be calculated? Then there are those cases of technologies or products which continuously reduce or eliminate environmental impacts, but are sold for some other purpose. Examples are solvent-free painting lines, energy-saving combustion techniques, low-energy engines, and refrigerators free of ozone depleting substances (OECD, 2001; see also UNEP, 2014). Yet it is these more complicated cases that normally governments should wish to encourage, since they minimise the pollution and waste generated and resources consumed during use, rather than deal with the pollution and wastes once they are generated.

In the area of trade, the trend is to create lists of certain goods and services which will enjoy lower tariffs for being considered environmental goods and services. In 2012, the Asia-Pacific Economic Cooperation (APEC)[1] agreed on a list of environmental goods on which they would cut tariffs to 5% or less by 2015. This was the first time that trade negotiations had produced such tariff cuts on environmental goods. The APEC List of Environmental Goods contains 54 items, including such items as renewable and clean energy technologies; wastewater treatment technologies; air pollution control technologies; solid and hazardous waste treatment technologies; and environmental monitoring and assessment equipment (APEC, 2016; see also ICTSD, 2016 for a review of progress). Following up on this, in January 2014, 14 members of the World Trade Organization (WTO) pledged to launch negotiations in the WTO on liberalising trade in green goods. In a joint statement, countries promised to find an agreement to "eliminate tariffs for goods that we all need to protect our environment and address climate change". They would build on the APEC List. They would apply the 'most favoured nation' principle. They would design a 'living agreement' that will evolve and reflect future needs and address other barriers to trade in green goods (US Department of State, 2014). Negotiations on an Environmental Goods Agreement were launched in 2014 within the WTO. Those negotiations, now involving 18 WTO members, are ongoing (WTO, a).

The 'list approach' may be the most practical way for governments to come up with an actionable set of products and services which they will consider to make up the EGS sector for their country. It can be constructed on the basis of the national strategy suggested previously. As in the case of the commitment made by the 18 WTO members, it is critical that any such list should be considered a 'living list', which can be changed with time to take into account changed circumstances: priority environmental goods and services today may no longer be so in the future, and should not continue to obtain support from the government.

Creating the enabling environment for industry support institutions for green industrialisation

It is generally recognised that enterprises, especially SMEs, need access to support institutions which can help them build up the knowledge and skills they need to adopt new procedures, processes, and products. This is equally the case for SMEs wishing to become greener. They need support to build up the skills they require to green themselves. This is an area where governments have often intervened to create such support institutions, either fully-funded or partially-funded by public funds.

An example of such an industry support institution which is very relevant to green industrialisation is the National Cleaner Production Centres (NCPCs). In 1994, UNIDO and UNEP launched a joint programme to establish NCPCs in the developing countries. The programme is ongoing. In each country where it operates, its objective is to establish a small centre whose staff, along with a broader set of national experts, are trained to undertake in-plant CP assessments in a series of pilot facilities. The centre staff can use the results of these assessments, along with later investments in CP by the pilot facilities, in information dissemination campaigns whose aim is to encourage other facilities to also undertake CP assessments, using the services of the centre and the trained national experts to do this. Relevant government agencies are part of the centre's oversight body, and centre staff can work with these agencies to promote the adoption of CP in other ways. With time, the NCPCs can add other CP-related services to their menu of services to broaden their relevance and appeal to industry. Initially, the services of the centre are fully subsidised by the project, but by the end of the project the objective is for the centre to have diversified sources of funding, relying on payments for services by enterprises but also on projects from the government or from the international community. As of 2015, the programme had implemented 58 projects to develop NCPCs. The regional distribution of the centres is as follows: 12 in Sub-Saharan Africa, 9 in Asia, 11 in Europe, 8 in the NIS countries, 13 in Latin America, and 5 in the Middle East and North Africa (UNIDO/UNEP, 2015).

Similar 'service centres' are to be found in the energy field. For instance, experience in countries with energy management standards or specifications has shown that the appropriate application of energy management standards requires significant training and skills. The implementation of an energy management standard within a company or an industrial facility requires a change in existing institutional approaches to the use of energy, a process that can benefit from assistance from a source of external expertise. Such service centres can also create and disseminate relevant technical information through energy efficiency assessment and self-auditing tools, case studies, reports, guidebooks, and benchmarking tools. These services can be provided by government entities through energy efficiency centres. In addition, or alternatively, governments can encourage other entities in the private sector, such as utilities, consulting engineers, equipment manufacturers or vendors, or ESCOs to offer these services (for a global overview of the ESCO market, see IEA, a).

Another type of industry support institution which is important for green industrialisation is the bodies related to private standards. Two very important sets of standards in this field are the ISO 14000 family of standards on environmental management systems and the ISO 50000 family of standards on energy management systems.[2] To function correctly, private standards which have been agreed to at the international level need to be adopted at the national level, normally through an existing national standards body. There also need to be entities which can certify that enterprises are meeting the standards. In cases where physical standards need to be met, there must be laboratories which can certify that the standard is met. Finally, there need to be bodies which can accredit all of these certification entities. While much of this standards infrastructure is run by the private sector, governments do have an important role to play in the running of the infrastructure. For instance, standards bodies tend to be public-private institutions.

Depending on the definition of the EGS sector chosen by the government, there could be other types of industry support institutions for green industrialisation which the government might wish to develop.

Developing local EGS

Once a government has determined through the development of a national strategy what environmental services it requires, it can go about developing these services. In doing this, governments can use approaches which have been used previously to grow any industry or service sector. The discussion here will therefore be brief.

The first issue which a government must tackle is to support the necessary local research and development (R&D) to develop green technologies, systems, and business models that currently do not exist or are weak. Doing fundamental research is expensive and requires a long-term commitment by the government to the necessary education, infrastructure, etc. For countries which do little or no R&D, it is more viable to start with adapting existing technologies from elsewhere to local conditions and needs through applied R&D. Applied R&D, if well used, can help to build the necessary skill sets that allow a country to later move to more fundamental research. The Republic of Korea built up its R&D programmes this way. China appears to be taking the same route. Whether a government supports applied and/or fundamental R&D in environmental services, several instruments can be used to support and encourage R&D. The most basic requirement is to have sufficient people who can do green research. This requires good STEM education throughout the educational system – see the next section. There has to be budgetary support for green R&D (normally in Ministries of Science and Technology or Education budgets). However, it is important to ensure that eventual users of the R&D in the private sector co-finance the research to ensure ownership (with the level of co-financing normally depending on how fundamental/applied the research is: the more fundamental, the more the government pays). It is critical that R&D should strongly link research institutions and industry. A big weakness of much R&D is that it is done in an 'ivory tower', with little connection to the real world and real problems. The government should link its disbursement of funds to evidence of close working relationships. Governments can use instruments like science parks, formal clusters, incubators, and the like as a good way to get people who are working on the same or similar problems to be aware of what each is doing. Many of the spill-over effects of R&D come through serendipitous contacts between researchers. Once research ideas are ready to be commercialised, governments can use incubators and accelerator programmes as good instruments to nurture start-ups in environmental services.

Developing the necessary skills base

As just mentioned, R&D for new environmental services, even the simpler applied R&D, cannot be undertaken successfully if there are not enough people trained in the STEM disciplines and in skills needed to change behaviour in firms. Therefore, governments need to ensure that its universities are turning out graduates with the necessary STEM skills. If necessary, curricula in relevant disciplines may have to be modified and new courses created in environmentally related disciplines. In particular, courses in product eco-design need to be introduced; product adaptation for environmental purposes requires designers who have been trained in eco-product design. Having the necessary STEM disciplines at the university level in turn requires good science and mathematics teaching at the secondary level. Skills related to the delivery of environmental services also need to be developed, which can best be done through vocational training. This could require modifications to the curricula of the country's technical vocational education and training schools. Finally, lifelong training should be offered. The state-of-the-art is changing all the time, and the countries' needs in environmental services will be changing all the time, too. All of this needs to be done in close consultation with the business community to ensure that the necessary skills are being developed.

Supporting the import of technologies, products, and systems required for EGS

While it is good for a country's overall economic growth to develop local solutions for the environmental services it needs, it is also true that the technologies, products, and systems needed for many environmental services already exist elsewhere. It could therefore be a valid strategy to encourage their import. The following seven-step process can be used as a guideline for this.

1   The government can start by helping the stakeholders in this process to obtain information on what green technologies, products, and systems are available and where. The government can help the stakeholders to connect with relevant global networks.

2   The government can then support technical assistance programmes which help companies (and other technology and product users) to properly define what their green needs are.

3   The government should ensure that its trade agreements have favourable regimes for the import of the green technologies, products, and systems which the government believes are a priority.

4   The government should take steps to make it easy to do business in the country (customs, taxation, and company law, intellectual property protection; good infrastructure [ports, roads]).

5   The government should support foreign direct investment (FDI), the creation of joint ventures, subcontracting arrangements, etc., which are relevant to environmental services that the country needs, so that as much of the incoming technologies/products as possible are eventually manufactured locally – this also exposes the local workforce to the new products/technologies.

6   The government can use demonstration programmes and similar instruments to show potential users what the technologies/products are capable of, and how they work – this lessens the risks perceived by potential users of adopting a (for them) untried product/technology.

7   The government can also use fiscal instruments to lessen the risk of first use.

Easing access to capital

One of the biggest problems for any enterprise, and SMEs in particular, is access to capital, and this is no different for enterprises wishing to offer environmental services. Governments can adopt a number of policies which make access easier for enterprises to access the capital they need. For start-ups, governments can reduce the need for initial capital through incubation programmes, cluster programmes, etc. They can make green credit lines available through the commercial banking system (although they need to make sure that the terms are more favourable than market terms). They can have loan guarantee programmes for green loans (this reduces the risks for the banks and leads to lower interest rates). They can also guarantee venture capital funds.

Note that these programmes – indeed, all support programmes where public monies are used to fund them – are forms of subsidies to enterprises wishing to enter the EGS sector. Earlier, it was stated that other subsidies – subsidies on fossil fuels, mining, water, etc. – should be eliminated. This leads to the question of whether subsidies should be used at all, even to support green industrialisation. It is true to say that there is no objective way to determine if a subsidy is economically a good thing or a bad thing. It is also true to say that many subsidy programmes which started out with good intentions were quickly subverted by the subsidies' recipients to further their own ends rather than to meet societal objectives. As has been stated elsewhere, "whether subsidies are positive or negative is typically a normative judgement" (OECD, 2007). If a government uses any type of subsidy programmes, several points need to be kept in mind. There needs to be a clear exit strategy, where programmes are time-bound from the outset. There should be clear and agreed objectives. Careful consideration should be given to who gets assistance, who pays, etc. When designing several programmes, these should be mutually consistent and integrated.

Supporting the export of technologies, products, and systems
required for EGS

Once a country has created an active EGS sector, the government can start considering how to support the export of the goods and services of this sector. The following six-step process can be used as a guideline for this.

1   The government can start by helping companies obtain information on overseas markets (for instance, by undertaking market research, holding country-market seminars, etc.).
2   The government can train its companies in the mechanics of export (which is very important for companies which have not previously exported).
3   The government can help the companies make the necessary connections through investment promotion activities (trade fairs, trade missions, etc.).
4   The government should ensure that its trade agreements have favourable regimes for the export of the country's green technologies, products, or systems.
5   The government can offer export financing and export insurance through an export-import bank.
6   The government should take steps to protect its companies' intellectual property rights abroad.

Government support may be most needed in the early stages of a company's export strategy. Companies see increased risks at this time: currency exchange rates, greater distances, new transportation modes, new government regulations, new legal and financial systems, new languages, and cultural diversity. At the same time, they see more costs: information acquisition, market research, trade financing. Government export assistance can help firms over this rough patch to the point where profits increase and risk heads downward.

The case in SSA countries

As was shown in Table 4.1, Africa is the region with the smallest EGS sector. This small size is reflected in the paucity of data on the sector in Africa. Taking waste management as a good indicator of the development of environmental services in a country – waste collection, treatment, and disposal being one of the earliest environmental services to develop in most countries, tracking urban development – data collected by the World Bank show that the SSA region is the region with the lowest collection rate for municipal solid waste (MSW), with, on average, 46% of MSW being collected (World Bank, 2012) (note that in many developing countries and in most low-income countries, industrial waste is not kept separate from wastes from households and other sources). This indicates that most SSA countries do not have enough service providers to collect all the municipal waste being generated (which in turn suggests that municipal authorities do not have sufficient funds, or are unwilling to commit sufficient funds, to MSW collection). Furthermore, the municipal wastes which are collected are almost exclusively dumped or sent to landfills, with few other disposal methods being used (World Bank, 2012). Here too, then, there is a lack of environmental services enterprises which could be recycling various fractions of the MSW stream (plastic, glass, metal, etc.). It should also be noted that since the MSW streams in the SSA region tend to be high in organic material, dumping or even formalised landfilling is not a good strategy since it can generate methane as well as organic acids which can pollute groundwater. Environmental services such as composting would be more sustainable. This lack of waste infrastructure had already been noted in Section 3.7 on Hazardous Waste Management, where reporting to the Basel Convention Secretariat shows that very few of the SSA countries have the infrastructure to manage hazardous wastes. The same reporting shows that some enterprises exist in the formal sector to deal with non-hazardous waste fractions like glass, plastics, and metal, although the number reported is quite low.

Centralised wastewater treatment in urban agglomerations is another indicator of the growth of environmental services in a country. In and of itself, the operation of treatment plants is an environmental service. It also generates ancillary environmental services: construction of the necessary infrastructure, sale of treatment chemicals, sale of treatment technologies, generation of biogas from the sludges, testing of water quality by laboratories, etc. The SSA region is characterised by poor sewerage connection, with only 7% of the population connected to sewers (WWAP, 2017). The wastewater treatment plants that do exist often do not work properly due to lack of investments in newer, more efficient removal technologies, lack of laboratory equipment to perform all the necessary water quality tests, lack of reliable sources of power, poor operating practices, etc. (Wang *et al.*, 2014). This shows that this key environmental service is also still undeveloped in the SSA countries.

Some other environmental services more directly relevant to green industrialisation also exist in the SSA countries. For instance, as mentioned earlier, since 1994, UNIDO and UNEP have established 12 National Cleaner Production Centres (NCPCs) in SSA countries: Cape Verde, Ethiopia, Ghana, Kenya, Mauritius, Mozambique, Rwanda, Senegal, South Africa, Tanzania, Uganda, and Zimbabwe. However, these centres, like other NCPCs in the less developed countries, have struggled to become financially sustainable, often having to rely on international funding to cover a significant portion of their operating costs. Some centres appear to be no longer functioning. Various entities or projects in SSA countries are also offering energy-related services, often in the form of subsidised energy audit programmes: the NCPC and the Private Sector Energy Efficiency initiative in South Africa, the Kenya Centre for Energy Efficiency and Conservation, the Zambia Energy Efficiency Management programme, as well as the Zambian Association of Manufacturers (CCEE, 2015). The South African electrical utility Eskom is running a successful demand side management programme. It provides subsidies to customers to implement verified electricity savings, with the funding coming from a levy on the electricity tariff (CCEE, 2015).

4.3. Eco-industrial parks

Introduction

Industrial parks (IP) are known by different names, including industrial estates, industrial regions, industrial areas, industrial zones, industrial investment regions, special economic zones, industrial corridors, etc. that are planned and developed for the purposes of industrial activities and supportive commercial, infrastructure, and service activities.

Industrial parks typically involve a collection of businesses undertaking manufacturing and processing, whose aims are to maximise profitability. These activities can produce significant negative environmental externalities, which either come from point sources or dispersed sources principally in the form of air emissions, water pollution, and land contamination.

Best environmental management practices for industrial estates and industrial clusters in urban areas have always included proper siting to avoid disruption or destruction of unique environmental areas and to create buffer zones between industrial activates and human settlements. They have also included requirements to have in place collective waste-water treatment plants, collection systems for solid and hazardous waste, and air pollution control technologies where necessary.

An eco-industrial park (EIP) is an IP where the management practices go beyond the traditional practices. These more advanced practices include resource inputs being recycled and/or exchanged with other plants (industrial symbiosis) in the same EIP, individual plants improving the efficiency of resource use with the implementation of cleaner production programmes, consideration of backward linkages outside the IP to ensure protection of the natural resource base (e.g., forest stewardship programmes), and use of common environmental management practices by input providers and a quantitative commitment to low carbon production. Low-carbon, green special economic zones are thought to be the most comprehensive and advanced concept of environmental sustainability (Yeo and Akinci, 2011).

Policies and programmes

There is extensive literature about industrial parks and eco-industrial parks known by their various names. A highly selective review summaries part of this literature.

FIAS (2008) examines 30 years of experience in zones, reviewing development patterns and economic impacts of zones worldwide. The experience shows that while zones have been effective in addressing economic growth and development objectives, they have not been uniformly successful; successes in East Asia and Latin America have been difficult to replicate, particularly in Africa, and many zones have failed. Moreover, since the onset of zone development in developing countries, concerns have been raised about the impact of zones on employment (in terms of gender, wage levels and benefits, worker rights, and work conditions), the environment, and related social factors.

GIZ (2015) focuses on the management level of an industrial zone or park. They intend to guide the industrial area to become more sustainable and are less dealing with the individual companies. The sustainability performance of companies inside the area is assumed to be guided by respective sectors or company-related rules or standards. However, a sustainability framework on the park level is likely to initiate and promote also positive changes on company level.

UNCTAD (2015) explores whether Export Processing Zones (EPZs) can undergo a 'role reversal': repositioning themselves to more systematically support the environmental and social objectives of sustainable development, and by doing so assist in addressing 'governance gaps' in the regulation of markets and enable trade and investment to more closely align with the SDGs. This involves a significant role reversal: transforming EPZs from a largely single-minded focus on increasing exports through lower social and environmental standards and conventional commercial benefits such as fiscal incentives ('first generation' EPZs) to instead creating zones that provide cost benefits but are also centres of excellence for sustainable development, in alignment with international social and environmental standards ('second generation' EPZs, or 'Sustainable Economic Zones').

UNIDO (2016a) documents, in comparable manner, 33 examples of EIPs in 12 developing and emerging economies, including their policy context (Cambodia, China, Colombia, Costa Rica, Egypt, El Salvador, India, Morocco, Peru, South Africa, Tunisia, and Vietnam). The report provides an in-depth comparative analysis of the results of the country case studies to understand the environmental, social, and economic benefits. This allows the extracting of good practices and success factors and the subsequent formulation of future recommendations. This study contributes to the understanding and scaling-up of the environmental and economic benefits to a larger number of industrial parks and their occupant companies. The full details of each case can be found in separate online publications.

UNIDO, the World Bank, and GIZ (2017) aim to assist a range of organisations and public institutions working in this field by providing an internationally recognised and commonly agreed framework for EIP requirements and to encourage continuous improvement processes for their environmental, social, managerial, and economic performance. The guidelines aim to complement rather than replace existing tools and standards. They seek to establish minimum good international industrials policy and practice performance guidelines based on the partners' expertise and experience. Partners and external parties can lean upon these guidelines as a reference point when working with industrial park stakeholders to establish minimum expectations and improve performance (see also UNIDO, 2017).

The World Bank (2014) aims to assist practitioners in understanding low-carbon zones (LCZs) and the systematic process required to eventually develop and operate such zones. Interested readers may include owners, managers, and engineers of the private enterprises located in the zone, as well as the relevant officials of the zone authority, developer, or co-developer of the zone. It presents a detailed explanation of the five key steps and activities involved in a low-carbon zone initiative, both for transforming an existing economic zone and for establishing a new LCZ. It then goes on to explore the policy and institutional requirements for developing an LCZ and offers recommendations on how the LCZ-specific policies and institutions can be effectively integrated with national policies and institutions to accelerate further reforms to promote sustainable industrialisation. It concludes with a set of practical tools for that can be used by the relevant practitioners to make key decisions and/ or plans and develop projects and programmes related to LCZs.

Industrial parks in SSA countries

We found only two studies that inventory industrial parks in SSA countries. FIAS (2008) identifies 29 export processing zones in 11 SSA countries. It classifies them by type of zone by public or private ownership and key sectors. IPRCC and UNDP (2015) identify 11 special economic zones in Ethiopia, 29 in Nigeria, and 10 in Zambia.

The Hawassa Industrial Park in Ethiopia, opened in 2016, is said to be one of the most advanced EIPs in SSA. It is designed around energy and conservation principles. It is powered by hydroelectricity and has zero effluent discharge. It is mainly designed for textile manufacture, garment products, and agro-industry (IPDC, a).

SSA research and reports

Monga (2011) critically reviews special economic zones (SEZs) development in Africa. He establishes a common point of reference for those who believe in the virtues of SEZs, explains why the many existing ones have not delivered the expected outcomes, and summarises the key issues on the agenda. He then suggests cluster-based industrial parks as the most effective tool for developing competitive industries and generating employment and provides some practical guidance to development practitioners and policy makers on the road ahead.

Farole (2011) investigates the economic performance of economic zone programmes in six African countries and four developing countries outside the region. He finds that African zones on the whole are underperforming in terms of attracting investments, facilitating exports, and creating jobs compared to those outside the African region.

IPRCC and UNDP (2015) look at both Africa's and China's SEZ experiences to date with a focus on SEZs in three African countries – namely Ethiopia, Nigeria, and Zambia – and two SEZ case studies in China. This study starts with a brief overview of definitions and a summary of the types and theoretical benefits of SEZs. A synopsis of the historic development and current status of SEZs in Africa is followed by an outline and analysis of SEZ policies and institutional frameworks as well as current and anticipated SEZs in Ethiopia, Nigeria, and Zambia. For each case study country, two operational SEZs are reviewed in detail. Additional chapters present an overview on SEZs in China using Shenzhen SEZ and the Suzhou Industrial Park as case studies to show how African countries might benefit from China's experience in SEZ development and management. Several conclusions are drawn, and recommendations are offered for consideration by African and Chinese policy makers as well as SEZ developers and managers on specific actions to do and to avoid. Specific actions to be taken for green industrialisation are setting high environmental standards at the beginning of SEZ development and putting in place a system for enforcement of these standards. Specific actions to avoid are approval of SEZs without a strong business case and approval of too many competing SEZs within a region.

4.4. Eco-design

Introduction

Both the International Organization for Standardization (ISO) and the European Commission define eco-design in the same way, namely as the "integration of environmental aspects into product design and development, with the aim of reducing adverse environmental impacts throughout a product's life cycle" (ISO, 2011; EC, 2009). Broadly speaking, then, the objectives of eco-design are to design (or redesign) products so that they

- are made with less materials and/or less toxic materials;
- are made with low-impact materials, or with parts that are made with low-impact materials (i.e., materials whose extraction and/or processing minimises impacts to human health and the environment);
- generate less pollution/waste and are safer for workers during their manufacture;
- consume less/less toxic materials and less energy during their use;
- last as long as possible (i.e., are durable and can be remanufactured/ refurbished/repaired);
- can be easily recycled at the end of their useful life.

Eco-design is a key component of any country's move towards a circular economy. It is principally through their design that products can have longer lifetimes in the market (being more durable and easier to remanufacture, refurbish, and repair) and can be easier to recycle once they have reached the end of their useful lives.

An eco-design process will generally go through the following steps:

1   Set the design objectives. Ideally, an eco-design process should apply all of the principles listed above when (re)designing a product. However, often the design team will decide on a particular objective (e.g., energy consumption) for the eco-design process and will (re)design the product around that.
2   Define the scope of the design exercise.
3   Prepare a life cycle inventory (i.e., an inventory of material and energy flows from the point where the raw materials are extracted to the point where the product is discarded).
4   Undertake a life cycle assessment to determine where the biggest impacts are occurring.
5   (Re)design the product to reduce the largest impacts.

Tools are available to help guide design groups wishing to undertake eco-design. The best known of these is the ISO document 14006 *Guidelines for Incorporating Eco-design*, part of the ISO 14000 series of standards on environmental management systems (ISO, 2011).

Large companies will often have their own internal product design department. Smaller companies will need to rely on external product design companies for their product design needs.

Services rather than products can also be subjected to an eco-design process. All service delivery will involve, to a greater or lesser extent, the use of products, so choices can be made about which products to use to lessen a service's environmental impacts.

Policies and programmes to promote eco-design

No legislation directly requires eco-design to be carried out on products. However, there is a considerable body of legislation establishing environmentally-related performance standards to which products must adhere; for instance:

•   Energy consumption standards for many products (see Section 3.4), e.g., the large number of EU regulations which implement the 2009 EU Directive "establishing a framework for the setting of eco-design requirements for energy-related products" (EC, 2009).
•   Standards which ban the use of certain toxic chemicals from products (see Section 3.6), e.g., the US standards banning the use of ozone

depleting substances in certain product categories like aerosol products (US EPA, a).

While such standards do not require companies to use eco-design, using the methodologies of eco-design can be an effective way for them to redesign their products to meet the standard.

The European Commission, aware of the strong role which eco-design plays in bringing about circular economies, has considered exploring the possibility of establishing new product-specific performance requirements in areas such as durability (e.g., minimum lifetime of products or critical components), ease of repair (e.g., availability of spare parts and repair manuals, design for repair), upgradeability, design for disassembly (e.g., easy removal of certain components), information (e.g., marking of plastic parts), and ease of reuse and recycling (e.g., avoiding incompatible plastics) (EC, 2016).

A government programme that can encourage eco-design in a less direct way is public procurement. By inserting green specifications in the overall product specifications, public procurement can create markets for green products and so encourage product designers to design products which meet these green specifications. The European Union has been one of the most active governments in this area (EC, a).

Governments can also use their research and development budgets to encourage research into, and the development of, green (energy efficient or resource efficient) products and technologies. The use of subsidy instruments – grants, loan guarantees, etc. – can also be used by governments to encourage the private sector to develop such products and technologies through the use of eco-design. An example is the European Commission's use of various types of funding to support eco-innovation (EC, b).

Finally, governments can make information available on how to perform eco-design through the publication of manuals and so on, and/or can run training programmes on eco-design. It can also make information available to consumers about the existence of products designed to be more sustainable. One such type of programmes are those offering voluntary eco-labels to companies whose products meet certain environmental criteria. (See UN Environment, a, for an overview of such labelling schemes, and Blue Angel, a, for information on the German eco-labelling scheme, one of the earliest such schemes.) See OECD (2008) for another example of how the government can inform consumers about sustainable products.

SSA research and reports

Little has been done to date to promote eco-design in the SSA countries, and most of that has been through development aid initiatives. For instance, an eco-design manual (design for sustainability manual), which was prepared specifically for developing economies, was pilot tested in SSA countries among other places (UNEP, a). The Technical University of Delft helped to establish a curriculum on the broader concept of product innovation at the University of Dar es Salaam in Tanzania, and a dozen product innovation projects were carried out in local industries. In addition, needs assessments were later made for the need for eco-design in Uganda, Tanzania, Kenya, and Zimbabwe (Crul and Diehl, 2008). Training on eco-design was given by the Uganda NCPC, which resulted in the redesign of the cardboard packing boxes by a local firm (however, as a sign of the practical difficulties facing implementation in Africa, as of 2004 the company had not been able to make the necessary investments) (UNIDO, 2004).

Nevertheless, eco-design is taking place in SSA countries, as individuals and companies understand the merit of this approach to design. The eco-design movement is particularly strong in the field of the built environment, where there is growing interest in eco-design applied to buildings (CR, 2017). Other eco-products have been designed by individuals. For instance, the Kenyan engineer and businessman Evans Wadongo has designed and commercialised a solar lamp, the MwangaBora solar lamp, for use in rural areas. For his work, he was nominated as one of CNN's Heroes in 2010 (Design Indaba, 2014 – this site gives other examples).

4.5. Recycling

Introduction

To the extent that materials recovery and recycling involve some form of transformation during production, they are part of the manufacturing sectors where this transformation occurs (e.g., transforming scrap metals into new metals, remanufacturing car engines). If the activities being carried out mainly refer to sorting activities, they are classified under waste management activities or wholesale of waste and scrap. Recycling was previously classified under manufacturing in ISIC 3, but this did not reflect its production process well. Given its importance, recycling merits particular attention in green industrialisation.

There is an increasing need for recycling, with increasing population and urbanisation driving increases in volumes of waste, on the one hand, and driving resource consumption, on the other. Waste is not only a volume problem. There is also the complexity of waste streams to be considered, with mixing of different types of material in the design of products as well as the mixing of waste streams after use. There are also increasing quantities of hazardous waste.

Recycling is an essential element in the 4Rs – reducing, reusing, recycling, and recovering waste (Japan first introduced the concept of '3Rs' – reduce, reuse, recycle – in the 1990s [METI, 2004], to which a fourth 'R' – recover – was later added[3]). Priority should always be given to activities which reduce and reuse waste, using the various cleaner production options as described in Section 3.3. Recycling should start with separation at source to ensure that high quality secondary materials are not lost and to avoid 'downcycling'. Finally, it may be possible to recover materials or energy from waste which cannot be reduced or reused.

A material can be recycled when there is both a treatment technique and a market for the final product. Any recycling process will generate basic materials and new residues that need to be dealt with appropriately.

Aluminium and steel recycling are well-established industrial activities. Aluminium is infinitely recyclable; two-thirds of the aluminium ever produced since 1886 (when the first commercially-viable extraction processes commenced) is still in use. Recycling saves 95% of the energy used to refine aluminium from bauxite and separation rates are high (80–90%). Steel is also infinitely recyclable and is the world's most recycled material. Two out of every three tonnes of steel produced is from secondary materials. Recycling one tonne of steel saves 1,200 kg of iron ore, 7 kg of coal, and 51 kg of limestone.

Recycling of plastics is an environmental concern in SSA countries, where much recycling is done by the informal sector. According to the Bureau of International Recycling, 20 times more plastic is used today than 50 years ago (BIR, a). Recycling plastics is a challenge for several reasons. Some products contain as many as 20 different plastics and on average 20,000 bottles are needed to obtain one tonne of plastic material. Obtaining sufficient amounts of high quality materials is difficult because of the use of additives, dyes, and fillers, some of which can be toxic substances.

Recycling of end-of-life vehicles (ELVs) is another recycling opportunity for some SSA countries. The potential of such recycling is not as well known in SSA countries as it is in the European Union, where every year ELVs generate between 7 and 8 million tonnes of waste. The EU Directive on ELV aims at making dismantling and recycling of ELVs more environmentally friendly. It sets clear quantified targets for reuse, recycling, and recovery of ELVs and their components (EC, 2000). The EU also pushes producers to manufacture new vehicles without hazardous substances (in particular lead, mercury, cadmium, and hexavalent chromium), thus promoting the reuse, recyclability, and recovery of waste vehicles.

Recycling of electronic waste (e-waste), also known as waste electrical and electronic equipment (WEEE), is a major environmental concern in SSA countries. While e-waste contains many valuable and precious materials, like palladium, gold, and silver, it also contains various hazardous materials, such as mercury and cadmium or brominated flame retardants. In a personal computer or a mobile phone, up to 60 elements from the periodic table can be found. This two-sided nature of e-waste requires well-structured regulations, a well-organised and managed collection, dismantling and treatment system, capable stakeholders and operators, and properly operating markets. However, even in industrialised countries the collection rates are still rather low and from some of them large amounts of discarded electric and electronic devices and e-waste are exported to countries that do not have proper e-waste management or treatment facilities.

Most African countries impacted by e-waste lack inventory data on e-waste; face illegal imports of e-waste under the category of second-hand goods; are unable to track the flow of products over borders in personal luggage or other smuggling operations; have unclear or poor labelling standards for countries exporting to them; keep under-paid and under-trained customs staff; have weak or non-existent legislation, regulation, and policies; lack financial resources to enforce authority where it exists; and face toxic compounds in the WEEE stream, including heavy metals, persistent, bio-accumulative, and toxic substances, and brominated flame retardants (World Bank, 2017).

A recent study commissioned by the World Bank indicates that Ghana, Kenya, and Nigeria have the highest levels of e-waste in the SSA region due to their steadily growing involvement in the importing, recycling, and refurbishing of ICT goods. The growth of ICT goods inevitably leads to the growth in e-waste and, given that 50–80% of the global e-waste flow is handled by informal sectors in developing countries, the recycling process itself generates environmental and human health impacts (World Bank, 2018).

Policies and support programmes

This section will focus on e-waste, which, as just mentioned, is a major environmental concern in SSA countries. To address e-waste, SSA countries need to consider both European and SSA country policies and programmes:

- The European Commission issued a Directive on WEEE, which entered into force in February 2003 (EC, 2002). The Directive provided for the creation of collection schemes where consumers return their WEEE free of charge. These schemes aim to increase the recycling of WEEE and/or reuse. In December 2008, the European Commission proposed to revise the Directive in order to tackle this rapidly increasing waste stream. The new WEEE Directive (EC, 2012) entered into force on 13 August 2012 and became effective on 14 February 2014.

- Ghana has a National Strategy for e-waste (finalised in 2011), draft e-waste legislation, and guidelines for the importation of useable electrical and electronic equipment. Yet there is no formal e-waste collection system, but rather a vibrant informal sector collections system with inappropriate disposal.
- Kenya has prepared guidelines specifically for e-waste management and in 2013 further completed the development of draft e-waste regulations, which are yet to come into force. Further, the Environmental Management and Coordination Regulations, which came into force in 2006, may apply to electronic waste where they can be classified as hazardous waste.

An overall approach to e-waste management in SSA countries should focus on the establishment of e-waste management strategies at national and regional levels. An e-waste management strategy includes all stages of the e-waste recycling chain, i.e., the design of collection schemes; the establishment of sustainable business models to set-up new dismantling facilities or to up-scale existing facilities to operate more efficiently; and the connection of the facilities with national, regional, and international downstream markets for appropriate end-processing of each fraction and to ensure a high recovery rate of precious materials.

SSA research and reports

Nnorom and Osibajo (2010) discuss the influence of product design on product end-of-life scenario and review the recovery options available for end-of-life electronics. Remanufacturing is a viable option in electronic waste management, reducing e-waste generation and increasing reuse of equipment and components. The authors describe the remanufacturing operation for mobile phones in Nigeria. The prospects, challenges, and opportunities in adopting remanufacturing in developing countries are also discussed. The problems of product design and product obsolescence need to be addressed if a global solution to e-waste generation and management is to be rapidly found. The globalisation of producer responsibility is critical in achieving this.

In the UN Economic Commission for Africa's 2016 Economic Report for Africa (UNECA, 2016), Schmitz describes a vehicle repair and metal working cluster located in Suame/Kumasi in Ghana. It repairs and recycles cars, lorries, and small buses. Some 200,000 people work in this industrial cluster, spread over 12,000 businesses. Local workshops are finding ever newer ways of prolonging the life of vehicles. Most interestingly, producers and traders are highly specialised in particular operations or products and some small engineering workshops produce new or reconditioned old parts.

UNIDO (2013) investigated the situation with regard to WEEE imports, use, and e-waste generation in Uganda. The assessment established that there are several challenges in management of WEEE, from importation and distribution as well as e-waste management strategies within Uganda. The country has put in place specific regulations for the management of e-waste.

UNIDO (2016b) conducted a project to assist the Akaki dismantling facility in Ethiopia to upscale its operations and to conduct a regional training on environmentally sound e-waste dismantling methods.

The World Bank (2017) describes the recently approved GEF project, which is a comprehensive overview of e-waste management issues in the SSA region and more specifically in five countries: Ghana, Kenya, Senegal, Tanzania, and Zambia.

Notes

1 APEC has 21 members, mostly on the Pacific Rim, but also including many of the Southeast Asian countries. APEC regional trade in environmental goods totalled USD 185 billion in 2010, accounting for 60% of world exports.
2 The Quality Management Standard, ISO 9000, and affiliated quality tools can also play an important if indirect role in greening of enterprises since running a high-quality process will often result in a more efficient, less wasteful process.
3 In the context of the management of hazardous or toxic wastes, the 4Rs often become replace, reduce, reuse, and recycle, to stress the need to move away from the use of the hazardous and toxic materials giving rise to such wastes.

References

APEC (2016). APEC cuts environmental goods tariffs. *Press Release.* 28 January. Asia-Pacific Economic Cooperation. Retrieved from: www.apec.org/Press/News-Releases/2016/0128_EG.aspx. Last accessed: 30.07.2019.

BIR (a). *Plastics.* Bureau of International Recycling. Retrieved from: https://bir.org/industry/plastics/. Last accessed: 04.08.2019.

Blue Angel (a). *Blue-Angel Website.* Retrieved from: www.blauer-engel.de/en. Last accessed: 30.07.2019.

BMU (2014). Büchele, R., Henzelmann, T., Panizza, P., Wiedemann, A., Roland Berger Strategy Consultants. Transl. by Robinson, N., Ukiah, N., Jokubauskas, C. *GreenTech Made in Germany 4.0: Environmental Technology Atlas for Germany.* July.

Bundesministerium für Umwelt, Naturschutz und nukleare Sicherheit (Federal Ministry for the Environment, Nature Conservation, and Nuclear Safety) (BMU).

CCEE (2015). *Accelerating Energy Efficiency: Initiatives and Opportunities, Africa*. ISBN: 978-87-93130-50-0. Copenhagen Centre on Energy Efficiency. Copenhagen. Retrieved from: https://unepdtu.org/wp-content/uploads/2015/08/african-regional-report. pdf. Last accessed: 04.08.2019.

CR (2017). Africa shows rising interest in green building design. *Construction Review Online*. 13 July. Retrieved from: https://constructionreviewonline.com/2017/07/africa-shows-rising-interest-in-green-building-design/. Last accessed: 30.07.2019.

Crul, M., Diehl, J. (2008). Design for Sustainability (D4S): Manual and tools for developing countries. 7th Annual ASEE Global Colloquium on Engineering Education Track 2, Practice Track: Successful Practices in Engineering Education, Session 4: Sustainable Development Curriculum. Cape Town, 19–23 October. Retrieved from: www.researchgate.net/publication/258278093_Design_for_Sustainability_ D4S_Manual_and_Tools_for_Developing_Countries. Last accessed: 30.07.2019.

Design Indaba (2014). *Evans Wadongo: The Little Light That Could*. 4 November. Retrieved from: www.designindaba.com/videos/interviews/evans-wadongo-little-light-could. Last accessed: 30.07.2019.

EC (2000). *Directive 2000/53/EC of the European Parliament and of the Council of 18 September 2000 on End-of-Life Vehicles*. European Commission. Retrieved from: https:// eur-lex.europa.eu/legal-content/EN/TXT/PDF/?uri=CELEX:02000L0053-20130611&qid=1405610569066&from=EN. Last accessed: 04.08.2019.

EC (2002). *Directive 2002/96/EC of the European Parliament and of the Council of 27 January 2003 on Waste Electrical and Electronic Equipment (WEEE)*. European Commission. Retrieved from: https://eur-lex.europa.eu/resource.html?uri=cellar:ac89e64f-a4a5-4c13-8d96-1fd1d6bcaa49.0004.02/DOC_1&format=PDF. Last accessed: 04.08.2019.

EC (2009). *Directive 2009/125/EC of the European Parliament and of the Council of 21 October 2009 Establishing a Framework for the Setting of Ecodesign Requirements for Energy-Related Products (Text with EEA Relevance)*. 21 October. European Commission. Retrieved from: https://eur-lex.europa.eu/legal-content/EN/ALL/?uri= CELEX%3A32009L0125. Last accessed: 30.07.2019.

EC (2012). *Directive 2012/19/EU of the European Parliament and of the Council of 4 July 2012 on Waste Electrical and Electronic Equipment (WEEE)*. European Commission. Retrieved from: https://eur-lex.europa.eu/legal-content/EN/TXT/PDF/?uri= CELEX:32012L0019&from=en. Last accessed: 04.08.2019.

EC (2016). *Communication from the Commission*. Ecodesign Working Plan 2016–2019. COM(2016) 773 final. Brussels, 30 November. European Commission. Retrieved from: https://ec.europa.eu/energy/sites/ener/files/documents/com_2016_773. en_.pdf. Last accessed: 30.07.2019.

EC (a). European Commission website. *Green Public Procurement, to Be Found at European Commission > Environment > Green Public Procurement*. Retrieved from: https://ec.europa.eu/environment/gpp/index_en.htm. Last accessed: 30.07.2019.

EC (b). European Commission website. *EU Funding for Eco-Innovation, to Be Found at European Commission > Environment > Eco-Innovation Action Plan > Policy and Funding > Funding Programmes*. Retrieved from: https://ec.europa.eu/environment/ecoap/ about-action-plan/union-funding-programmes_en. Last accessed: 30.07.2019.

Environmental Business Journal (2012). Global environmental markets. XXV:6, 7.

Eurostat (2009). *The Environmental Goods and Service Sector: A Data Collection Handbook.* Eurostat Methodologies and Working Papers. p. 23. Unit E3 – Environmental Statistics and Accounts, Eurostat, European Commission. Retrieved from: http://ec.europa.eu/eurostat/documents/3859598/5910217/KS-RA-09-012-EN.PDF/01d1733e-46b6-4da8-92e6-766a65d7fd60?version=1.0. Last accessed: 30.07.2019.

Fankhauser, S., Bowen, A., Calel, R., Dechezlepretre, A., Grover, D., Rydge, J., Sato, M. (2013). Who will win the green race? In search of environmental competitiveness and innovation. *Global Environmental Change*, 23:5:902–913.

Farole, T. (2011). *Special Economic Zones in Africa: Comparing Performance and Learning from Global Experiences.* Report Number 60059. ISBN: 978-0-8213-8638-5. The World Bank. Washington, DC. Retrieved from: http://documents.worldbank.org/curated/en/996871468008466349/pdf/600590PUB0ID181onomic09780821386385.pdf. Last accessed: 14.08.2019.

FIAS (2008). *Special Economic Zones: Performance, Lessons Learned and Implications for Zone Development.* Report Number 45869. Foreign Investment Advisory Service, the Multi-Donor Investment Climate Advisory Service Managed by the International Finance Corporation (IFC) and Supported by the Multilateral Investment Guarantee Agency (MIGA) and the World Bank (IBRD). Retrieved from: http://documents.worldbank.org/curated/en/343901468330977533/pdf/458690WP0Box331s0April200801PUBLIC1.pdf. Last accessed: 14.08.2019.

GIZ (2015). *Guidelines for Sustainable Industrial Areas: Version 1.0.* October. Deutsche Gesellschaft für Internationale Zusammenarbeit GmbH. Eschborn. Retrieved from: https://tuewas-asia.org/wp-content/uploads/2017/05/7-Guidelines-for-Sustainable-Industrial-Areas.pdf. Last accessed: 14.08.2019.

ICTSD (2016). Vossenaar, R. *Reducing Import Tariffs for Environmental Goods: The APEC Experience.* September. International Centre for Trade and Sustainable Development. Geneva. Retrieved from: www.ictsd.org/sites/default/files/research/reducing_import_tariffs_for_environmental_goods_the_apec_experience.pdf. Last accessed: 30.07.2019.

IEA (a). International energy agency website. *Energy Service Companies, to Be Found at Home > Topics > Energy Efficiency > ESCOs.* Retrieved from: www.iea.org/topics/energyefficiency/escos/. Last accessed: 30.07.2019.

IISD (2011). Charles, C. *Irrigation Country Case Studies, Measuring Irrigation Subsidies: Policy Recommendations from a Spanish Case Study.* Global Subsidies Initiative (GSI). International Institute for Sustainable Development. Winnipeg. Retrieved from: www.iisd.org/library/measuring-irrigation-subsidies-policy-recommendations-spanish-case-study. Last accessed: 30.07.2019.

IISD (2013). Beaton, C., Gerasimchuk, I., Laan, T., Lang, K., Vis-Dunbar, D., Wooders, P. *A Guidebook to Fossil-Fuel Subsidy Reform for Policy-Makers in Southeast Asia.* Global Subsidies Initiative (GSI). International Institute for Sustainable Development. Winnipeg. Retrieved from: www.iisd.org/gsi/sites/default/files/ffs_guidebook.pdf. Last accessed: 30.07.2019.

IISD (a). Steenblik, R. *Subsidy Primer.* Chapter 3 "Subsidy Types", pp. 18–27. Global Subsidies Initiative (GSI). International Institute for Sustainable Development. Retrieved from: www.iisd.org/gsi/sites/default/files/primer.pdf. Last accessed: 30.07.2019.

IPDC (a). *Hawassa Industrial Park (HIP)*. Industrial Parks Development Corporation. Retrieved from: www.ipdc.gov.et/index.php/en/industrial-parks/hawasa. Last accessed: 14.08.2019.

IPRCC/UNDP (2015). *If Africa Builds Nests, Will the Birds Come? Comparative Study on Special Economic Zones in Africa and China*. International Poverty Research Center in China and the United Nations Development Programme. Retrieved from: www.undp.org/content/dam/china/docs/Publications/UNDP-CH-Comparative%20Study%20on%20SEZs%20in%20Africa%20and%20China%20-%20ENG.pdf. Last accessed: 14.08.2014.

ISO (2011). *Environmental Management Systems: Guidelines for Incorporating Ecodesign*. ISO 14006:2011(E). International Organization for Standardization. Geneva. Retrieved from: www.ehslaws.com/Public/upload/201701/5869eedfa46f6.PDF. Last accessed: 30.07.2019.

ITC (2014). Bucher, H., Drake-Brockman, J., Kasterine, A., Sugathan, M. *Trade in Environmental Goods and Services: Opportunities and Challenges*. Technical Paper. International Trade Centre. Geneva. Retrieved from: www.intracen.org/uploaded Files/intracenorg/Content/Publications/AssetPDF/EGS%20Ecosystems%20 Brief%20040914%20-%20low%20res.pdf. Last accessed: 30.07.2019.

METI (2004). *Toward a Sustainable Asia Based on the 3Rs*. Working Group on Enhancing International Recycling, Waste Prevention and Recycling Sub-Committee, Industrial Structure Council. October. Ministry of Economy, Trade and Industry. Retrieved from: www.meti.go.jp/policy/recycle/main/english/council/reports/report_sutainableasia_en.pdf. Last accessed: 05.08.2019.

Monga, C. (2011). *Cluster-Based Industrial Parks: A Framework of Action*. Policy Research Working Paper 5900. December. The World Bank. Washington, DC. Retrieved from: http://documents.worldbank.org/curated/en/574921468332054782/pdf/WPS5900.pdf. Last accessed: 14.08.2019.

Nnorom, I., Osibajo, O. (2010). Overview of prospects in adopting remanufacturing of end-of-life electronic products in the developing countries. *International Journal of Innovation, Management and Technology*, 1:3.

OECD (2001). *Environmental Goods and Services: The Benefits of Further Global Trade Liberalisation*. Trade Directorate, Organisation for Economic Cooperation and Development. Paris. Retrieved from: https://read.oecd-ilibrary.org/trade/environmental-goods-and-services_9789264193611-en#page1. Last accessed: 30.07.2019.

OECD (2007). Subsidy reform and sustainable development: Political economy aspects. Proceedings of the Workshop Subsidy Reform and Sustainable Development: Political Economy Aspects, held in Helsinki, Finland, 20–21 June. Retrieved from: https://read.oecd-ilibrary.org/environment/subsidy-reform-and-sustainable-development_9789264019379-en#page5. Last accessed: 30.07.2019.

OECD (2008). *Eco-Innovation Policies in Australia*. Environment Directorate, Organisation for Economic Cooperation and Development. Paris. Retrieved from: www.oecd.org/australia/42876903.pdf. Last accessed: 30.07.2019.

Ricardo (2017). Haydock, H., McCullough, A., Nuttall, C., Evans, L., Kaar, A., Bonifazi, E., Sibille, R., Houghton, M., Nair, S. *UK Business Opportunities of Moving to a Low Carbon Economy*. 15 March. Ricardo Energy & Environment. Retrieved from:

www.theccc.org.uk/wp-content/uploads/2017/03/ED10039-CCC-UK-Bus-Opportunities-Draft-Final-Report-V7.pdf. Last accessed: 14.08.2019.

TAI (2013). Grudnoff, M. *Pouring More Fuel on the Fire: The Nature and Extent of Federal Government Subsidies to the Mining Industry.* Policy Brief # 52. ISSN: 1836-9014. June. The Australia Institute. Retrieved from: www.tai.org.au/sites/default/files/PB%2052%20Pouring%20more%20fuel%20on%20the%20fire.pdf. Last accessed: 30.07.2019.

UNCTAD (2015). *Enhancing the Contribution of Export Processing Zones to Sustainable Development Goals: An Analysis of 100 EPZs and a Framework for Sustainable Economic Zones.* United Nations Commission on Trade and Development. Geneva. Retrieved from: https://unctad.org/en/PublicationsLibrary/webdiaepcb2015d5_en.pdf. Last accessed: 14.08.2019.

UNECA (2016). *Economic Report on Africa: Greening Africa's Industrialization*, pp. 197–98. United Nations Economic Commission for Africa. Addis Ababa. Retrieved from: http://repository.uneca.org/bitstream/handle/10855/23017/b11560861.pdf?sequence=1. Last accessed: 04.08.2019.

UN Environment (a). UN Environment website. *Eco-Labelling.* Retrieved from: www.unenvironment.org/explore-topics/resource-efficiency/what-we-do/responsible-industry/eco-labelling. Last accessed: 30.07.2019.

UNEP (2014). *Measuring the Environmental Goods and Services Sector: Issues and Challenges.* Green Economy Working Paper No. 1. United Nations Environment Programme. Nairobi. Retrieved from: www.greengrowthknowledge.org/sites/default/files/downloads/resource/WorkingPaperEGSSWorkshop.pdf. Last accessed: 30.07.2019.

UNEP (a). *Design for Sustainability: A Practical Approach for Developing Economies.* United Nations Environment Programme, Delft University of Technology (TU Delft), Inwent, German Federal Ministry for Economic Cooperation and Development. Retrieved from: www.d4s-de.org/manual/d4stotalmanual.pdf. Last accessed: 30.07.2019.

UNIDO (2004). *Integrated Programme in Uganda: Enhanced Competitiveness and Sustainability of Industrial Development with Particular Emphasis on Agro-Industries and Micro and Small-Scale Enterprises.* 27 February. Evaluation Unit, United Nations Industrial Development Organization. Vienna. Retrieved from: www.unido.org/sites/default/files/2007-11/23820_Uganda_Integrated_Programme_Feb_2004_0.pdf. Last accessed: 30.07.2019.

UNIDO (2013). Uganda Cleaner Production Centre. *Inventory On e-Waste Management Practices in Uganda.* Final Report. UE/UGA/1/2/001. October. United Nations Industrial Development Organization. Vienna. Retrieved from: https://open.unido.org/api/documents/4783827/download/Inventory%20on%20e-waste%20management%20practices%20in%20Uganda%20-%20Final%20report. Last accessed: 14.08.2014.

UNIDO (2016a). *Global Assessment of Eco-Industrial Parks in Developing and Emerging Economies: Achievements, Good Practices and Lessons Learned from Thirty-Three Industrial Parks in Twelve Selected Emerging and Developing Countries.* November. United Nations Industrial Development Organization. Vienna. Retrieved from: www.unido.org/sites/default/files/2017-02/2016_Unido_Global_Assessment_of_Eco-Industrial_

Parks_in_Developing_Countries-Global_RECP_programme_0.pdf. Last accessed: 14.08.2019.

UNIDO (2016b). *Investment Promotion on Environmentally Sound Management of Electrical and Electronic Waste in East Africa with Focus on Ethiopia.* Independent Terminal Evaluation. April. United Nations Industrial Development Organization. Vienna. Retrieved from: www.thegef.org/sites/default/files/project_documents/GEF%2520ID-5040_GFETH-120227_TE%2520report%25202017.pdf. Last accessed: 14.08.2019.

UNIDO (2017). *Implementation Handbook for Eco-Industrial Parks.* United Nations Industrial Development Organization. Vienna. Retrieved from: www.unido.org/sites/default/files/files/2018-05/UNIDO%20Eco-Industrial%20Park%20Handbook_English.pdf. Last accessed: 14.08.2019.

UNIDO/UNEP (2015). *National Cleaner Production Centres Twenty Years of Achievement: Towards Decoupling Resource Use and Environmental Impact from Manufacturing Growth.* October. United Nations Industrial Development Organization and United Nations Environment Programme. Retrieved from: www.unido.org/fileadmin/user_media_upgrade/What_we_do/Topics/Resource-efficient__low-carbon_production/NCPC_20_years.pdf. Last accessed: 30.07.2019.

UNIDO/World Bank/GIZ (2017). *An International Framework for Eco-Industrial Parks.* December. United Nations Industrial Development Organization, the World Bank, GIZ. Retrieved from: https://openknowledge.worldbank.org/bitstream/handle/10986/29110/122179-WP-PUBLIC-AnInternationalFrameworkforEcoIndustrialParks.pdf?sequence=1&isAllowed=y. Last accessed: 06.08.2019.

US Department of Commerce (2010). *Measuring the Green Economy.* US Department of Commerce, Economics and Statistics Administration. April. Retrieved from: www.commerce.gov/sites/default/files/migrated/reports/greeneconomyreport_0.pdf. Last accessed: 30.07.2019.

US Department of Commerce (a). *Bureau of Economic Analysis.* Industry Data, Underlying Detail of Industry Economic Accounts Data: GDP by Industry. Retrieved from: https://apps.bea.gov/iTable/iTable.cfm?reqid=56#reqid=56. Last accessed: 04.08.2019.

US Department of State (2014). *World Economic Forum Joint Statement on Environmental Goods Trade.* Retrieved from: https://kr.usembassy.gov/p_econ_012414b/. Last accessed: 30.07.2019.

US EPA (a). *Code of Federal Regulations, Part 82 Protection of Stratospheric Ozone, Subpart a Production and Consumption Controls.* US Environmental Protection Agency. Retrieved from: www.gpo.gov/fdsys/pkg/CFR-2016-title40-vol21/xml/CFR-2016-title40-vol21-part82.xml#seqnum82.4. Last accessed: 30.07.2019.

Wang, H., Wang, T., Zhang, B., Li, F., Toure, B., Bosire Omosa, I., Chiramba, T., Abdel-Monem, M., Pradhan, M. (2014). Water and wastewater treatment in Africa: Current practices and challenges. *CLEAN: Soil, Air, Water,* 42:8:1029–1035.

World Bank (2012). Hoornweg, D., Bhada-Tata, P. *What a Waste: A Global Review of Solid Waste Management.* Urban Development Series, No. 15. March. The World Bank. Washington, DC. Retrieved from: https://siteresources.worldbank.org/INTURBANDEVELOPMENT/Resources/336387-1334852610766/What_a_Waste2012_Final.pdf. Last accessed: 04.08.2019.

World Bank (2014). *Low Carbon Zones: A Practitioner's Handbook*. Report Number 90511. May. The World Bank. Washington, DC. Retrieved from: http://documents. worldbank.org/curated/en/406281468149388758/pdf/905110WP0Box380arbo n0Zones0Handbook.pdf. Last accessed: 14.08.2019.

World Bank (2017). *Environmental Health and Pollution Management Programme in Africa*. GEF-6 Program Framework Document (PFD). 10 April. The World Bank. Retrieved from: www.thegef.org/sites/default/files/project_documents/Revised_ PFD_EHPMP_10_April_2017-final.pdf. Last accessed: 14.08.2019.

World Bank (2018). *Environmental Health and Pollution Management Programme in Africa*. Project Information Document (PID). The World Bank.

WTO (a). World Trade Organization website. *Environmental Goods Agreement (EGA), to Be Found at Home > Trade Topics > Trade and Environment > Ega*. Retrieved from: www.wto.org/english/tratop_e/envir_e/ega_e.htm. Last accessed: 30.07.2019.

WWAP (2017). *Wastewater: The Untapped Resource*. The United Nations World Water Development Report 2017. United Nations World Water Assessment Programme. March. UNESCO. Paris. Retrieved from: www.unido.org/sites/default/files/2017-03/UN_World_Water_Development_Report_-_Full_0.pdf. Last accessed: 04.08.2019.

Yeo, H., Akinci, G. (2011). Low-carbon, green special economic zones. In Farole, T., Akinci, G. (eds.) *Special Economic Zones: Progress, Emerging Challenges and Future Directions*, pp. 280–305. World Bank. Washington, DC. Retrieved from: http:// documents.worldbank.org/curated/en/752011468203980987/pdf/638440PUB0 Exto00Box0361527B0PUBLIC0.pdf. Last accessed: 14.08.2019.

5 Green industry indicators[1]

5.1. Introduction

The UN General Assembly's Resolution 70/1, 'Transforming our World: The 2030 Agenda for Sustainable Development', puts economic development on the global development agenda. At the core of the new development agenda are the 17 Sustainable Development Goals (SDGs) (UN, 2015).

Of these 17 goals, five address economic development and environmental concerns whereas other goals address social, political, and agricultural development. Goal 9 sees industry (herein defined as manufacturing) as the primary engine not only for job creation and economic growth but also technology transfer, investment flows, and skills development. Industry is also central in contributing to goal 6 (ensuring availability and sustainable management of water and sanitation for all), goal 7 (affordable and clean energy), and goal 12 (responsible consumption and production). The 17 goals are accompanied by 169 targets that constitute the substance of the goals; most of them take the form of objectives to be met. Achievement of the 169 targets is monitored through 230 indicators. Of the 169 targets and 230 indicators, 4 targets and their 12 associated indicators will be directly impacted by industrial development (Table 5.1) (we treat 9.2.1 as two indicators [9.2.1a and 9.2.1b] because it contains percent and per capita estimates that are significantly different[2]).

This chapter has three objectives: (i) to assess the quality dimensions of data for monitoring industry-related SDG progress in one sector, industry, and for one geographic region, the 47 countries in the SSA region, (ii) to question the feasibility of meeting even the most basic economic and employment industry-related targets, and (iii) to identify additional indicators for monitoring industry-related progress in meeting SDG targets.

Table 5.1 SDGs impacted by industrial development

Goals	Targets*	Indicators*
6. Ensure availability and sustainable management of water . . .	6.3 By 2030, improve water quality by reducing pollution, halving the proportion of untreated wastewater.	6.3.1 Proportion of wastewater safely treated
	6.4 By 2030, substantially increase water-use efficiency across all sectors and ensure sustainable withdrawals . . .	6.4.1 Change in water-use efficiency over time
7. Affordable, reliable, and modern energy	7.3 By 2030, double the global rate of improvement in energy efficiency.	7.3.1 Energy intensity measured in terms of primary energy and gross domestic product (GDP)
9. Infrastructure, industrialisation, and innovation	9.2 Promote inclusive and sustainable industrialisation and, by 2030, significantly raise industry's share of employment and GDP, in line with national circumstances, and double its share in least developed countries.	9.2.1 Manufacturing value-added (MVA) as a percent of GDP and per capita MVA
		9.2.2 Manufacturing employment as a percent of total employment
	9.3 Increase the access of small-scale industrial and other enterprises, in particular in developing countries, to financial services, including affordable credit, and their integration into value chains and markets.	9.3.1 Proportion of small-scale industries in total industry value-added
		9.3.2 Percent of small-scale industries with a loan or line of credit
	9.4 By 2030, upgrade infrastructure and retrofit industries to make them sustainable, with increased resource efficiency . . .	9.4.1 CO_2 emission per unit of value added
	9.b Support domestic technology development, research, and innovation in developing countries . . .	9.b.1 Proportion of medium and high-tech industry value-added in total value-added
12. Responsible consumption and production	12.2 By 2030, achieve the sustainable management and efficient use of natural resources.	12.2.2 Domestic material consumption (DMC), DMC per capita, and DMC per GDP*
	12.4 By 2020, achieve the environmentally sound management of chemicals and wastes throughout their life cycle . . . and significantly reduce their release to air water and soil . . .	12.4.2 Treatment of waste, generation of hazardous waste, hazardous management by type of treatment

* The 169 targets are identified by two numbers or one number and one letter. The 230 indicators are identified by three numbers or letters.

Source: Information extracted from UN 2016

The chapter starts with a brief summary of the literature about the African data deficit, which to date has focused almost exclusively on macro socio-economic variables, before turning to the methodology we use to define the quality dimensions of data reviewed here. We then assess the quality dimensions in terms of completeness, relevance, accuracy, timeliness, and coherence. Next, we question the feasibility of meeting industry-related targets proposed by the Inter-Agency and Expert Group on Sustainable Development Goal Indicators. We end by endorsing the recommendations of others and propose one way to improve data quality for energy-related targets.

5.2. Literature review

To the best of the authors' knowledge, the quality of the data in the SSA countries with respect to industry-related SDG indicators has hardly been addressed nor have the targets been questioned in the published literature. Rather, the literature, both journal articles and publications by those monitoring the SDG process, has focused on macro socio-economic variables and the limited capacity of national statistical offices to collect and disseminate SDG-relevant data. The challenges for national statistical offices are well described by Diaz-Sarachaga *et al.* (2018), who finds that 60% of the indicators set for tracking progress towards SDGs are lacking information and therefore their assessment is questionable, and by Spangenberg (2016), who writes that only 29% of the 169 targets are well defined in the Final List of Indicators (UN, 2016).

The most widely cited critique of the overall data quality in the SSA region is by Jerven (2008, 2010, 2013). He describes in considerable detail data weaknesses in terms of quality for monitoring gross domestic product (GDP) in SSA countries. More recently, he argues that economists have misinterpreted the African experience at the macro-economic level as one of long-term economic failure (Jerven, 2015). In none of his critiques does he address data quality limitations for monitoring manufacturing-related economic, employment, and environmental performance.

The Center for Global Development addresses the data quality issue by widening the focus from economic parameters to social and environmental parameters, such as birth and death rates, poverty, land use, environment, health, education, and safety (CGD/APHRC, 2014; CGD, 2014, 2015a, 2015b). The Center also describes the more important challenges facing national statistical offices and options for addressing those challenges. It recommends that improving the quality of the current data categories should have priority over expanding data categories. However, the Center does not comment on industry-related data.

In its general review of development data, the Sustainable Development Solutions Network (SDSN, 2015a, 2015b, a) includes a brief description of environmental issues. Furthermore, it offers a comprehensive analysis of the costs for improving the global statistical system. Along the same lines, Kiregyera (2015) puts forward suggestions on how to improve data collection. Again, most reviews do not discuss the data quality for manufacturing output, employment, and environmental impact. A more recent report by the Sustainable Development Goals Center for Africa and the Sustainable Development Solutions Network states that industry-related data should be excluded because different countries specialise in different sectors, so there is no common threshold of manufacturing as a share of GDP for which all countries should aim. In the same report, they also present an extensive review of Ghana that reveals that 30 indicators are lacking data and overall at least 33% of the data is of questionable quality (SDGCA/SDSN, 2018).

UNIDO, which has the mandate of collecting and disseminating international industrial statistics and, more recently, the responsibility to report on a number of SDG 9 indicators, is keenly aware of the data quality issues in industrial statistics. Many years before the formulation of the SDGs, UNIDO documented that many SSA countries have not collected industry-related data for a long time and have no regular programme for updating industrial statistics (UNIDO, 2009). UNIDO recently reviewed the availability of statistical indicators for assessing progress in meeting industry-related SDG 9 targets (UNIDO, 2017). For other indicators, UNIDO relies partly on its own data set and partly on data provided by other international organisations responsible for industry-related data. The review finds that in developing countries, data are not yet available for many indicators, particularly for Least Developed Countries (LDCs). While data for basic manufacturing production and employment are available for most developing countries, there are problems with even the basic production and employment indicator data for manufacturing sub-sectors and a critical data gap in many developing countries for the remaining indicators.

In sum, the available literature has yet to address the SSA data quality issues for monitoring progress in meeting industry-related SDG indicators other than offering generic advice for upgrading the capacity of statistical offices. Nor does the literature provide specific guidance to the UN Inter-Agency and Expert Group on Sustainable Development Goal Indicators on tasks it needs to undertake to improve the quality of data necessary to the monitor progress in meeting targets.

5.3. Methodology

We started our assessment of the quality dimensions (components) of data for monitoring progress in meeting industry-related SDG targets by reviewing several data quality assessment frameworks which have been proposed. Two of these are mentioned here. The UN National Quality Assessment Framework (NQAF), proposed by the United Nations Statistics Division (UNSD), is made up of five dimensions: (1) relevance; (2) accuracy and reliability; (3) timeliness and punctuality; (4) accessibility and clarity; and (5) coherence and comparability (chapter 3 of UNSD, 2019). UNSD also presented a detailed mapping of NQAF with other frameworks, both those of international and national organisations. After reviewing the NQAF and several of these other frameworks, we decided to adopt a similar framework proposed by UNIDO because it is focused on the quality dimensions of data related to industrial activity (UNIDO, 2009). In addition to the five quality dimensions proposed in the NQAF, UNIDO adds the quality dimension of completeness. Thus, its six quality dimensions are:

- Completeness – country and activity coverage;
- Relevance – data are central to assessing progress;
- Accuracy – correctly describes the phenomena it is designed to measure;
- Timeliness – the lag between the reference year of the most recently reported data and their publication;
- Comparability – national data comply with various UN recommendations related to industrial statistics;
- Coherence – terms in one dataset have exactly the same meaning in another data set.

Given the overwhelming task of assessing the quality dimensions of SDG indicator data, we limited our review to five of the six quality dimensions proposed by UNIDO: completeness, relevance, accuracy, timeliness, and coherence, with most attention paid to completeness. The latter is what hindered monitoring progress in meeting the indicators of the Millennium Development Goals (MDGs) (UNSD, a) and what is now hindering monitoring progress in meeting the SDG targets. We did not consider comparability because it is not a data quality issue for SSA countries.

5.4. Data quality

Completeness

Data for indicators 9.2.1a, manufacturing value added (MVA) as percent of GDP, and 9.2.1b, MVA per capita, are available from the MVA database of the United Nations Industrial Development Organization (UNIDO, a). Data are reported for all 47 SSA countries for the period 2000 to 2018 (Table 5.2).

Table 5.2 MVA and employment in the SSA countries, 2000–2018

Country	MVA share in GDP		Growth	MVA per capita		Growth	Manufacturing employment share		Absolute growth	MVA growth	Manufacturing employment growth
	2000	2018		2000	2018		2000	2018			
Angola	3	8	142.6	73	262	259.3	3	2	−39.3	572.1	38.2
Benin	23	12	−46.9	157	110	−29.7	10	15	51.7	17.7	157.6
Botswana	6	6	−0.8	314	486	54.7	9	2	−75.1	108.8	−55.5
Burkina Faso	10	7	−35.9	46	48	4.2	3	15	372.0	77.0	582.5
Burundi	13	11	−15.3	29	23	−19.4	2	2	12.7	41.3	102.2
Cabo Verde	8	6	−28.9	189	213	12.6	5	5	−17.9	43.2	29.5
Cameroon	15	14	−7.8	176	213	21.0	7	6	−18.8	95.5	41.5
Central African Republic	14	24	64.7	68	81	20.6	6	7	14.8	52.2	43.9
Chad	7	6	−13.4	30	49	60.2	6	4	−30.2	195.0	30.4
Comoros	5	6	13.2	78	99	26.0	8	9	14.6	93.6	95.4
Congo, Republic of	2	4	75.7	52	101	95.7	19	21	11.0	227.4	109.3
Côte d'Ivoire	14	15	3.9	190	254	33.9	5	6	15.4	99.9	56.2
Democratic Republic of Congo	32	16	−48.6	92	67	−27.3	9	10	13.0	29.7	99.7
Djibouti	4	3	−15.2	35	54	52.8	13	16	20.6	106.8	84.6
Equatorial Guinea	9	30	248.8	562	3076	447.1	7	3	−49.0	1070.2	14.7
Eritrea	10	6	−44.7	70	35	−49.5	7	6	−18.2	−22.8	33.9
Eswatini	32	34	4.2	952	1320	38.7	12	10	−15.9	81.9	21.7
Ethiopia	4	6	30.3	8	30	293.3	3	5	58.8	532.5	201.1
Gabon	3	5	50.9	301	414	37.4	3	4	19.2	130.8	131.0
Gambia	5	5	−16.7	29	25	−11.9	9	9	1.3	54.6	86.5
Ghana	8	5	−37.5	77	92	20.3	12	8	−31.5	87.1	26.9
Guinea	13	9	−28.2	74	74	−0.5	3	3	7.5	47.5	62.8
Guinea-Bissau	13	10	−20.2	68	61	−10.7	6	6	−0.8	37.1	62.3
Kenya	13	10	−22.9	105	118	12.5	11	11	−5.7	82.2	51.9
Lesotho	10	11	9.8	85	144	68.4	5	12	158.3	104.0	189.6

(Continued)

Table 5.2 (Continued)

Country	MVA share in GDP 2000	2018	Growth	MVA per capita 2000	2018	Growth	Manufacturing employment share 2000	2018	Absolute growth	MVA growth	Manufacturing employment growth
Liberia	0	4	1024.2	1	15	1566.7	4	7	87.7	2581.4	238.9
Madagascar	11	12	5.8	57	59	3.1	5	7	31.3	71.6	146.6
Malawi	7	10	29.4	28	46	65.9	8	8	-7.9	179.3	66.8
Mali	15	13	-10.3	61	133	119.0	12	5	-60.7	281.6	-7.7
Mauritania	12	6	-49.8	122	81	-33.6	6	6	-13.2	11.3	48.8
Mauritius	19	12	-36.0	1072	1276	19.0	29	13	-53.5	27.4	-46.2
Mozambique	11	9	-20.1	28	45	62.7	1	1	-36.6	175.0	-4.2
Namibia	11	11	-5.1	427	621	45.5	5	7	25.0	98.2	92.9
Niger	6	6	3.3	18	24	31.3	6	7	11.4	158.5	114.8
Nigeria	6	9	46.8	84	223	165.2	7	8	19.7	324.5	85.8
Rwanda	6	6	-3.9	20	48	135.5	1	2	57.2	266.3	159.8
Sao Tome and Principe	9	8	-13.4	77	99	29.3	8	5	-32.2	94.7	13.1
Senegal	14	9	-32.2	122	112	-8.4	9	14	53.1	51.2	192.9
Seychelles	12	7	-39.1	1190	1066	-10.4				5.2	
Sierra Leone	3	2	-33.2	7	9	30.3	3	3	-2.9	119.7	53.5
Somalia	2	2	1.4	2	2	0.0	7	7	5.1	65.5	74.5
South Africa	15	12	-15.8	848	913	7.6	13	11	-16.6	35.1	9.7
Togo	7	10	41.9	37	64	70.2	15	13	-11.3	173.9	42.0
Uganda	11	9	-20.1	43	57	32.7	6	4	-32.0	144.1	33.3
United Republic of Tanzania	6	7	19.0	28	60	117.0	3	3	-22.7	275.3	38.8
Zambia	10	8	-18.5	92	131	42.9	3	5	67.7	138.9	190.8
Zimbabwe	18	8	-56.5	113	73.2	-35.2	8	4	-44.8	-10.4	-9.3
Total SSA	**11**	**10**	**-9.6**	**130**	**165**	**26.6**	**7**	**7**	**1.7**	**105.9**	**73.7**

Notes: Countries in italics are LDCs. Abbreviations: MVA, manufacturing value added; SSA, Sub-Saharan Africa

Source: Data extracted from UNIDO, a; ILO 2018

The potential of even this most basic data (GDP and MVA) as long-term baseline indicators is problematic because of the growing trend among African countries to revise their methods and base year data to calculate GDP. In the year 2014 alone, five countries (Kenya, Nigeria, Tanzania, Uganda, and Zambia) undertook rebasing exercises (Sy, 2015). Not only are there massive upward revaluations of GDP, there are significant changes in GDP composition. The 2013 revised figures for the five countries show increases in services, declines in industry, and relatively stable levels of agriculture. Revision of Ghanaian macro-economic accounts in 2010 shows that the service sector is now larger than agriculture, and that industry contributes less to GDP than had been reported in the old series. The reduced industry contribution in the rebased database, however, is most likely because of slow economic growth in the 2000s rather than correction of its weight in the national accounts (Jerven and Duncan, 2012).

Data for indicator 9.2.2 (manufacturing employment as a percent of total employment) are available from the International Labour Organization's (ILO) Trends Econometric Models and the UNIDO Industrial Statistics Database (INDSTAT) (ILO, 2018; UNIDO, b). ILO reports data for both formal and informal manufacturing and total employment for 43 of the 47 SSA countries for the period 2000 to 2015, whereas UNIDO reports data only for formal manufacturing employment for 22 out of 47 SSA countries and does not report total employment.

Data for indicator 9.3.1 (the percent share of small-scale industries in industry value added) are not yet available. There is no consensus about the various definitions of industry, some of which are broad (manufacturing, construction, and mining) and others are narrow (only manufacturing). Nor is there a consensus about how to define small-scale industry. Lastly, there is a scarcity of data collected by SSA countries with a common definition of small-scale industry.

Data for indicator 9.3.2 (the percent of small-scale industries with a loan or line of credit) are reported in the World Bank Enterprise Surveys (World Bank, a). The data for small-scale industries (5 to 19 employees) are reported at irregular intervals (between five and ten years) for 35 out of 47 SSA countries in the period 2006 and 2017. For two countries, there are data for three points in time; for 23 countries, for two points in time; and ten countries, for one point in time.

Data for indicator 9.4.1 carbon dioxide (CO_2) emissions per unit of value added) combine CO_2 emissions from total fuel combustion reported by the International Energy Agency (IEA) with MVA data from UNIDO (IEA, 2018a; UNIDO, a). What is not included in the IEA data are CO_2 process emissions (mainly from cement production) reported by the Carbon Dioxide Information Analysis Center (CDIAC, 2016). The CO_2 emission data from total fuel combustion are available for 23 out of the 47 SSA countries for the period 1990 to 2016.

Data for indicator 9.b.1 (proportion of medium and high-tech industry value added in total value added) are important for determining value-added shifts in economic activity from low-tech to medium and high-tech industry in total value added. UNIDO INDSTAT is the only database with information about manufacturing sub-sectors (UNIDO, b). Unfortunately, in the case of Africa, only 13 out of 47 countries reported sub-sector value-added data for the period 2000 to 2014; for the remainder there are hardly any data. For those 13 countries, there are significant variations in the reported number of sub-sectors and in yearly coverage.

Data for industry-relevant water indicators 6.3.1 (proportion of wastewater safely treated) and 6.4.1 (change in water use efficiency) are not available in AQUASTAT (FAO, a). It reports only more general water withdrawal and municipal wastewater treatment. AQUASTAT does report industry water withdrawal, which combines self-supplied industries not connected to the public distribution and water for the cooling of thermoelectric power plants. AQUASTAT reports industrial water use data for 47 SSA countries in some but not all periods between 2000 and 2017. The data-rich periods are 1996–2002 (28 countries) and 2003–2007 (28 countries); there are virtually no country-specific industrial water data for SSA countries for the period 2008–2012 and no country-specific industrial data for the period 2013–2017.

Data for indicator 7.3.1 (energy intensity defined as energy use per unit of MVA) for industry are available in the IEA Extended World Energy Balances and UNIDO's INDSTAT database (IEA, 2018b; UNIDO, b). It is the most comprehensive (over 100 developing countries) and complete (1971 to the present) data source. Unfortunately, it reports total final consumption data for industry (manufacturing, mining, and construction) for only 22 out of the 47 African countries; there are no data for the remainder of the countries. There is no data category for manufacturing, but there are data categories for 11 manufacturing sub-sectors. Only six out of the 22 countries have data for more than five out of the 11 manufacturing sectors and for at least three out of four years (1990, 2000, 2010, and 2014).

Data for indicator 12.2.2 (domestic material consumption by the industry sector) are not yet available in the Material Flow database put together by Sustainable Europe Research Institute and Vienna University of Business and Economics (SERI/VUBE, a). The current database comprises data for more than 200 countries (including the 47 SSA countries) and more than 300 different materials aggregated into four main material groups of material flows. The most important indicators are domestic material extraction and consumption. The materials flow database reports domestic material consumption by country. The data can be disaggregated by the four main material groups (biomass, metal ores, minerals, and fossil fuels), but not yet by sectors such as agriculture and industry.

Data for indicator 12.4.2 (hazardous waste) are extremely limited and there is no agreed upon methodology for measuring this indicator. The United Nations Statistics Division (UNSD, b) reports hazardous waste generation for only ten out of 47 SSA countries (Burkina Faso, Cabo Verde, Cameroon, Madagascar, Mauritius, Niger, South Africa, Togo, Zambia, and Zimbabwe) for the period 1995 to 2014. For some of these countries the data are only for one year or one part of the country. Moreover, the definition of hazardous waste varies from country to country and one cannot discern the proportion of hazardous waste generated by the manufacturing sector (UNSD, b).

Relevance

We find that the data set for monitoring industry-related progress fails to provide an adequate assessment of potential progress and needs to be expanded to include changes in absolute levels of MVA and of manufacturing employment.

Keeping MVA as a percent of GDP as an economic indicator (9.2.1) is essential but it is of limited value because it is more likely to decrease rather than increase over time due to the rapid expansion of the service sector in most SSA countries. Consequently, we propose including growth in the absolute value of MVA as an essential and complementary measure to the percent share of MVA in GDP. For most SSA countries, the absolute value increased during the past 15 years and most likely will continue to do so in the next 15 years.

Keeping manufacturing employment as a percent of total employment (9.2.2) is essential but it too most likely will show a decline over the next 15-year period if the past 15-year trend is a guide. For the 47 African countries for which we have data, the percent declined in 32 countries and increased in 21 countries in the period 2000–2016. By contrast, the number increased in 41 countries and decreased slightly for six countries the number of manufacturing jobs decreased slightly. Considering past trends and expansion of the service sector, it is unlikely that most of the SSA countries will be able to double the share as originally proposed by the IAEG-SDGs (ILO, 2019; Dasgupta *et al.*, 2019). Consequently, we propose including growth in manufacturing employment as an essential and complementary measure to the percent share of manufacturing employment in total employment.

The GDP measure of energy intensity (7.3) needs to be complemented by MVA energy intensity. We support adding this indicator even though there are data quality concerns about the data for monitoring progress. Specifically, IEA data for the most part are too aggregated (only industry and not separated for the most part into the three sectors within industry (manufacturing, construction, and mining). An even better complementary measure would be energy efficiency but there are no manufacturing sector data to measure improvements in energy efficiency at that level. We also recommend adding energy decoupling as an indicator for the manufacturing sector, which is in line with but not clearly specified as an indicator for target 7.3.

Along the same lines, the GDP measure of CO_2 intensity (9.4.1) needs to be complemented by MVA CO_2 intensity. We propose adding this indicator even though there are data quality concerns about the data for monitoring progress. Specifically, there is a need to reconcile different estimates of industrial CO_2 emissions. We also recommend adding CO_2 decoupling as an indicator for the manufacturing sector, which is in line with but not clearly specified as an indicator for target 9.4.1.

Accuracy

A comparison of percent changes in MVA and employment over the period 2000 to 2018 calls into question the accuracy of employment data for 11 out of 46 countries (excluding Seychelles because there are no employment data). The ILO employment database for those countries shows there are large (more than 100%) changes in MVA, but only small or negative changes in employment. For other countries the changes in MVA and employment are reasonably consistent.

Timeliness

Our review of the timeliness of industry-related data is limited to subsector value-added needed to monitor progress in meeting 9.b.1. UNIDO is solely responsible for collecting this data and considers data timely if there is only a three-year lag between a reference year of the most recently reported data and their publication. Our review of value-added data in UNIDO's INDSTAT database finds that there is only a three-year lag (2016–2018) for only six SSA countries. There are lags of six years for six SSA countries and greater than six years for 14 countries. There are no value-added data for the remaining 21 SSA countries (UNIDO, b).

Coherence

Coherence, which requires that terms and concepts used in one dataset have the same meaning in another dataset, is an issue in estimating the accuracy of some industry-related indictors. The more significant issues are those for comparing changes in MVA and employment and estimating both energy intensity and CO_2 intensities. Comparisons of changes in MVA and employment need additional verification because UNIDO value-added data are collected for the formal sector with ten or more employees whereas ILO data combine employment in both the formal and informal sectors. Estimates of manufacturing energy intensity (7.3.1) are challenging because there is no IEA data category for total manufacturing energy consumption that can be combined with UNIDO data for MVA to estimate intensities. Estimates of CO_2 intensity (9.4.1) are questionable because of the differences in reported industry CO_2 emissions by IEA, the Carbon Dioxide Information Analysis Center, and the United Nations Framework Convention on Climate Change.

5.5. Feasibility of meeting targets

We use the changes in five indicators over the past 15 years (2000–2015) as a basis for assessing the likelihood of meeting targets during the next 15-year period (2016 to 2030). These indicators are 9.2.1a (MVA as a percentage of GDP), 9.2.1b (per capita MVA), 9.2.2 (manufacturing employment), 9.4.1 (CO_2 intensity and decoupling), and 7.3.1 (energy intensity and decoupling).

Manufacturing value added

We first estimate how many countries doubled their share of MVA in GDP in the past 15 years because doubling the share is one of the proposed targets for LDCs (slightly more than two-thirds of SSA countries are LDCs) to meet in next 15-year period, 2016 to 2030. For the SSA region (47 countries), the share of MVA in GDP decreased from 11.1% in 2000 to 10.1% in 2018 (Table 5.2). The percent of MVA in GDP increased for 15 countries, decreased for 25 countries, and remained the same for 7 countries. In 2000–2018, two countries, Equatorial Guinea and Liberia, experienced a sharp upturn in their shares of MVA in GDP, more than doubling the percent shares.

We then estimate how many countries doubled the change in MVA per capita between 2000 and 2018, because doubling per capita is one of the proposed targets for LDCs in the next 15-year period. MVA per capita doubled over this period for four oil-rich countries (Angola, Congo, Equatorial Guinea, and Nigeria) and four other countries (Ethiopia, Liberia, Mali, and United Republic of Tanzania); increased for 34 countries; and declined for three countries (Eritrea, Seychelles, and Zimbabwe).

We propose an additional indicator that has the potential to tell a more positive story about progress in meeting target 9.2. This additional indicator would be the percent growth in MVA between 2016 and 2030. The percent increase for the whole of SSA was 96% over the period 2000 to 2018 and varied considerably among countries. The percent growth in MVA for 18 of the 47 countries was more than 100%. For 14 countries, the percent growth ranged from 50 and 100% and for 13 countries it ranged between 0 and 50%. MVA decreased for two countries (Eritrea and Zimbabwe).

Manufacturing employment

We first estimate how many countries doubled their share of manufacturing employment in the past 15 years because doubling the share is one of the proposed targets for LDCs (slightly more than two-thirds of SSA countries are LDCs) in next 15-year period, 2016 to 2030. For the period 2000–2018, the percent of manufacturing employment in total employment for SSA region remained the same (Table 5.2). For the 46 countries in the ILO database, the percent of manufacturing employment in total employment increased for 21 countries and decreased for 23 countries. Two countries (Burkina Faso and Lesotho) doubled their share.

We propose an additional indicator that has potential to tell a more positive story in meeting target 9.2. This indicator would be the percent change in total manufacturing employment. Total manufacturing employment increased by more than 100% for 12 countries, between 50 and 100% for 15 countries, between 0 and 50% for 13 countries; it deceased for five countries.

Energy intensity and decoupling

Energy use intensity and the relative decoupling of energy consumption from MVA could be estimated for only 22 SSA countries. Manufacturing energy intensity (manufacturing energy consumption per unit of MVA) in SSA remained the same between 2000 and 2016. SSA average intensity is comparable with the world average as well as the average intensities for other regions. The energy intensities of four SSA countries were higher than the SSA average in 2016 and of 22 countries were lower. For the period 2000 to 2016, relative decoupling of energy from industrial output for SSA countries was −0.2 compared to the world average of 0.0 (Table 5.3). Relative decoupling occurred for 12 of the 22 countries for which we found data.

Indicators Country	MVA growth	Energy growth	Energy intensity (manufacturing) 2000	Energy intensity (manufacturing) 2016	Growth	Relative decoupling	CO$_2$ emission intensity 2000	CO$_2$ emission intensity 2016	Growth	Relative decoupling
Angola	512.5	64	0.6	0.16	-73	-0.7	1.24	0.27	-78	-1.0
Benin	11.7	287	0.05	0.17	240	2.5	0.12	0.51	325	2.8
Botswana	93.5	115	0.04	0.05	25	0.1	0.13	0.08	-38	-0.7
Cameroon	84.3	71	0.07	0.07	0	-0.1	0.07	0.05	-29	-0.6
Côte d'Ivoire	63.9	146	0.1	0.15	50	0.5	0.23	0.3	30	-0.2
Democratic Republic of Congo	29.6	22	0.67	0.63	-6	-0.1	0.01	0.01	0	-0.2
Eritrea	-28.4	-25	0.08	0.08	0	0.0	0.16	0.11	-31	0.0
Ethiopia	414.7	346	0.59	0.51	-14	-0.1	1.58	1.44	-9	-0.8
Gabon	111.7	763	0.98	3.99	307	3.1	1.41	1.5	6	-0.5
Ghana	74.9	5	0.88	0.53	-40	-0.4	0.47	0.66	40	-0.2
Kenya	69.1	124	0.19	0.25	32	0.3	0.45	0.62	38	-0.2
Mauritius	22.1	-17	0.2	0.13	-35	-0.3	0.28	0.21	-25	-0.4
Mozambique	160.6	144	1.48	1.38	-7	-0.1	0.13	0.23	77	-0.3
Namibia	75.9	2141	0	0.04	0	11.7	0.01	0.02	100	0.1
Niger	148.2	251	0.12	0.17	42	0.4	0.2	0.39	95	-0.2
Nigeria	307.0	120	0.31	0.17	-45	-0.5	0.29	0.16	-45	-0.9
Senegal	44.3	206	0.15	0.32	113	1.1	0.42	1	138	0.6
South Africa	35.2	23	0.44	0.4	-9	-0.1	0.97	0.85	-12	-0.4
Togo	137.9	-16	0.5	0.18	-64	-0.6	1.42	0.4	-72	-0.9
United Republic of Tanzania	229.3	188	1.3	1.13	-13	-0.1	0.5	0.43	-14	-0.7
Zambia	125.2	114	1.13	1.07	-5	0.0	0.48	0.24	-50	-0.8
Zimbabwe	-8.7	-53	0.79	0.41	-48	-0.5	2	0.79	-61	-0.6
Total SSA	**96.5**	**59**	**0.5**	**0.5**	**12**	**-0.2**	**0.65**	**0.47**	**-28**	**-0.6**
World	**55.1**	**45.7**	**0.24**	**0.22**	**-6.0**	**0.0**	**0.49**	**0.51**	**4.1**	**-0.1**

Calculation of RDuse = [(Energy Use 2014/MVA2014) − (Energy Use 2000/MVA2000)] / (Energy Use 2000/MVA 2000)
Calculation of RDCO$_2$ = [(CO$_2$ 2014/MVA2014) − (CO$_2$ 2000/MVA2000)] / (CO$_2$ 2000/MVA 2000)

Source: Data extracted from IEA 2018a, IEA 2018b, and UNIDO b

CO_2 emission intensity and decoupling

CO_2 emission intensity and the relative decoupling of CO_2 emissions from MVA could be estimated for only 22 SSA countries. For the period 2000 to 2016, CO_2 manufacturing intensity decreased from 0.7 kg per unit of MVA to 0.5 kg per unit of MVA, resulting in a relative decoupling of CO_2 emissions from manufacturing of −0.6% (Table 5.3). Eighteen countries experienced relative decoupling of CO_2 emissions from MVA. Other countries, particularly Benin, Senegal, and Namibia, experienced significant increases in manufacturing CO_2 emission intensity.

5.6. Recommendations

Our recommendation for improving data quality seconds that of others that call for additional financial and technical support national statistical offices. The General Assembly Resolution 70/1 calls for an intensification of efforts to strengthen statistical capacities and to support capacity-building capacities in developing countries, particularly African countries (UN, 2015). The individual capacities of the national statistical offices in terms of technical, financial, and labour force mean that they are simply unable to deliver all relevant data. Jerven (2013) as well as the Center for Global Development (CGD, 2014) find that national offices are "caught within a vicious cycle". They have insufficient resources to collect and properly process data. The resulting low output and accuracy results in a lower demand, which in turn minimises the resources available needed to break out of the cycle. More recently, the Sustainable Development Goals Report 2018 reiterates that additional resources are required to monitor not just industry-related targets, but for all proposed SDG targets. Based on a pilot project in six countries – three in Africa and three in Asia – data for only 40 (20%) of the global SDG indicators are currently available and another 47 global indicators (23%) have a data source and should be easily feasible. The remaining 57% of indicators could be feasible with enhancing country's statistical capacity through consultations with all components of the National Statistical Systems (UN, 2018).

The several ongoing private and public efforts to disseminate data in Africa should increase the demand for improved data quality. The most promising is the African Information Highway initiated by AfDB (AfDB, a). Its goal is to improve data availability and accuracy across the whole continent and to provide a platform that links all national statistical offices in Africa with each other and with important stakeholders. Data are now available for all African countries on economic, environment, and energy topics. Currently, the African Information Highway contains no relevant data for the industry-related SDG targets (AfDB, b). Other promising efforts that should increase the demand for quality data are OpenAFRICA and the African Data Initiative. The former is an independent open-source platform for the general public. It is a grassroots initiative supported by numerous stakeholders like Google and the World Bank Group (OpenAFRICA, a). The latter is a crowd funded project by the African Maths Initiative. It aims to support the data revolution in Africa with enough data training and the availability of suitable software (Chuffed, a).

Another industry specific opportunity for improving data accuracy and coverage is to initiate more energy decoupling programmes for the manufacturing sector. There are already ongoing industrial energy decoupling programmes in Africa that are yielding data about energy use and achieving commendable savings in energy use. Most impressive is the South African National Energy Efficiency Strategy first issued in 2005 and revised in 2008 (South Africa, 2008). The strategy set a national target for energy efficiency improvement for the industrial sector of 15% by 2015 relative to projected consumption, and annual reduction targets for five energy-intensive industrial sectors. The Department of Energy recently announced that the programme has exceeded its target, achieving an overall 19% reduction in energy use by 2015 (A. Hartzenburg, personal communication, 2017). More recently, Ethiopia, with its Climate-Resilient Green Economy Strategy (Ethiopia, 2011), and Kenya, with its Green Economy Strategy and Implementation Plan (Kenya, 2016), have formulated green economy strategies, both of which benchmark industrial energy consumption and set energy decoupling targets. Five countries (Ghana, Kenya, Mauritius, South Africa, and Uganda) have implemented sustainable consumption and green production policies and adopted green national strategies under the SWITCH-Africa Green project launched by UN Environment in 2014 (SWITCH Africa Green, a).

5.7. Conclusions

This chapter expands the data-deficit literature by focusing on the data quality for monitoring industry-related progress in meeting SDG targets. We find that there are international databases for monitoring only a few of industry-related SDG targets set for SSA countries. Clearly, additional sector-specific efforts are needed for data collection and verification. Moreover, meeting the conventional economic and employment industry-related targets, which is not questioned in the literature, will be a challenging task for many SSA countries based on our review of their track record over the past 15 years, a finding which is in line with the observations by the UN Economic Commission for Africa: "Achieving and following up on all these goals and targets (with more than 200 indicators) will obviously be difficult, requiring states to have the capacity to identify interventions with multiplier effects on other goals and targets" (UNECA, 2016). Policy makers in individual SSA countries need to give serious consideration to improving data collection, revising the IAEG-SDGs proposed indicators, and adding additional indicators for absolute levels of MVA and employment. Admittedly, this task will be difficult given that current statistics lag considerably behind real time and, if not carefully constructed, may not reflect what is happening in their countries. Still, setting achievable targets supported by reasonably accurate data avoids creating unrealistic expectations.

Note

1 This chapter reproduces an article published in *Sustainable Development* (Luken *et al.*, 2019), with kind permission from the publisher.
2 We exclude two potential industry related indicators for target 9.5, which calls for enhancing scientific research and upgrading the technological capabilities of industrial sectors, because data cannot be disaggregated by sectors, in our case manufacturing.

References

AfDB (a). *The Africa Information Highway Initiative: How Information Facilitates GDP Growth*. African Development Bank. Retrieved from: www.afdb.org/en/news-and-events/the-africa-information-highway-initiative-how-information-facilitates-gdp-growth-12433. Last accessed: 14.08.2019.

AfDB (b). *African Development Bank Group Data Portal*. Retrieved from: http://dataportal.opendataforafrica.org/. Last accessed: 14.08.2019.

CDIAC (2016). *Database for Total CO_2 Emissions*. Carbon Dioxide Information Analysis Center. Retrieved from: https://cdiac.ess-dive.lbl.gov/. Last accessed: 14.08.2019.

CGD (2014). Glassman, A., Sandefur, J. *The Political Economy of Bad Data: Evidence from African Survey & Administrative Statistics*. Working Paper 373. July. Center for Global Development. Retrieved from: www.cgdev.org/sites/default/files/political-economy-bad-data.pdf. Last accessed: 14.08.2019.

CGD (2015a). Glassman, A., Post, L. Fueling the data revolution: An African data consensus. *CGD Policy Blogs*. 1 April. Center for Global Development. Retrieved from: www.cgdev.org/blog/fueling-data-revolution-africa-data-consensus. Last accessed: 14.08.2019.

CGD (2015b). Glassman, A. Springtime for the data revolution. *CGD Policy Blogs*. 17 April. Center for Global Development. Retrieved from: www.cgdev.org/blog/springtime-data-revolution. Last accessed: 14.08.2019.

CGD/APHRC (2014). *Delivering on the Data Revolution in Sub-Saharan Africa: Final Report of the Data for African Development Working Group*. Center for Global

Development and African Population and Health Research Center. Retrieved from: www.cgdev.org/sites/default/files/CGD14-01%20complete%20for%20 web%200710.pdf. Last accessed: 14.08.2019.

Chuffed (a). *African Data Initiative*. Retrieved from: www.chuffed.org/project/african datainitiative. Last accessed: 14.08.2019.

Dasgupta, S., Kim-Beom, K., Pinedo-Caro, L. (2019). As much to be gained by merchandise as manufacture? The role of services as an engine of growth. *The Japanese Political Economy*. Retrieved from: www.tandfonline.com/doi/full/10.1080/23291 94X.2018.1544031.

Diaz-Sarachaga, J.M., Jato-Espino, D., Castro-Fresno, D. (2018). Is the Sustainable Development Goals (SDG) index an adequate framework to measure the progress of the 2030 agenda? *Sustainable Development*, 26:663–671. https://doi.org/10. 1002/sd.1735.

Ethiopia (2011). *Climate Resilient Green Economy: Green Economy Strategy*. Federal Democratic Republic of Ethiopia. Addis Ababa. Retrieved from: www.adaptation-undp.org/sites/default/files/downloads/ethiopia_climate_resilient_green_economy_ strategy.pdf. Last accessed: 14.08.2019.

FAO (a). *AQUASTAT*. Food and Agricultural Organization. Rome, Italy. Retrieved from: www.fao.org/nr/water/aquastat/data/query/index.html?lang=en. Last accessed: 14.08.2019.

IEA (2018a). *CO_2 Emissions from Fuel Combustion 2018*. International Energy Agency. Paris. Retrieved from: https://webstore.iea.org/co2-emissions-from-fuel-combustion-2018. Last accessed: 14.08.2019.

IEA (2018b). *World Energy Balances 2018*. International Energy Agency. Paris. Retrieved from: https://webstore.iea.org/world-energy-balances-2018. Last accessed: 14.08.2019.

ILO (2018). *Trends Econometric Models*. International Labour Organization. Geneva. Retrieved from: www.ilo.org.

ILO (2019). *Work for a Brighter Future*. International Labour Organization. Geneva. Retrieved from: www.ilo.org/wcmsp5/groups/public/-dgreports/-cabinet/ documents/publication/wcms_662410.pdf. Last accessed: 14.08.2019.

Jerven, M. (2008). *African Economic Growth Reconsidered: Measurement and Performance in East-Central Africa 1965–1995*. PhD Dissertation, London School of Economics. UMI Number: U615944. UMI Dissertation Publishing. London. Retrieved from: http://etheses.lse.ac.uk/2992/1/U615944.pdf. Last accessed: 14.08.2019.

Jerven, M. (2010). The relativity of poverty and income: How reliable are African economic statistics? *African Affairs*, 109:434:77–96. Simon Fraser University. London.

Jerven, M. (2013). *Poor Numbers: How We Are Misled by African Development Statistics and What to Do about It*. Cornell University Press. Ithaca, NY.

Jerven, M. (2015). *Africa: Why Economists Get It Wrong*. Zed Books. London.

Jerven, M., Duncan, M. (2012). Revising GDP estimates in Sub-Saharan Africa: Lessons from Ghana. *The African Statistical Journal*, 15:13–22.

Kenya (2015). *Green Economy Strategy and Implementation Plan: Kenya 2016–2030: A Low Carbon, Resource Efficient, Equitable and Inclusive Socio-Economic Transformation*. August 2016. Government of the Republic of Kenya. Nairobi. Retrieved from: www.environment.go.ke/wp-content/uploads/2018/08/GESIP_Final23032017. pdf. Last accessed: 13.08.2019.

Kiregyera, B. (2015). *The Emerging Data Revolution in Africa: Strengthening the Statistics, Policy and Decision-Making Chain.* Africa Sun Media. Stellenbosch, South Africa. Retrieved from: www.africansunmedia.co.za/Portals/0/files/extracts/9781920689568_extract. pdf. Last accessed: 14.08.2019.

Luken, R., Mörec, U., Meinert, T. (2019). Data quality and feasibility issues with industry-related Sustainable Development Goal targets for Sub-Saharan African countries *Sustainable Development*, 2019:1–10.

OpenAFRICA (a). *Homepage.* About. Retrieved from: https://africaopendata.org/ about. Last accessed: 14.08.2019.

SDGCA/SDSN (2018). *Africa SDG Index and Dashboards Report 2018.* July. The Sustainable Development Goals Center for Africa and Sustainable Development Solutions Network. Retrieved from: http://unsdsn.org/wp-content/uploads/2018/07/ AFRICA-SDGS-2018-Complete-Report-WEB.pdf. Last accessed: 14.08.2019.

SDSN (2015a). *Indicators and a Monitoring Framework for the Sustainable Development Goals: Launching a Data Revolution.* 15 May. Sustainable Development Solutions Network. Retrieved from: http://unsdsn.org/wp-content/uploads/2015/05/FINAL-SDSN-Indicator-Report-WEB.pdf. Last accessed: 14.08.2019.

SDSN (2015b). *Data for Development: A Needs Assessment for SDG Monitoring and Statistical Capacity Development.* 17 April. Sustainable Development Solutions Network. Retrieved from: http://unsdsn.org/wp-content/uploads/2015/04/Data-for-Development-Full-Report.pdf. Last accessed: 14.08.2019.

SDSN (a). *Counting on the World: Building Modern Data Systems for Sustainable Development.* Sustainable Development Solutions Network. Retrieved from: www.unsdsn. org/wp-content/uploads/2017/09/sdsn-trends-counting-on-the-world-1.pdf. Last accessed: 14.08.2019.

SERI/VUBE (a). *MaterialFlows.Net: The Material Flow Analysis Portal.* Sustainable Europe Research Institute and Vienna University of Business and Economics. Retrieved from: www.materialflows.net. Last accessed: 14.08.2019.

South Africa (2008). *National Energy Efficiency Strategy of South Africa.* First Review. October. Department of Minerals and Energy. Republic of South Africa. Pretoria. Retrieved from: www.energy.gov.za/EEE/Review%20of%20National%20 Energy%20Efficiency%20Strategy%202008.pdf. Last accessed: 14.08.2019.

Spangenberg, J.H. (2016). Hot air or comprehensive progress? A critical assessment of the SDGs. *Sustainable Development*, 2017:25:311–321.

Sy, A. (2015). *Are African Countries Rebasing GDP in 2014 Finding Evidences of Structural Transformation?* 3 March. Africa in Focus. Brookings. Retrieved from: www.brookings. edu/blog/africa-in-focus/2015/03/03/are-african-countries-rebasing-gdp-in-2014-finding-evidence-of-structural-transformation/. Last accessed: 14.08.2019.

SWITCH Africa Green (a). *Homepage.* About. Retrieved from: www.switchafricagreen. org. Last accessed: 14.08.2019.

UN (2015). *Transforming Our World: The 2030 Agenda for Sustainable Development.* Resolution adopted by the General Assembly on 25 September. A/RES/70/1. 21 October. United Nations. New York. Retrieved from: www.un.org/ga/search/ view_doc.asp?symbol=A/RES/70/1&Lang=E. Last accessed: 14.08.2019.

UN (2016). *Final List of Proposed Sustainable Development Goal Indicators.* [Annex IV of the Report of the Inter-Agency and Expert Group on Sustainable Development Goal Indicators. E/CN.3/2016/2/Rev.1]. United Nations. New York. Retrieved from: https://sustainabledevelopment.un.org/content/documents/11803Official-List-of-Proposed-SDG-Indicators.pdf. Last accessed: 14.08.2019.

UN (2018). *The Sustainable Development Goals Report 2018*. United Nations. New York. Retrieved from: https://unstats.un.org/sdgs/files/report/2018/TheSustainable DevelopmentGoalsReport2018-En.pdf. Last accessed: 14.02.2020.

UNECA (2016). *Economic Report on Africa 2016: Greening Africa's Industrialisation*. March. United Nations Economic Commission for Africa. Addis Ababa. Retrieved from: http://repository.uneca.org/bitstream/handle/10855/23017/b11560861.pdf? sequence=1. Last accessed: 13.08.2019.

UNIDO (2009). Upadhyaya, S., Todorov, V. *UNIDO Data Quality: A Quality Assurance Framework for UNIDO Statistical Activities*. Working Paper 06/2008. Research and Statistics Branch, United Nations Industrial Development Organization. Vienna. Retrieved from: https://unstats.un.org/unsd/unsystem/Documents/QAF-UNIDO.pdf. Last accessed: 14.08.2019.

UNIDO (2010). Upadhaya, P. *Towards a New Industrial and Business Statistics Programme for Developing Countries and Countries with Economies in Transition*. Working Paper 09/2009. Research and Statistics Branch, United Nations Industrial Development Organization. Vienna. Retrieved from: www.unido.org/api/opentext/documents/download/10081493/unido-file-10081493. Last accessed: 14.08.2019.

UNIDO (2017). *Statistical Indicators of Inclusive and Sustainable Industrialization: Baseline Scenario*. Policy Research and Statistics Department, United Nations Industrial Development Organization. Vienna. Retrieved from: https://stat.unido.org/content/publications/statistical-indicators-of-inclusive-and-sustainable-industrialization. Last accessed: 14.08.2014.

UNIDO (a). *UNIDO Statistics Data Portal*. Manufacturing Value Added (MVA). United Nations Industrial Development Organization. Vienna. Retrieved from: https://stat.unido.org/database/MVA%202019,%20Manufacturing. Last accessed: 14.08.2019.

UNIDO (b). *Industrial Statistics (INDSTAT): Value-Added Manufacturing Sub Sectors and Employment* [Data file]. United Nations Industrial Development Organization. Vienna. Retrieved from: https://stat.unido.org/. Last accessed: 14.08.2019.

UNSD (2019). *United Nations National Quality Assurance Frameworks Manual for Official Statistics*. Series M No. 100. Statistics Division, Department of Economic and Social Affairs. United Nations. New York. Retrieved from: https://unstats.un.org/unsd/methodology/dataquality/references/1902216-UNNQAFManual-WEB.pdf. Last accessed: 17.02.2020.

UNSD (a). *Millennium Development Goals Indicators*. United Nations Statistics Division. New York. Retrieved from: http://mdgs.un.org/unsd/mdg/Host.aspx?Content=Indicators/OfficialList.htm. Last accessed: 14.08.2019.

UNSD (b). *Environmental Indicators: Hazardous Waste Generation*. United Nations Statistics Division. New York. Retrieved from: https://unstats.un.org/unsd/environment/hazardous.htm. Last accessed: 14.08.2019.

World Bank (a). *Enterprise Surveys*. Retrieved from: www.enterprisesurveys.org/. Last accessed: 14.08.2019.

6   Green industry assessments

6.1. Introduction

This chapter starts by summarising the *Practitioner's Guide to Strategic Green Industrial Policy* (SGIP), which offers guidance on how to develop strategic green industrial policies. The next three sections describe the findings of three green industry assessments – Ghana, Nigeria, and Senegal. All three assessments were completed before the publication of the Practitioner's Guide. Both the Practitioner's Guide and the three green industry assessments are available online.

6.2. Practitioner's Guide

Introduction

The *Practitioner's Guide to Strategic Green Industrial Policy* was commissioned by UNIDO under the Partnership for Action on Green Economy (PAGE) to guide policy-makers in the development of their strategic green industrial policies as they advance their green economies (PAGE, 2016).

High-level, multi-sectoral, economy-wide policy-making will be required to tackle even just green industrialisation, which is the industrial piece of the puzzle to bring about circular economies.

Green industrialisation requires an integrated approach to policy-making, going beyond the industry sector itself and involving other policy-making areas such as economics, fiscal, environment, health and safety, science and technology, innovation, education, and trade.

Figure 6.1 is an overview of the planning process.

The individual steps of this planning process will now be discussed.

Initial activities

The process of developing, implementing, and monitoring a SGIP will require policy and institutional integration across government.

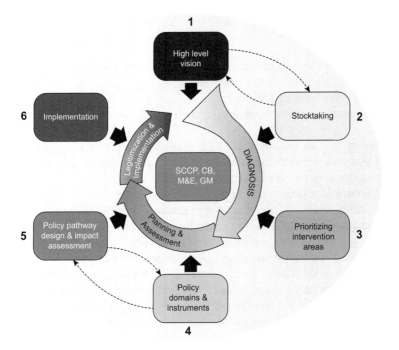

Figure 6.1 SGIP overview

SCCP: Stakeholder Coordination, Consultation, and Participation
CB: Capacity Building
M&E: Monitoring and Evaluation
GM: Gender Mainstreaming

Source: PAGE, 2016

Therefore, a strong lead agency needs to be chosen, which has an accepted leadership role throughout the government. Possible candidates are:

- Finance ministries;
- Economic development ministries;
- The Prime Minister's office.

There must also be strong support throughout the public sector. Senior representatives from relevant ministries should therefore be assigned to the task of developing the SGIP, and they will, under the leadership of the lead agency, form the SGIP team.

To manage the transition to green industrialisation, governments will need some key policy management capabilities. At a minimum, they need the capabilities to:

- Define a transition project and mobilise societal support;
- Establish clear rules of competition;
- Deliver services effectively;
- Create or remove protection as needed while avoiding political capture.

One of the first tasks of the SGIP team will therefore be to identify gaps in the government's capabilities. Where gaps are identified, the SGIP team needs to put in place a process to build them up.

Stakeholder coordination and consultation will permeate all phases of the policy cycle. It is therefore vital to ensure that the SGIP team identifies all the necessary stakeholders from the start. Stakeholder analysis can be used as a tool to decide who needs to participate. Particular care needs to be taken to ensure participation by women and under-represented groups.

When undertaking a stakeholder analysis, it is necessary to distinguish between key stakeholders, primary stakeholders, and secondary stakeholders. Key stakeholders are those without whose support and participation a policy cannot be achieved, or who can veto the policy ('veto players'). Primary stakeholders are those directly affected by a policy, either as beneficiary, because they lose/gain power, or in some other way are positively/negatively affected. Finally, secondary stakeholders are those whose involvement in the policy development/implementation is only indirect or temporary.

Potential key stakeholders for the SGIP include

- policy-making bodies;
- standards bodies/accreditation bodies;
- government organisations (ministries, agencies);
- subnational government bodies (e.g., local authorities);
- enforcement authorities;
- business membership organisations/labour organisations;
- consumer organisations and other relevant non-governmental organisations/civil society organisations;
- local communities impacted.

Potential primary stakeholders for the SGIP include

- industrial polluters, industrial energy, and water users;
- energy producers, energy distribution systems, and energy traders;

- industry, energy, and mining associations;
- industrial zones, industrial clusters, and innovation parks;
- inspection and supervision bodies/enforcing organisations;
- service organisations (e.g., laboratories, certification bodies);
- supranational bodies, regional networks, and subnational bodies;
- individuals and organisations affected by industrial pollution;
- individuals and organisations which will be affected by any measures to be developed and implemented under a SGIP.

Potential secondary stakeholders for the SGIP include

- expert groups/consultants;
- research bodies and education and training organisations;
- media;
- international organisations and technical assistance organisations.

One of the first tasks of the SGIP team will be to generate a 'status quo' document. This document could cover at least the following items:

- context of the initiative;
- preliminary internal capacity assessment;
- industry assessment.

The document should provide enough detail from which the lead agency and its partners can guide their activities. It should provide sufficient insight into what needs to be done and approximately by when. It must help to identify if allocated resources – human and financial – will be sufficient. The SGIP team should plan to revise and update the document as the policy development process continues; essentially, it turns into a road map for the whole process.

High level vision setting

Once the initial activities are ongoing, the SGIP team should turn its attention to defining a vision which states the long-term goal of the initiative. They should choose a vision that is easy to communicate, e.g., increasing industry's resource productivity by a factor of X within the next 20 years.

The SGIP team needs to consult in the development of the vision, whilst taking care not to come under undue influence from vested interests. It should also avoid raising false expectations.

Stocktaking

Once a high-level vision has been established, the SGIP team will under-take a stocktaking exercise. This stocktaking will have two main elements:

- On the one hand, the SGIP team needs to gather data, information, and other evidence on how the elements of the current industrial system interact with each other and with the natural environment.
- On the other hand, the SGIP team needs to undertake a detailed analysis of the policy instruments (rules, regulations, voluntary partnerships, support programmes, financial instruments, etc.) that the government (at all levels) has been using to promote industrial development. The SGIP team needs to assess if these are still all valid and – perhaps more important – if there are possible frictions between them and the concept of SGIP: will they act as a brake on the implementation of SGIP?

Gathering of evidence is vital because identifying the most significant resource use and pollution problems is a key aspect to determining the focus, the priorities, and the objectives of the SGIP. Evidence gather-ing needs to be both at sectoral and at sub-sectoral levels to reveal the most relevant sectors and sub-sectors within these sectors. The evidence gathered should be sufficiently detailed allow the setting of baselines and benchmarks and the setting of short- and medium-term goals.

The following are all areas where data/information/evidence relevant to the SGIP can emerge:

- key manufacturing plants and industrial zones;
- key industry support institutions: cleaner production centres, quality management organisations, energy efficiency/energy conservation centres;
- production statistics, export/import statistics – including the export and import of waste;
- labour statistics;
- natural resource inventories in areas affected by environmental damage;
- energy, water, sewage, and waste tariffs and costs;
- taxes and subsidies influencing the cost of energy, water, and materials;
- recycling sector economics, including informal systems;
- environmental funds and facilities;
- export market requirements.

As for policy stocktaking, this involves evaluating a broad range of policies. The exercise could cover at least the following:

- industrial policies/strategies/regulations, including sector-based strategies;
- environmental policies, laws, and regulations;
- energy policies, laws, and regulations;
- socio-economic policies;
- labour policies, including occupational health and safety;
- trade policies;
- science, technology, and innovation policies;
- land use/planning policies;
- infrastructure policies.

Note that the evidence gathered during the stocktaking exercise could lead to a refining of the high-level vision.

Prioritising intervention areas

Once the stocktaking exercise is completed, the SGIP team will be in a position to determine the issues and/or the (sub-)sectors where interventions are most required, or will be most effective, to reach (satisfy) the high-level vision. It will also identify the most relevant actors with whom the team will need to work. Finally, it will have available to it the data from which baselines can be established for future monitoring and evaluation.

With this information, and after stakeholder consultations, the SGIP team can develop the most relevant set of medium-term goals, and it can communicate them. The team can also create the relevant indicators which it can use to monitor progress and report to senior government officials and the public.

Policy domains and instruments

The SGIP team should now be in the position where they can identify the key policy instruments that they wish to use and the key policy domains that they wish to intervene in with these instruments.

The instruments can be implemented in any one of the following policy domains:

- the products manufactured, and services offered, by industry;
- the technologies that are used, and could be used, by industry;

- the capital invested in industry;
- the labour used by industry;
- the land occupied and used by industry.

As for the policy instruments, they can fall into any one of the following categories:

- they can mandate the necessary changes in behaviour;
- they can use the market to bring about the desired changes in behaviour;
- they can be voluntary/informational, supporting the actors to make the desired changes in behaviour.

Since SMEs make up the overwhelming share of all enterprises and employment, selection of instruments and domains should take their specificities into account.

Policy pathway design

Once the SGIP team has chosen the desirable policy-domain-instrument combinations, it can develop various policy pathways to see how to implement the chosen policy instruments in the chosen policy domains. Pathways can, and indeed often will, involve making changes to existing policies. The SGIP team will need to ensure that phase-in times will be gradual if departures from existing policies are significant, so as to give the affected enterprises the necessary time to adjust. The team can assess alternative pathways for any negative impacts.

Pathways can also involve developing 'trigger projects' or choosing 'pilot sectors' that can help demonstrate the benefits of the new policy instruments and accelerate stakeholder acceptance.

Where possible, pathways should integrate the chosen policies with national strategies, programmes, and frameworks. Some examples are

- national mechanisms for the implementation of the Sustainable Development Goals (SDGs);
- national sustainable development strategies;
- poverty reduction strategies;
- national strategies on sustainable consumption and production;
- integrated legal frameworks (e.g., China's circular economy promotion law);
- resource efficiency action plans (e.g., those developed by the EU).

Implementation and monitoring

Once the SGIP team has chosen the desired policy pathways, all the relevant government entities, at all levels, will begin to implement the chosen policy instruments. There is no discussion of this final phase in the Practitioner's Guide, but well-known, relatively standard approaches can be adopted. The SGIP team should become a monitoring and 'auditing' entity, following progress of implementation and taking any necessary steps to redress any failures in implementation and put it back on track. It should be reporting on progress to senior government officials and the public.

6.3. Green industry policy study: Nigeria

In 2012, in the framework of UNIDO's Green Industry Platform, a study was prepared on the status and challenges of green industrialisation in Nigeria (UNIDO, 2012). The study follows the guidance set out in *Policies for Supporting Green Industry* (UNIDO, 2011) and identifies policy gaps as was done in similar UNIDO studies for India and Vietnam. The following summarises the conclusions and recommendations of in the study.

The report describes environmental and energy issues, policies, and institutional arrangement that directly or indirectly limit the greening of industry in Nigeria. There is a significant need to reduce the discharge of environmental pollutants and to improve industrial energy efficiency. In particular, water quality is severely degraded in those states with significant concentrations of industry, and efforts to reduce this degradation by locating firms on industrial estates which have the potential for cost-effective effluent treatment is failing because common effluent treatment plants (CETPs) are not being built or if built do not operate properly.

Despite the notable efforts by the government to introduce a conventional industrial environmental management programme with supporting institutional arrangements, deterioration of the environment continues and inefficiencies in resource utilisation, particularly energy use, are likely to persist. The report identified several policy gaps that need to be addressed to move along the path towards the green industrialisation.

Policy integration

Although Nigeria has a comprehensive policy and regulatory framework to support the greening of industries, the policies and plans related to green industry are peripheral or subordinate to dominant dynamics of industrialisation and urbanisation. It was found that the institutional mandates for development, environment, and energy are not really integrated. Nowhere is this lack of integration more evident than in the chapters on manufacturing and SMEs in the National Implementation Plan. The chapters describe support for establishing industrial clusters and model enterprise zones with no mention of environmental safeguards either in those chapters or in the chapter on environment. Another telling example of the lack of integration is failure to include the imperative for energy conservation and efficiency.

Low productivity

Overcoming Nigerian manufacturers' low productivity (both labour and factor productivity) is both a challenge to, and an opportunity for, improving their resource efficiency. The challenge to improving productivity is formidable because: (i) existing process equipment is old and depends mostly on manual loading of raw materials; (ii) imported equipment and spare parts are very costly; (iii) capacity is under-utilised due to power stoppages, lack of funds for timely procurement of inputs, long delays at the ports, and limited demand for products that are more costly than imported ones; and (iv) the workforce is poorly skilled.

Industrial energy efficiency

A green industry policy needs to focus on improvements in the efficiency of energy use. Admittedly, it cannot address the need to improve the consistent delivery and supply of energy needed by the industrial sector, but it could help mitigate what is considered the major constraint on industrial production. More efficient use of available electricity would help to some extent but certainly not eliminate this constraint. In addition, improving industrial energy efficiency often comes about by reducing material and water use and improving the quality of material inputs, all of which would be positive contributions to green industry.

A survey of industrial energy efficiency policy measures in place in 31 developing countries (including Nigeria) found that only four out of 21 potential measures were in place in Nigeria. These were training for firm personnel, government agency for energy efficiency, international financing for industrial energy efficiency, and industrial energy efficiency research and development.

Clearly the current energy policy mix lacks many of the measures that have been used in other countries to improve energy efficiency. These measures include setting quantified and achievable efficiency targets, benchmarking the current energy use per unit of output for specific subsectors and identifying opportunities for improving energy efficiency. Once realistic targets are set, various known and successful policy approaches can be implemented. These include laws and regulations, negotiated agreements (energy efficiency contracts between government and industry), information-based instruments, new technology and innovation support, and market-based instruments.

Financing the greening of industries

Firms in Nigeria have more difficulties than those in many other SSA countries in accessing finance and then obtaining it at a reasonable cost. They have trouble in putting up the needed collateral or finding acceptable cosigners, being sufficiently profitable to qualify for a loan, or even completing an application. Thus, for them obtaining working capital for adoption and adaption of green technologies is a major challenge. SMEs as distinct from larger firms also have difficulties accessing other financial sources such as venture capital, foreign funds, and capital markets, and are therefore heavily dependent upon informal credit sources. The assessment did not identify any significant government-led financing schemes targeted at industry of any size which promote investment in resource efficiency measures – e.g., favourable loan and loan guarantees.

Improved infrastructure

Inadequate infrastructure for waste and water management is a serious problem in Nigeria, particularly given the country's rapid growth and urbanisation. The situation is critical in the four urban areas with the greatest concentration of industrial activity and with limited if any treatment of industrial wastewaters – Lagos, Rivers, Kano, and Kaduna. For example, of the five industrial estates in Lagos that contain the majority of medium and large industries, only one estate has a CETP and that one is reported to not operate properly.

To keep pace with Nigeria's growing emphasis on clustering firms on industrial estates or in common facility centres, finance will need to come from the government or the private sector to build CETPs and to ensure collection and proper disposal of solid wastes. Given the difficulties of securing financing for productive investments, the private sector will be challenged to secure the needed finance. Rather, the owner/ managers of industrial estates, usually the government, must organise and finance construction of CETPs and then recover the costs by collecting user fees.

Creating business incentives

State and community pressures are often not enough on their own to encourage resource efficient practices and responsible environmental management. Motivations, opportunities, resources, and processes are all important in driving environmental improvements. Unfortunately, industry-led initiatives, such as corporate social responsibility (outside of the oil producing region), eco-labelling, ISO standards, and voluntary agreements, have yet to gain any foothold in Nigeria.

There is scope for the government to promote the greater use of these instruments as a means of encouraging sound environmental practices. The government could publicise the requirements by multinationals for firms to adopt codes of practice and standards that have resulted in significant benefits from the utilisation of resource efficient technologies. It could also publicise community efforts that are becoming important catalysts of environmental change, through environmental complaints and citizen actions.

Policy implementation and enforcement

Nigeria has several national laws, regulations, and standards that seek to protect the environment and ensure sustainable development. It also has put in place federal and state institutions that are responsible for their implementation. However, having laws on the books and implementing those laws are two very different things. Issues of capacity, coordination, and conflicts of interest all hinder effective policy implementation.

Although Nigeria has a comprehensive range of strict environmental quality and pollutant discharge standards that are in line with those put forward in the World Bank guidelines, there remains the problem of limited enforcement. Only in the case of Lagos state is there a noticeable enforcement effort. Otherwise the government's inability to implement its laws has served to undermine the credibility of the environmental standards and enforcement. It is much cheaper to pay a fine or offer a bribe than to change a production process or install effluent abatement equipment.

Commitment to systematic data collection

An effective green industry policy needs to be designed based on systematic and routinely collected data about the industrial sector, its energy and water use, and its pollutant generation and discharge. Currently, none of these data are available. Even the most basic economic data on the number and location of establishments in each subsector and their output have not been collected since 1996 by the National Bureau of Statistics. Energy use by subsector is also not known, as is pollutant discharge. These data are essential for designing a cost-effective strategy for greening industry and for monitoring its implementation.

Overall potential for resource efficient and cleaner production (RECP)

On the one hand, implementing a RECP policy and programme in Nigeria will be a challenge. The industrial sector itself is confronted with so many problems just to be competitive that any new effort would be rejected. For many firms, securing a regular power supply, accessing credit at a reasonable cost, sourcing raw materials and spare parts, and finding and retaining skilled workers take all the time and talent of management.

On the other hand, a smart RECP policy and programme could offer firms a path for improving their competitive position by reducing their high levels of waste. A smart RECP policy and programme, perhaps under the National Productivity Centre, could be an essential component of a national effort to increase the productivity in the industrial sector. It could be similar to the UNIDO programme to improve energy and resource efficiency in the Vietnamese steel industry. A well organised and managed demonstration of the potential of RECP within the context of subsector upgrading programmes and a realistic dissemination strategy have the potential to spark a greening of industry in Nigeria.

6.4. Ghana green industry and trade assessment

In 2015, in the framework of the Programme of Action for a Green Economy (PAGE), a report was prepared on the status and challenges of green industrialisation in Ghana (PAGE, 2015a). The following summarises the conclusions and recommendations of the assessment.

Findings

Several policy arenas have the potential to accelerate green industry and trade in Ghana. One is industrial policy with its provisions for electricity and water efficiency programmes and several dimensions of cleaner production – efficient use of materials, technology promotion, voluntary standards, and self-regulatory measures. A second is trade policy, at the national and regional level, which is geared towards delivering a strategic expansion of Ghana's productive base and promoting exports of non-traditional products with a view to diversifying Ghana's export base. A third is environmental policy with the comprehensive permitting requirements (energy and cleaner production audits) under the 1994 Environmental Protection Law, and the upcoming environmental fiscal reform policy that could use the Ghana Green Fund resources to promote greening of industry and environmental activity more broadly. A fourth is energy policy with a number of energy efficiency and conservation options such as energy audits and energy management practices, as well as the 'energy economy' vision, put forth in the Strategic National Energy Plan. A fifth is the National Science, Technology, and Innovation Policy with its support for development of alternative energy sources and of more energy efficient industrial process technologies.

A major constraint in implementing these potentially useful policy options is identifying manufacturing sectors that have the most potential for improved resource efficiency and pollutant reduction because of the vacuum of economic, environmental, and resource use data. Missing economic data are plant-size distribution as well as number and current sub-sector value added. The last industrial census was 2013. Missing environmental data are comprehensive industrial pollutant discharge and indicators of where industrial pollutant discharge is severely impairing environmental quality. Missing resource data are manufacturing sector estimates of energy, water, and material consumption. The only energy consumption data are for the manufacturing sector as a whole and not for sectors. There are no data on material or water consumption even at the level of the manufacturing sector. Consequently, identification of the subsectors that are more inefficient in resource use and thus targets for greening industry was not possible for this assessment.

The lack of essential economic, environmental, and resource data for an assessment was anticipated because of the data problems lamented in the Stocktaking Report for Ghana and Integrated Assessment of the Impacts of Green Investment and Policy Reforms in Ghana. As written in the Stocktaking Report (PAGE, 2015b):

> paucity of reliable data is a key challenge which cuts across the agricultural, energy, industry and environmental sectors. This is, however, more severe within the environmental realm, where data are either non-existent or missing for several years. An appreciable amount of statistics exists for the agricultural and energy sectors, but data for these sectors also lack information on vital indicators such as policy cost and yearly targeting.

In contrast, there are sufficient data on exports and imports and the institutional capacity of assisting certifying bodies to identify measures to green trade in manufactured goods. Concrete trade opportunities for manufactured goods are thereby identified in the manufacture of environmental and renewable energy technologies, in the institutional capacity for accreditation (national standards body) and conformity assessment, in firms complying with quality, health, and environmental standards (ISO 9000, HASP ISO 1400, and eco-labelling), in embedding sustainability as a core business strategy, in promoting the complete disassembly, recovery, and reuse of individual product components (re-manufacturing), and in exporting firms that are greening their supply chains, including transport.

In spite of these industry data deficiencies, more efficient use of electricity in the manufacturing sector ought to be a priority given the scarcity and unreliability of the supply of electricity. An electricity decoupling programme, essentially energy audits, should target the two high-energy consuming sectors: iron and steel, and cement. An expanded decoupling programme to reduce environmental impact should initially target those subsectors discharging the most water pollutants (food and beverage, textiles) and those emitting the most air pollutants (charcoal production, wood processing, metal fabrication).

Recommendations

Among the various measures identified for greening economy and trade, a resource decoupling initiative focused on one manufacturing sector is one of the most promising measures supportive of a transition to a green economy. The current industrial, environmental, and energy policies appear to have failed to decouple resource use and industrial output because they lack specificity; they do not target specific resources (such as electricity consumption) or pollutants (such as particulate matter), do not focus on a particular sector(s), and do not fix a date for achieving an agreed upon reduction target. A Resource Efficient Green Industry (REGI) initiative endorsed by the Ministry of Trade and Industry and the National Energy Commission (the carrot) and involving the Ghana National Cleaner Production Centre and the Ghana Climate Innovation Centre would be a modest step in addressing this failure. The National Cleaner Production Centre would work together with one manufacturing sector (steel rolling is a promising choice) to reduce resource use (energy) by a specific date as an example of the potential for improving resource efficiency and bringing about improved competitive performance.

The initiative would be backed up by the regulatory authority (the stick) of the Environmental Protection Agency (EPA) that would allow it to impose resource use standards if the sub-sector fails to meet its agreed target(s). Industrial associations would much prefer to collectively meet an association-set goal rather than to have each plant meet an imposed standard as doing so has the potential to reduce the collective cost of compliance.

If a REGI initiative is impossible and the government still wants to encourage the greening of industry, a reasonable recommendation is for the government to implement the legislative mandates of the various ministries/commissions. Clearly, there is scope for the relevant ministries to be more aggressive in implementing environmental standards. For example, the EPA could expand its permitting activity to all medium and large plants. Currently the EPA has permitted only 250 to 300 plants out of an estimated population of 500 to 600 medium and large plants.

Along the same lines as expanded permitting is a recommendation to expand the AKOBEN programme. Currently there around 200 participating plants out of a population of 300 to 500 plants. Many more plants should be enrolled in the programme.

Essential to all of the above is a recommendation that the Ghana Statistical Service, the EPA, and the National Energy Commission collect timely and comprehensive economic, environmental, and energy use data. Such data, which are currently not available, are essential for identifying the most promising subsector for improved resource efficiency, and determining whether decoupling is actually happening. Without such data, it is not possible to measure success or failure of greening initiatives.

Another recommendation is that the government enforce industrial zoning regulations. Effective enforcement would reduce populations exposed to industrial pollution. Successful confinement of industrial activity to specific geographic areas would also allow for use of a common wastewater treatment plant and common collection and disposal of solid and hazardous wastes.

Another recommendation is selective banning of imported resource inefficient (dirty) technologies. If not a ban, then there should be a requirement for firms importing technologies to undertake a technology audit. The current importation and use of resource inefficient technologies clearly increases the challenge of greening industry.

Another recommendation, important in light of the call for expansion of the use of renewable energy technology in the draft Green Economy Report for Ghana, is government support for manufacturing accessories for renewable energy technology and for setting up assembly plants for solar panels. This support could come in the form of finance from the proposed Ghana Green Fund and tax exemptions.

Supportive of all of this would be an expanded public advocacy for a green economy. As of November 2015, there was an important need to promote dialogue amongst stakeholders and to strengthen the national capacity for communication on a green economy and sustainable development.

Out of the assessed measures for green manufactured trade, two recommendations are feasible and within the current capacity of governmental organisations. One is enhancement of the capacity of the Ghana Standards Authority to issue ISO 14001 certificates that would be internationally recognised. The Authority would be able to issue these certificates as a much lower cost than conformity assessment bodies in Europe or North America. Another recommendation is to support the greening of selected supply chains. An easy first target for a government initiative would be to work with the eight major exporters of wood products. Such an effort would ensure that they are using certified logs, recycling wood wastes, complying with air pollution standards, and not using child labour. A second target would be greening of the supply chain of the second largest export of manufactured goods, essential oils. Greening of this supply chain would ensure processing efficiency of raw material and use of the residual biomass for energy generation. At this time, a third green industry trade category, export of pollution control and renewable energy technologies, is not feasible because these technologies are not yet being manufactured in Ghana.

6.5. Senegal green industry assessment

In 2015, in the framework of the Programme of Action for a Green Economy (PAGE), a report was prepared on the status and challenges of green industrialisation in Senegal (PAGE, 2015c). The following summarises the conclusions and recommendations of the assessment.

Conclusions

Without industrialisation, it will be difficult for Senegal to overcome poverty. However, this industrialisation must benefit the whole country, taking into account the needs of local industrial stakeholders (SMEs) as well as consumers, while at the same time preserving the health of the country's ecosystems and its population: it must be a green industrialisation.

Implementing green industrialisation involves many stakeholders (the government, enterprises, technical and financial partners, consumers, etc.) who each have a specific role to play, but who must play their roles in a synergistic and coherent manner.

For the most part, Senegal currently has in place the essential political mechanisms necessary to leverage the transition to a green economy, of which green industrialisation is one of the principal components. Three other major factors appear to be required for this successful transition.

Firstly, improvements are required in the policies and programmes which create the enabling environment for the successful implementation of a green industrialisation. Here, the government is a key actor. Specifically, it must pursue its efforts to install a business-friendly climate. This will come about by, among other things, resolving the issues surrounding energy. This in turn requires expanding the programmes aimed at increasing energy efficiency, but also showing an unshakable support for a transition towards clean and reliable alternative sources of energy. The government also has a key role to play on issues regarding the legal and regulatory framework. It will need to bring about those reforms which are necessary to promote private investment in green industrialisation. In this regard, the government should pay particular attention to a speedier implementation of the Environmental Code, especially with respect to the application of Environmental Impact Assessments. From this perspective, there needs to be a significant strengthening of the technical capacities as well as the communication skills of the Directorate for the Environment and Classified Establishments (Direction de l'Environnement et des Etablissements Classés [DEEC]), which is responsible for the implementation of the Environmental Code and all other related instruments.

Secondly, an expansion in financial incentives is necessary. Currently, the Upgrading Office is having difficulties responding to all the requests being submitted to it. In addition, it is necessary to reinforce the synergies between, on the one hand, this Office (as well as any other entities with similar missions which could be created in the future), and, on the other, their stakeholders (the DEEC, the Ministry of Industry, etc.).

Thirdly, the awareness of enterprises of what is at stake must be raised and they must receive the necessary training to analyse both their financial and their technical needs, of which one is technology choices. This need for support to adopt a clean and green upgrading is that much more acute for SMEs, multinationals being able to obtain support for this from their headquarters.

In addition to these three key factors, if Senegal's potential is to be effectively exploited and an effective transition to green industrialisation to take place, it seems essential to resolve issues related to the decentralisation of industrial units, to the support given to research and to the policies for sharing its results, and to the involvement of civil society (consumers, defenders of human rights, etc.).

Recommendations

With this in mind, the following recommendations are made to the main stakeholders:

The government should

- strengthen the necessary capacities to offer detailed diagnostics to industrial enterprises, particularly SMEs, using green industry criteria, and to define with them, and in partnership with the Upgrading Office, a programme for their upgrading;
- support an evaluation of the *Plan Sénégal Émergeant* (the country's framework document for its development), in light of the challenges of green industrialisation and climate change;
- strengthen the efficiency and effectiveness of the legislative and regulatory framework, and, in partnership with the private sector, define the modalities which will allow the latter to better master the framework's requirements;
- identify the new challenges posed by the transition to green industrialisation and integrate them into the legislative and regulatory framework;
- support an increase in financial incentive schemes, taking into account the specific needs of industrial actors – in particular, the SMEs;
- undertake a detailed analysis to the barriers to the development and scale-up of renewable energies, and establish the necessary corrective measures as well as a timetable for their implementation;
- raise the awareness of the private sector, in particular the SMEs, about the need for sustainable development and the use of green industrialisation as the principal tool for implementing it in the industrial sector;
- raise the awareness of the other stakeholders (consumers, civil society organisations, the informal sector, etc.) about green industrialisation, and support the development of a programme of action.

Some of these action points fall under the direct responsibility of technical entities within the government, while for the others it is more a question of prioritising know-how, with the government limiting itself to putting in place the enabling conditions.

Company management and industrial associations should

- create the conditions for a greater openness to the issues of sustainable development in general and green industrialisation in particular;
- with the support of the government and financial and technical partners, draw up an action plan for the transition to a green industrialisation, with clearly defined milestones.

References

PAGE (2015a). *Ghana Green Industry and Trade Assessment*. Copyright © United Nations Industrial Development Organization, 2015, for Partnership for Action on Green Economy. Retrieved from: www.greengrowthknowledge.org/sites/default/files/downloads/resource/GhanaGreenIndustryAndTradeAssessment_PAGE_0.pdf. Last accessed: 13.08.2019.

PAGE (2015b). *Ghana's Transition to A Green Economy: A Stocktaking Report*. Copyright © United Nations Industrial Development Organization, 2015, for Partnership for Action on Green Economy. Retrieved from: https://www.un-page-.org/files/public/ge_stocktaking_ghana_2015_page.pdf. Last accessed: 16.02.2019.

PAGE (2015c). *L'industrie verte au Sénégal: Évaluation et perspectives de développement*. Copyright © United Nations Industrial Development Organization, 2015, for Partnership for Action on Green Economy. Retrieved from: https://isid.unido.org/files/GreenIndustry/Green%20Industry%20Assessment%20-%20Senegal%20-%20PAGE,%202015%20(French).pdf. Last accessed: 15.08.2019.

PAGE (2016). *Practitioner's Guide to Strategic Green Industrial Policy*. Copyright © United Nations Industrial Development Organization, 2016, on behalf of Partnership for Action on Green Economy. Retrieved from: www.unido.org/sites/default/files/2016-11/practitioners_guide_to_green_industrial_policy_1__0.pdf. Last accessed: 15.08.2019.

UNIDO (2011). *UNIDO Green Industry: Policies for Supporting Green Industry*. May. United Nations Industrial Development Organization. Vienna. Retrieved from: www.unido.org/sites/default/files/2011-05/web_policies_green_industry_0.pdf. Last accessed: 13.08.2019.

UNIDO (2012). *Nigeria Green Industry Policy Assessment*. March. United Nations Industrial Development Organization. Vienna. Retrieved from: https://www.greenindustryplatform.org/sitest/default/files/downloads/resource/Nigeria%20green%2013%2003%202012b.pdf. Last accessed: 16.02.2020.

7   Green industrialisation
       research

7.1. Introduction

Previous chapters in this book about policies and programmes to support green industrialisation in SSA countries covered four substantive areas. Chapter 2 is a summary of the various definition of green industrialisation, which is closely related to several other terms – green economy, green growth, and green jobs. Chapters 3 and 4 summarise the policy and support programme literature focused on green industrialisation. Chapter 5 assesses, to the extent that data allow it, the process of green industrialisation in SSA countries, as characterised by the industry-related Sustainable Development Goals' targets between 2000 and 2016, using international databases. Chapter 6 summarises technical guidance for undertaking green industrialisation assessments and the policy and support programme findings/implications identified in three SSA green industry assessments (Ghana, Nigeria, and Senegal). This seventh and final chapter identifies areas for further research that could be undertaken about policies and support programmes needed to accelerate green industrialisation in SSA countries and to monitor progress in meeting industry-relevant SDG targets.

While recommendations are presented for each substantive area, two recommendations cut across all areas. First, there is a paucity of information both about the economic and environmental dimensions of green industrialisation and about the implementation of existing policies and support programmes that have the potential to drive green industrialisation. The lack of information about the industrial economic structure and its environmental impacts is a central finding in all three green industry assessments summarised in Chapter 6 and in the review of the past progress of SSA countries meeting SDG industry-related targets in Chapter 5. The lack of information about the barriers to policy and programme implementation and successful actions by some countries to overcome them is evident in the limited number of SSA case studies. Second, there is a need to recognise that greening industry requires more than a focus on reducing GHG emissions, to which African industry is a minor contributor in the global context. Successful greening of industry also requires significant reductions in conventional pollutants in urban areas with concentrated industrial activity, improvements in energy efficiency needed to reduce the energy intensity of outdated technologies and effective management of chemical and hazardous waste, as well as attention to the social dimensions (this same point is made in UNECA, 2016).

Regarding definitions of green industrialisation, covered in Chapter 2, research is needed to describe more fully its understanding of the concept of green industrialisation in order to focus its research efforts. We suggest defining green industrialisation as being made up of two distinct but interactive processes – 'greening industry', which is what any enterprise can do to green itself; and 'creation of greening services', which is making available those goods and services required by enterprises, primarily SMEs, to green themselves. The policy and support dimensions of greening industry are separated into four complementary and, to some extent, overlapping regimes – pollution control for abating conventional pollutants released from industrial plants into the environment; resource efficiency and cleaner production measures implemented to improve resource efficiency; energy management for energy efficiency and use of renewable energy to reduce GHG emissions; and chemical and hazardous waste management inside and outside of a plant but for which firms are responsible. The policy and support dimensions of greening services are four separate regimes – environmental services, eco-industrial parks, eco-design, and remanufacturing/recycling.

We suggest potential research activities for five of these regimes, four of which are described in Chapter 3 and one in Chapter 4, in the following paragraphs. We do not suggest research activities for the other three greening service regimes (eco-industrial parks, eco-design, and remanufacturing and recycling) described in Chapter 4 because these regimes are less important for greening industrialisation in SSA countries and we could not find relevant SSA reports. However, these greening services regimes should be considered as potential research areas given their potential to reduce the impacts of products and services in SSA countries.

7.2. Pollution control

Regarding pollution control, we suggest the following potential research topics:

- Information is needed about the extent to which SSA countries are implementing the basic activities of command-and-control regulation (standards, permitting, monitoring, and, most importantly, enforcement). To the extent that these essential activities are not being undertaken, there is a need to know for specific countries the barriers limiting these activities and the measures required to overcome them.
- Information is needed about the capital and operating costs to factories of implementing pollution control measures. Studies done many years ago by the US Environmental Protection Agency and the OECD suggest that the annual operating costs are in the range of 2–3% of production costs. If that is also the case for SSA firms, could they cover this cost without undue financial burden?
- Are SSA countries using economic incentives to encourage firms to reduce pollution discharge? Have any countries tried to use economic incentives (or their converse, elimination of subsidies) and given up the effort?
- Are SSA countries using any transparency and disclosure programmes other than the public disclosure programme in Ghana? If so, what has been done, and if not why have countries not tried any of these programmes? What lessons can be learned from the AKOBEN disclosure programme in Ghana?

7.3. RECP

Regarding resource efficient and cleaner production, we suggest the following potential research topics, perhaps done in collaboration with UNIDO:

- There are currently 11 UNIDO/UNEP National Cleaner Production Centres operating in SSA countries, yet little is known about their accomplishments in working with specific industrial plants. UNIDO has collected only a few poorly documented case studies. Perhaps researchers could collaborate with UNIDO in collecting more information about the benefits and costs of RECP interventions at specific industrial plants.
- Researchers could consider undertaking, with a few of the longest running NCPCs in SSA countries, a survey of the extent to which manufacturing firms are aware of the RECP concept or more broadly the benefits of implementing resource efficiency measures. This research is proposed in light of findings from two studies, one in South Africa (Morris *et al.*, 2011) and the other in Vietnam

(UNIDO, 2012b), that show limited awareness of RECP potential in spite of active and well-funded centres in both countries.

- There is a need to understand which policy mix to apply in SSA countries to promote RECP. A discussion and/or analysis on how to best mix the policies would be desirable as a reference for policy-makers in developing countries. On the other hand, many factors influence the choice of policy instruments, so it might also be a good starting point to analyse which instruments are lacking in a particular country or region, and – depending on the particular circumstances – to introduce new instruments in order to fill those gaps.

7.4. Energy management

Regarding energy management, we suggest a slightly different approach to identifying potential research topics because so much has already been written about African energy issues. We are referring particularly to the IEA African Energy Outlook (IEA, 2014) and the IRENA African Roadmap for a Renewable Energy Future (IRENA, 2015). These agencies need to be consulted before undertaking any research activities in the field of industrial energy management. Because neither report discusses industrial energy management, we tentatively suggest a few potential research topics as follows, perhaps done in some cases in collaboration with IEA and IRENA:

- A survey needs to be undertaken of the extent to which SSA countries have set industrial energy targets in National Energy Plans and have promulgated industrial energy management, industrial equipment, and systems assessment standards.
- There is a need to document and disseminate the productivity, energy security, and environmental benefits of improving industrial energy efficiency in SSA countries.
- There is a need to design a model programme that would support medium-sized and large companies to adopt energy management systems (ISO 50001).
- There is a need to investigate the reasons why there is so much variation among countries in the adoption of policy mechanisms to promote renewable energy, and what guidance countries need to become proactive in this field. Of particular importance would be to understand the limited adoption of feed-in tariffs which would encourage industries to adopt renewable energy technologies.

7.5. Chemicals and hazardous waste management

Regarding chemical and hazardous waste management, we suggest the following potential research topics:

- Since most of the SSA countries are importers of chemicals, often as part of formulated products, a key source of information for them about the possible hazards of these chemicals comes through the proper labelling of chemicals or products containing chemicals, as well as the provision of Material Safety Data Sheets with the imported products. Researchers could research the 'state of play' in terms of labelling and MSDS requirements, especially with respect to the Globally Harmonized System of Classification and Labelling of Chemicals.
- Researchers, if possible together with the SAICM Secretariat and using the SAICM reporting format as a template, could undertake an updated mapping of where SSA countries stand in their implementation of the Strategic Approach to International Chemicals Management, complementing and completing the rather weak reporting which there has been to date by the SSA countries.
- Researchers, if possible together with the Basel Convention Secretariat, could undertake to complement and complete the rather weak reporting to the Secretariat by SSA countries regarding their implementation of the Basel Convention.
- Researchers could also research the implementation status of the Bamako Convention. In principle, since its adoption, there should have been no further importation of hazardous wastes into Africa. Yet that does not seem to have been entirely the case.

7.6. Environmental services

Regarding environmental services, we suggest the following potential research topics:

- Research related to 'levelling the playing field', namely adoption and enforcement of pollution control legislative framework and the elimination of subsidies, has already been touched upon earlier. Their great relevance to ensuring financially viable environmental services should be kept in mind during any research on these topics.
- Since there are very few formal environmental services in place in SSA countries, researchers could consider working with one or more SSA countries to develop, as pilot cases, national strategies for

developing green services. The dissemination of the results of such pilot cases could encourage other SSA countries to do the same.

7.7. Industry-related SDG indicators

Chapter 5 reviews the extent to which industry-related targets in the UN Sustainable Development Goals are measurable with currently available data and whether it is feasible for most SSA countries to meet the targets by 2030. The review found that there are international databases for measuring progress for some but not all industry related SDG targets. For many targets, there are no industry-related data yet. The review also suggests that meeting the conventional economic and employment industry-related targets, for which there are some quantitative indicators, will be a challenging task for many SSA countries based on an assessment of their track record over the past 15 years. We suggest that research about the extent of green industrialisation in SSA use an enhanced number of industry-related SDG indicators as a metric for measuring progress. There are currently 12 associated indicators for the four industry-related targets. Two additional indicators should be added to the list. One is the growth in the absolute value of MVA as an essential and complementary measure to the percent share of MVA in GDP for which there are data for 47 countries. The other is the absolute growth in manufacturing employment as an essential and complementary measure to the percent share of manufacturing employment in total employment for which there are data for 47 countries. In addition, researchers would need to collaborate with IEA to expand the number of countries reporting fuel consumption data for industry. Currently, only 22 out of the 47 SSA countries report this data to the IEA.

Researchers could evaluate the feasibility of constructing a composite index for green industrialisation using industry-related SDG indicators. A composite index is useful because it summarises complex, multi-dimensional data into a single number. A performance composite index, such as the UN Human Development Index (UNDP, a) and the UNIDO Competitive Industrial Performance Index (UNIDO, 2019), documents the levels of performance of countries in terms of a specific set of outcomes. A progress composite index, such as the UNEP Green Economy Progress Index (PAGE, 2017), documents trends over time among countries. In other words, a progress composite index would concentrate not on the levels but on the changes in achievements.

To illustrate the potential of composite indexes, we have constructed SDG9 performance and progress indexes (SDG9per and SDG9pro) for 16 SSA countries. Only 16 have been included because of limited country data; even then, we have used only five of the seven industry-related SDG indicators, because there are no data for the remaining two indicators. The indexes show that countries can be ranked differently on their performance (level of achievement) and progress (movement towards a target). For example, South Africa ranks number 1 on performance as of 2015 but it ranks last on progress between 2000 and 2015, while Angola ranks number 12 on performance but ranks number 1 on progress between 2000 and 2015. We have then grouped the 16 countries into four categories (advanced-active, advanced-passive, backward-active, and backward-passive) by combining their rankings on both indexes and have used the country groupings to identify policies which have the potential to improve their rankings. See Annex 1 for more details on the country rankings, the four-category grouping, and suggested policy implications.

A more limited option for measuring the extent of green industrialisation is to work with some of the 11 UNIDO/UNEP National Cleaner Production Centres in SSA countries to gather baseline data for monitoring improvements in resource efficiency and reductions in pollutant discharge from the manufacturing sector.

Another area of potential area of research is to explore avenues for cooperation with the several ongoing private and public efforts to disseminate SDG-relevant data about SSA countries. The most prominent is the African Information Highway initiated by AfDB. Its goal is to improve data availability and accuracy across the whole continent and to provide a platform that links all national statistical offices in Africa with each other and with important stakeholders. Data are now available for all African countries on economic, environment, and energy topics. At this time, there are no data available in the African Information Highway relevant for the industry-related SDG targets. Other potential partners in data dissemination are OpenAFRICA and the African Data Initiative. The former is an independent open-source platform for the general public, while the latter is an ongoing effort – initially funded through a crowd-funding campaign – to help design and build statistical software that can easily be used throughout the developing world.

7.8. Green industry assessments

Chapter 6 summarises four reports about green industry assessments. The first report, the *Practitioner's Guide to Strategic Green Industrial Policy*, offers guidance on how to undertake a green industry assessment. The other three reports describe the findings of three green industry assessments – Ghana (PAGE, 2015a), Nigeria (UNIDO, 2012a), and Senegal (PAGE, 2015b). In addition, the energy management regime of Chapter 3 describes strategies that are like green industry assessments. These are the Ethiopia Climate-Resilient Green Economy Strategy (2011), Kenya Green Economy Strategy and Implementation Plan (2015), Mozambique's Green Economy Roadmap (AfDB, 2015), the Rwanda Green Growth and Climate Resilience Strategy, (2011) and the South Africa Green Economy Accord (2011).

A recommended research effort here is a comparative review of the extent to which the industry-related targets and policy recommendations in these assessments and strategies have the potential to encourage green industrialisation. A cursory review of these assessments and strategies reveals that there are noticeable differences and similarities in these documents. A comparative assessment could provide useful guidance to those involved in implementing the recommendations in the assessments and the targets and policies in the strategies. It could also provide useful guidance for other SSA countries in undertaking assessments and formulating strategies.

References

AfDB (2015). *Transition towards Green Growth in Mozambique: Policy Review and Recommendations for Action*. African Development Bank. Abidjan. Retrieved from: www.afdb.org/fileadmin/uploads/afdb/Documents/Generic-Documents/Transition_Towards_Green_Growth_in_Mozambique_-_Policy_Review_and_Recommendations_for_Action.pdf. Last accessed: 13.08.2019.

Ethiopia (2011). *Climate Resilient Green Economy: Green Economy Strategy*. Federal Democratic Republic of Ethiopia. Addis Ababa. Retrieved from: www.adaptation-undp.org/sites/default/files/downloads/ethiopia_climate_resilient_green_economy_strategy.pdf. Last accessed: 14.08.2019.

IEA (2014). *Africa Energy Outlook: A Focus on Energy Prospects in Sub-Saharan Africa*. International Energy Agency. Paris. Retrieved from: www.iea.org/publications/freepublications/publication/WEO2014_AfricaEnergyOutlook.pdf. Last accessed: 13.08.2019.

IRENA (2015). *Africa 2030: Roadmap for a Renewable Energy Future*. October. International Renewable Energy Agency. Bonn. Retrieved from: www.irena.org/publications/2015/Oct/Africa-2030-Roadmap-for-a-Renewable-Energy-Future. Last accessed: 13.08.2019.

Kenya (2015). *Green Economy Strategy and Implementation Plan: Kenya 2016–2030: A Low Carbon, Resource Efficient, Equitable and Inclusive Socio-Economic Transformation*. August. Government of the Republic of Kenya. Nairobi. Retrieved from: www.environment.go.ke/wp-content/uploads/2018/08/GESIP_Final23032017.pdf. Last accessed: 13.08.2019.

Morris, M., Barnes, J., Morris, J. (2011). *Energy Efficient Production in the Automotive and Clothing/Textiles Industries in South Africa*. Working Paper 04/2011. Development Policy, Statistics and Research Branch, United Nations Industrial

Development Organization. Vienna. Retrieved from: https://open.unido.org/api/documents/4814916/download/Energy%20efficient%20production%20in%20the%20automotive%20and%20clothing-textiles%20industries%20in%20South%20Africa. Last accessed: 13.08.2019.

PAGE (2015a). *Ghana Green Industry and Trade Assessment.* Copyright © United Nations Industrial Development Organization, 2015, for Partnership for Action on Green Economy. Retrieved from: www.greengrowthknowledge.org/sites/default/files/downloads/resource/GhanaGreenIndustryAndTradeAssessment_PAGE_0.pdf. Last accessed: 13.08.2019.

PAGE (2015b). *L'industrie verte au Sénégal: Évaluation et perspectives de développement.* Copyright © United Nations Industrial Development Organization, 2015, for Partnership for Action on Green Economy. Retrieved from: https://isid.unido.org/files/Green-Industry/Green%20Industry%20Assessment%20-%20Senegal%20-%20PAGE,%202015%20(French).pdf. Last accessed: 15.08.2019.

PAGE (2017). *The Green Economy Progress Measurement Framework: Methodology.* Copyright © United Nations Environment Programme, 2017, for Partnership for Action on Green Economy. Retrieved from: www.un-page.org/files/public/general/gep_methodology.pdf. Last accessed: 15.08.2019.

Rwanda (2011). *Green Growth and Climate Resilience: National Strategy for Climate Change and Low Carbon Development.* October. Republic of Rwanda. Kigali. Retrieved from: https://cdkn.org/wp-content/uploads/2010/12/Rwanda-Green-Growth-Strategy-FINAL1.pdf. Last accessed: 13.08.2019.

South Africa (2011). *Green Economy Accord.* 17 November. Economic Development Department, Republic of South Africa. Pretoria. Retrieved from: www.sagreenfund.org.za/wordpress/wp-content/uploads/2015/04/Green-Economy-Accord.pdf. Last accessed: 13.08.2019.

UNDP (a). *Human Development Report.* United Nations Development Programme. New York. Retrieved from: www.hdr.undp.org/. Last accessed: 15.08.2019.

UNECA (2016). *Economic Report on Africa 2016: Greening Africa's Industrialisation.* March. United Nations Economic Commission for Africa. Addis Ababa. Retrieved from: http://repository.uneca.org/bitstream/handle/10855/23017/b11560861.pdf?sequence=1. Last accessed: 13.08.2019.

UNIDO (2012a). *Nigeria Green Industry Policy Assessment.* March. United Nations Industrial Development Organization. Vienna. Retrieved from: https://www.greenindustryplatform.org/sitest/default/files/downloads/resource/Nigeria%20green%2013%2003%202012b.pdf. Last accessed: 16.02.2020.

UNIDO (2012b). *UNIDO Support to the National Cleaner Production Center in Vietnam.* Independent Ex-Post Evaluation. Evaluation Group, United Nations Industrial Development Organization. Vienna. Retrieved from: www.unido.org/sites/default/files/2012-06/VNCPC%20Ex%20post%20evaluation%20final%201206 13_0.pdf. Last accessed: 14.08.2019.

UNIDO (2019). *Competitive Industrial Performance Report 2018.* Biennial CIP report, edition 2018. United Nations Industrial Development Organization. Vienna. Retrieved from: www.unido.org/sites/default/files/files/2019-05/CIP.pdf. Last accessed: 15.08.2019.

Annex 1

Composite indexes

A.1.1 Introduction

Composite indicators are useful because they summarise complex, multi-dimensional data into a single indicator. They facilitate the interpretation of many separate indicators by reducing the set of indicators without losing the underlying information. For composite indicators to facilitate interpretation, it is critical to have enough indicators so that multidimensionality is captured but limited in number for ease of interpretation. To understand a complex phenomenon like green industrialisation, composite measures are better suited than a single indicator to capture its multi-dimensional nature and synthesise the information captured by the aggregated indicators (OECD, 2008).

In some cases, researchers and policy-makers are interested in evaluating the performance of countries in terms of a specific set of outcomes. For this type of composite index, the focus of the analysis is on performance. An example of this type of composite index is the UN Human Development Index (UNDP, 2019). This kind of composite index focuses on status or achievement. In other cases, researchers and policy-makers are more interested in specific rates of progress of countries. For this type of composite index, the focus is on relative changes in country efforts over time. An example of this type of composite index is the UNEP Green Economy Index (PAGE, 2017). This type of composite index focuses on changes in achievements. While useful, both of these indexes have their limitations. First, no single indicator embodied in them can adequately represent the complex phenomenon they purport to capture. Second, their values may vary depending on the statistical method used to compile the index using the same underlying data.

In this Annex, we summarise four composite indexes that benchmark the progress of SSA countries in meeting SDG targets and introduce performance and progress indexes strictly limited to industry-related SDG9 targets.

A.1.2 Four global sustainable development indexes

Lin *et al.* (2019) construct an Inclusive Sustainable Transformation (IST) index for 198 countries, including 45 SSA countries, over a 15-year period (2000–2015). This index distinguishes itself from other indicators that track the structural characteristics of the economy by ensuring that the comparisons between countries account for differences in their level of development. The primary source of indicator data are two UN reports on the monitoring of the SDGs: Indicators and a Monitoring Framework for the SDGs (SDSN, 2015) and the report of the Inter-Agency and Expert Group on SDG Indicators (ECOSOC, 2017); these are supplemented by other sources. The authors expand the country data using multiple imputation techniques and transform the variables using a simple arithmetic mean to create the IST index. The index includes 27 indicators, three-quarters of which are included in the previously-mentioned UN reports. Five of the indicators are identical to the five industry-related indicators in goal 9. The 2015 IST Index ranked 29 of the 45 SSA countries in the lower half of all ranked countries. The highest ranked SSA countries are Chad, Guinea, and Kenya, whereas Angola, Tanzania, and Djibouti are the lowest ranked SSA countries (first two columns of Table A.1.1).

Sachs *et al.* (2018) construct an SDG Index and Dashboard for 156 countries, including 40 SSA countries, as of 2017. The SDG Index for 156 countries consists of 88 indicators for the 17 SDGs with additional indicators for OECD countries. The indicators used differ significantly from the SDG indicators. None of the industry-relevant SDG9 targets and indicators are among the 88 indicators. The SDG Index is computed by first estimating scores for each goal using the arithmetic mean of indicators for that goal and then averaging across all 17 SDGs to obtain the SDG Index score. The global SDG Index score and scores by goal can be interpreted as the percentage of achievement. The difference between 100 and a country's score is therefore the distance in percentage that needs to be completed to achieve the SDGs. The SDG Index ranked 32 of the 40 SSA countries in the lowest quartile. The highest ranked SSA countries are Cabo Verde, Mauritius, and Gabon, whereas Central African Republic, Chad, and the Democratic Republic of Congo are the lowest ranked SSA countries (second set of columns in Table A.1.1).

UNIDO (2019) constructs for the first time on and an experimental basis a CO_2-Adjusted Competitive Industrial Performance (CO_2-Adjusted

Table A.1.1 Rankings of the SSA countries according to four different global sustainable development indexes

Lin et al. (2019)		Sachs et al. (2018)		UNIDO (2019)		Moll de Alba and Todorov (2018)	
IST Index rank (2015)	Country	SDG Index rank (2017)	Country	CO_2-Adjusted CIP Index rank (2016)	Country	GIP Index rank (2014)	Country
52	Chad	88	Cabo Verde	53	Botswana	42	South Africa
52	Guinea	90	Mauritius	59	Nigeria	64	Mauritius
57	Kenya	100	Gabon	60	South Africa	80	Senegal
60	Comoros	101	Ghana	67	Mauritius	81	Tanzania
65	Lesotho	107	South Africa	83	Cameroon	86	Cameroon
68	Guinea–Bissau	114	Namibia	87	Congo	92	Ghana
68	Togo	115	Zimbabwe	97	Zambia	93	Ethiopia
73	Ghana	116	Botswana	99	Côte d'Ivoire	96	Botswana
79	Benin	118	Senegal	103	Kenya	98	Kenya
81	Malawi	119	Kenya	104	Senegal	101	Nigeria
81	Sao Tome and Principe	120	Rwanda	105	United Republic of Tanzania	104	Eritrea
86	Liberia	121	Cameroon	110	Mozambique		
87	Eritrea	122	Côte d'Ivoire	111	Gabon		
88	Mozambique	123	Tanzania	113	Angola		
90	South Africa	125	Uganda	115	Zimbabwe		
99	Rwanda	128	Ethiopia	116	Ghana		
100	Congo, Republic of	129	Zambia	117	Niger		
100	Zimbabwe	130	Congo, Republic of	123	Ethiopia		
102	Zambia	131	Guinea				
103	Burundi	132	Togo				
107	Gambia	133	Gambia				
107	Sierra Leone	134	Mauritania				
112	Central African Republic	135	Lesotho				
114	Côte d'Ivoire	136	Burkina Faso				

#	Country		#	Country
115	Seychelles		137	Eswatini
116	Namibia		138	Mozambique
119	Senegal		139	Djibouti
120	Uganda		140	Malawi
131	Mauritius		141	Burundi
132	Cameroon		142	Mali
133	Democratic Republic of Congo		144	Angola
143	Gabon		146	Sierra Leone
149	Mauritania		147	Benin
151	Madagascar		148	Niger
158	Botswana		149	Liberia
165	Mali		150	Nigeria
167	Burkina Faso		153	Madagascar
168	Ethiopia		154	Democratic Republic of Congo
171	Niger		155	Chad
174	Equatorial Guinea		156	Central African Republic
176	Nigeria			
177	Somalia			
178	Djibouti			
184	Tanzania			
188	Angola			

Source: Data extracted from Lin *et al.* 2019), Sachs *et al.* 2018, UNIDO 2019, and Moll de Alba and Todorov 2018

CIP) for 123 countries, including 18 SSA countries, as a complement to its Competitive Industrial Performance Index for 150 countries, as of 2016. The CIP Index covers three main dimensions of industrialisation, each consisting of two indicators. These dimensions are: i) the capacity to produce and export manufactured goods, ii) technological deepening and upgrading, and iii) world impact. The CO_2-Adjusted CIP Index incorporates CO_2 emissions intensity that combines data from the International Energy Agency and UNIDO. Both CIP indexes have their limitations for reporting on industry-related SDG9 targets: there are no indicators in the indexes for employment, and – the same limitation of all indexes reviewed – they use only CO_2 emissions to represent the multiple negative environmental effects of industrialisation. The CO_2-Adjusted CIP index ranked 15 out of the 18 in the lower half and 12 in the lowest quartile (UNIDO, 2019). The highest ranked SSA countries are Botswana, Nigeria, and South Africa, whereas Ethiopia, Niger, and Ghana are the lowest ranked SSA countries (third set of columns in Table A.1.1).

Moll de Alba and Todorov (2018) construct a Green Industrial Performance (GIP) Index that encompasses 107 countries, including 11 SSA countries, as of 2014. They use a list of green products and services based on both energy conservation and environmental goals, primarily derived from the US Department of Commerce (2010), to identify green manufacturing and employment within total manufacturing value added (MVA) and employment (UNIDO, INDSTAT) and green exports as a share of total exports (UN Comtrade). They also use data from IEA to estimate CO_2 emissions from manufacturing. Their three dimensional indicators are capacity to produce and export green manufactures (green MVA per capita and green exports per capita); role of green manufacturing (share of green MVA in total MVA and share of green manufactured exports in total exports); and social and environmental aspects of green manufacturing (share of green manufacturing employment in total manufacturing employment and CO_2 emissions from manufacturing per unit of MVA). Each of the six indicators are normalised in the range of $(0,1)$ and aggregated by their geometric means to create the GIP Index. The 2014 GIP Index ranked ten of the 11 SSA countries (excluding South Africa) in the lowest quartile. South Africa, Mauritius, and Senegal are the highest ranked SSA countries whereas Eretria, Nigeria, and Kenya are the lowest ranked SSA countries (last two columns in Table A.1.1).

Kynčlová *et al.* (2020) construct an SDG-9 performance index for 128 countries over the period 2000-2016; all 16 countries in our analysis are included in their analysis. Among the SSA countries ranked in 2016, South Africa, Mauritius and Nigeria are at the top, whereas Ghana,

Eritrea and Niger rank at the bottom. Biggeri *et al.* (2019) construct an Integrated Sustainable Development Index for the same time period (as of 2017) and same countries (156 countries) as Sachs *et al.* (2018).

A.1.3 Industry-related SDG9 performance and progress indexes

The UN General Assembly adopted Resolution 70/1, 'Transforming our World: The 2030 Agenda for Sustainable Development', and so put economic development on the global development agenda. At the core of the new development agenda are the 17 Sustainable Development Goals (SDGs). Goal 9 sees industry (herein defined as manufacturing) as the primary engine not only for job creation and economic growth but also technology transfer, investment flows, and skills development. There are four industry-related targets and seven industry-related indicators (Table A.1.2).

Indexes for SDG9 performance (SDG9per) and for SDG9 progress (SDG9pro) could be constructed for only 16 out of 47 SSA countries because of limited country data; even then, only five rather than all seven indicators could be used, because there are no data for the two indicators for target 9.3 (proportion of small-scale industries in total value added and percentage of small-scale industries with a loan or line of credit). The SDG9per and SDG9pro indexes show that countries can be ranked differently on their performance (level of achievement) and progress (movement towards a target) (Table A.1.3).

Whereas South Africa ranks number 1 on performance as of 2016, it ranks 11th on progress between 2000 and 2016 and whereas Angola ranks 13th on performance, it ranks number 3 on progress between 2000 and 2016.

Figure A.1.1 is a scatter diagram with values of SDG9per and SDG-9pro for 16 SSA countries. It is divided into four quadrants based on the median values of the SDG9 Progress Index (0.288) and SDG9 Performance Index (0.1235). Definitions of these two indexes suggest characteristic words to describe each of the four quadrants. For SDG-9per, a country is described as leading if its SDG9per value is higher than the median, and lagging if its value is lower than the median. For SDG9pro, a country is described as active if its value is higher than the median, and passive if its value is lower than the median. Therefore, the top right quadrant includes leading and active countries in green industrial transformation, represented by 'leading-active'. The top left quadrant includes lagging but active countries that are represented as 'lagging-active'. The bottom left quadrant includes lagging and passive

Table A.1.2 SDG9 targets and indicators related to industrialisation

Targets	Indicators
9.2 Promote inclusive and sustainable industrialisation and, by 2030, significantly raise industry's share of employment and gross domestic product, in line with national circumstances, and double its share in least developed countries.	9.2.1a Manufacturing value added as a proportion of GDP 9.2.1b Manufacturing value added per capita 9.2.2 Manufacturing employment as a proportion of total employment
9.3 Increase the access of small-scale industrial and other enterprises, in particular in developing countries, to financial services, including affordable credit, and their integration into value chains and markets.	9.3.1 Proportion of small-scale industries in total industry value added 9.3.2 Proportion of small-scale industries with a loan or line of credit
9.4 By 2030, upgrade infrastructure and retrofit industries to make them sustainable, with increased resource-use efficiency and greater adoption of clean and environmentally sound technologies and industrial processes, with all countries taking action in accordance with their respective capabilities.	9.4.1 CO_2 emissions per unit of value added
9.b Support domestic technology development, research, and innovation in developing countries, including by ensuring a conducive policy environment for, inter alia, industrial diversification and value addition to commodities.	9.b.1 Proportion of medium and high-tech industry value added in total value added

Source: Information extracted from UN 2016

countries represented as 'lagging-passive'. The bottom right quadrant includes countries that are leading but passive in green transformation, represented as 'leading-passive'.

Figure A.1.2 depicts policies and strategies for accelerating green industrialisation. Policies are characterised as hard and soft in terms of the flexibility of implementation and strategies as penalising, motivating, and supporting in terms of the stringency of application. For leading–active countries, governments should consider using supportive policies such as education and training whereas leading–passive countries should consider using voluntary agreements and extended producer responsibility. For lagging-active countries, governments should consider encouraging industries to adopt environmental management standards and clustering industrial activities, whereas for lagging-passive countries, governments

Table A.1.3 SDG9 performance and progress rank for 16 SSA countries

SDG9 performance rank	SDG9 Performance Index	Country	SDG9 progress rank	SDG9 Progress Index
1	0.265	South Africa	11	0.081
2	0.252	Mauritius	6	0.477
3	0.186	Nigeria	4	0.569
4	0.161	Côte d'Ivoire	14	−0.318
5	0.161	Namibia	10	0.095
6	0.158	Cameroon	1	0.846
7	0.142	Senegal	16	−1.346
8	0.131	Botswana	2	0.842
9	0.116	Kenya	15	−0.519
10	0.090	Congo	9	0.254
11	0.089	Mozambique	5	0.518
12	0.079	Ethiopia	8	0.322
13	0.074	Angola	3	0.718
14	0.074	Tanzania	7	0.365
15	0.067	Ghana	13	−0.316
16	0.055	Niger	12	−0.031

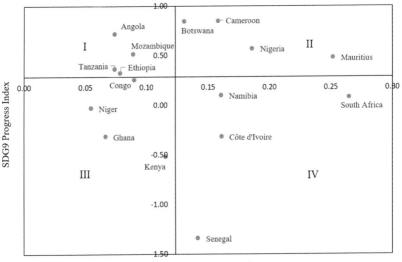

Figure A.1.1 Scatter plot of the SDG9per and SDGpro of 16 countries

Note: I, 'lagging-active' countries; II, 'leading-active' countries; III, 'lagging-passive' countries; IV, 'leading-passive' countries

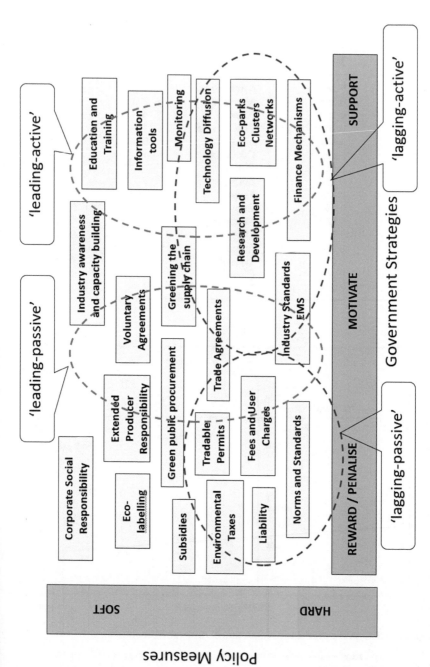

Figure A.1.2 Policy and strategy options for accelerating green industrialisation

need to use command-and-control regulation and various economic incentives.

Whereas the three green industry assessments summarised in Chapter 6 identified unique gaps, weakness, and opportunities for accelerating green industrialisation based on in-depth investigations in three countries, the green industry indexes constructed for this book provide a broad overview of potential policies and strategies. For the four leading-active countries (Botswana, Cameroon, Mauritius, and Nigeria), their governments need to focus on soft policies and supportive strategies. For the four leading-passive countries (Côte d'Ivoire, Namibia, Senegal, and South Africa), their governments need to focus on soft policies and motivating and supportive strategies. For the four lagging-active countries (Angola, Ethiopia, Mozambique, and Tanzania), their governments need to focus on hard policies and motivating and supportive strategies. For the four lagging-passive countries (Congo, Ghana, Kenya, and Niger), their governments need to focus on hard policies and penalising/rewarding strategies.

References

Biggeri M., Clark, D., Ferrannini, A. Mauro V. (2019). Tracking the SDGs in an 'integrated' manner: A proposal for a new index to capture synergies and trade-offs between and within goals. *World Development* 122:628–647.

ECOSOC (2017). *Report of the Inter-Agency and Expert Group on Sustainable Development Goal Indicators*. E/CN.3/2017/2. Statistical Commission Forty-eighth session 7–10 March. United Nations Economic and Social Council. New York. Retrieved from: https://unstats.un.org/unsd/statcom/48th-session/documents/2017-2-IAEG-SDGs-E.pdf. Last accessed: 15.08.2015.

Kynčlová P., Upadhyaya, S., Nice, T. (2020). Composite index as a measure on achieving SDG-9 industry-related targets: The SDG-9 index. Accepted for publication by Applied Energy.

Lin, J.Y., Monga, C., Standaert, S. (2019). The inclusive sustainable transformation index. *Social Indicators Research*, 143:47–80.

Moll de Alba, J., Todorov, V. (2018). Green industrial performance: The GIP index. *World Review of Science, Technology and Sustainable Development*, 14:266–293.

OECD (2008). *Handbook on Constructing Composite Indicators: Methodology and User Guide*. Organisation for Economic Cooperation and Development. Paris. Retrieved from: www.oecd-ilibrary.org/content/publication/9789264043466-en. Last accessed: 15.08.2019.

PAGE (2017). *The Green Economy Progress Measurement Framework: Methodology*. Copyright © United Nations Environment Programme, 2017, for Partnership for Action on Green Economy. Retrieved from: www.un-page.org/files/public/general/gep_methodology.pdf. Last accessed: 15.08.2019.

Sachs, J., Schmidt-Traub, G., Kroll, C., Lafortune, G., Fuller, G. (2018). *SDG Index and Dashboards Report 2018: Global Responsibilities Implementing the Goals*. July. Bertelsmann Stiftung and Sustainable Development Solutions Network (SDSN). New York. Retrieved from: https://s3.amazonaws.com/sustainabledevelopment. report/2018/2018_sdg_index_and_dashboards_report.pdf. Last accessed: 15.08.2019.

SDSN (2015). *Indicators and a Monitoring Framework for the Sustainable Development Goals: Launching a Data Revolution*. 15 May. Sustainable Development Solutions Network. Retrieved from: http://unsdsn.org/wp-content/uploads/2015/05/FINAL-SDSN-Indicator-Report-WEB.pdf. Last accessed: 14.08.2019.

UN (2016). *Final List of Proposed Sustainable Development Goal Indicators* [Annex IV of the Report of the Inter-Agency and Expert Group on Sustainable Development Goal Indicators. E/CN.3/2016/2/Rev.1]. United Nations. New York. Retrieved from: https://sustainabledevelopment.un.org/content/documents/11803Official-List-of-Proposed-SDG-Indicators.pdf. Last accessed: 14.08.2019.

UNDP (2019). *Human Development Report*. United Nations Development Programme. New York. Retrieved from: www.hdr.undp.org/. Last accessed: 15.08.2019.

UNIDO (2011). *UNIDO Green Industry: Policies for Supporting Green Industry*. May. United Nations Industrial Development Organization. Vienna. Retrieved from: www.unido.org/sites/default/files/2011-05/web_policies_green_industry_0.pdf. Last accessed: 13.08.2019.

UNIDO (2019). *Competitive Industrial Performance Report 2018*. Biennial CIP report, edition 2018. United Nations Industrial Development Organization. Vienna. Retrieved from: www.unido.org/sites/default/files/files/2019-05/CIP.pdf. Last accessed: 15.08.2019.

US Department of Commerce (2010). *Measuring the Green Economy*. US Department of Commerce, Economics and Statistics Administration. April. Retrieved from: www.commerce.gov/sites/default/files/migrated/reports/greeneconomyreport_0.pdf. Last accessed: 30.07.2019.

Yuan, Q., Yang, D., Yang, F., Luken, R., Saieed, A., Wang, K. (2020). Green industry development in China: An index base assessment from perspectives of both current performance and historical effort. *Journal of Cleaner Production*, 250. The article can be retrieved at: https://www.sciencedirect.com/science/article/pii/S0959652619343276?via%3Dihub.

Annex 2
Economic and technology policies

A.2.1. Introduction

Economic policies (broadly defined, and the boundaries are often blurred) can indirectly support green industrialisation in at least three ways – through conventional industrial policies, through trade policies, and finally through resource pricing policies. In addition, technology and innovation policies also have the potential to accelerate green industrialisation by directing the technological infrastructure to support plant-level adoption of more resource-efficient technologies. These families of policies and their impact on green industrialisation are discussed in more detail next.

A.2.2. Industrial policy

The recent publication by Altenburg and Assmann (2017) provides extensive information about various policy aspects and country case studies of green industrial policy. They define green industrial policy as encompassing sets of measures that governments use to accelerate the structural transformation towards a low-carbon, resource-efficient economy in ways that also enable productivity enhancements in the economy. The publication clarifies the conceptual foundations of green industrial policy; describes the economic and social co-benefits of green transformation; identifies key policies that have the potential to decouple industrial production from resource consumption and production; and presents four country experiences in implementing in key policies.

The industrial policies considered to have the most influence on green industrialisation are those that directing change in structural composition, supporting openness to foreign direct investment (FDI), export promotion, privatisation, and the creation of industrial estates. These policies work their way through the institutional network in different ways to influence the behaviour of individual enterprises. Directing change in structural composition can shift manufacturing to higher value-add and less polluting sectors and mandate the phase-out of more polluting sectors. Increased openness to FDI affects factor markets, in particular the availability of technology, finance, and skills, when foreign enterprises bring more advanced (usually cleaner) technologies and the skills needed to operate them into a country. Governmental incentives for export promotion affect product markets by supporting domestic producers in exporting, since this normally requires the producers to manufacture more competitive goods using more advanced techniques and technologies than those normally used in production for the domestic market. Privatisation of state-owned enterprises affects factor markets by forcing enterprises to be more efficient in their use of production inputs, which often results in the use of cleaner technologies. Finally, the creation of industrial estates affects factor markets by lowering the costs of basic services, such as communication and transport, as well as those of environmental services for collective abatement of pollutants.

A.2.3. Trade policy

Trade-related import policies, in particular the lowering or raising of tariffs and non-tariff restrictions (quotas), work their way through the institutional network via factor and product markets. Low tariffs and few quantitative restrictions on intermediate inputs affect factor markets by making imported, cleaner chemicals, goods, and technologies less costly. Low tariffs and few quantitative restrictions on finished goods affect product markets by putting cost pressure on domestic manufacturers to compete with imported goods, which gives them an incentive to use cleaner technologies to lower production costs.

IISD/UNEP (2014) is a comprehensive assessment of the interlinkages between international trade, the environment, and the green economy. It therefore focuses on national and international trade policy and rules, on environmental governance and principles, and the relationship between both. UNEP (2016) consists of an assessment of five national-level projects that identify green export opportunities, two of which are Ghana and South Africa. The Ghana case study assesses the potential for exporting solar energy to neighbouring countries. The South Africa case study identifies export opportunities resulting from a shift to organic farming in the agricultural and agro-processing sector. Both studies end with country recommendations and offer tailored policy objectives for harnessing countries production potential and their export activities.

A.2.4. Resource pricing policy

In general, higher resource prices – those that reflect full production cost and, in a limited number of cases, pollution damage – are incentives for green industrialisation, particularly the adoption of resource efficient technologies. Higher resource prices typically motivate the managers of enterprises to reduce total expenditure on resource inputs by using resource efficient technologies that lower raw material, water, and energy use per unit of output. The price effect depends on the share of resource costs in total production and the extent to which costs can be passed on to consumers.

Resource pricing policies work their way through factor markets to influence the behaviour of individual enterprises. Most often, resource pricing policies interfere with free market prices by subsidising the costs of production inputs, primarily for energy and water. In some cases, the policies are ones of neglect to the extent that they fail to set any price, which happens in the case of groundwater. Below market prices for these production inputs encourage their excessive use by enterprises.

Among other topics, the World Energy Outlook 2014 describes the energy outlook for SSA and the implications of subsided energy prices. Key elements in the energy outlook are the prospects for improving access to modern energy services and for developing the region's huge resource potential in a way that contributes not only to regional and global energy balances but also to local economic and social well-being. The Outlook describes in considerable detail how a subsidy involves a complex set of changes in economic resource allocation through its impact on costs or prices, or both. These shifts inevitably have wider ranging economic, social, and environmental effects (IEA, 2014). Chapter 5 in Altenburg and Assmann (2017) is informative about the need for disruptive industrial policies that eliminate subsidies and mandate phase-outs.

A.2.5. Technology and innovation policies

Science, technology, and innovation are of critical significance for green industrialisation in all its dimensions – economic, social, and environmental. Technological innovation and engineering solutions are main drivers towards green industrialisation through addressing environmental degradation and restoration, water scarcity, and energy needs of African countries. Science, technology, and innovation policies in Africa serve as a tool to promote economic diversification and manufacturing development (AUC, 2014).

Science, technology, and innovation policies are most effective when they are aligned with political and socio-economic evolution of any state. Policies should comprise all the necessary measures for creating, funding, and mobilising private and public scientific and technological resources and act as an enabler for the implementation of a well-designed development agenda. International and regional cooperation on technology and innovation policies is an important area for action. National innovation systems cannot be separated for a national economy; they need to be open for technology and information flows and for cooperation with technology and innovation actors in other regions to learn from their experiences and approaches (Alabi *et al.*, 2018).

Technology and innovation policies have the potential to increase the adoption of environmentally sound technologies, particularly clean technologies, by directing the technological infrastructure to support plant-level adoption of more productive technologies and to train workers to operate these technologies. Technology policies work their way through the institutional network to influence plant-level behaviour in two ways. One pathway empowers intermediary agencies, mostly manufacturing or technical extension services, to enhance plant-level capabilities to adopt or utilise newer technologies and to use their existing technology more efficiently. The other pathway affects factor markets by supporting training programmes that improve the skills of the labour force.

An article by Kemp and Never (2017) is particularly informative about phasing in technologies needed to enhance the successful uptake of resource efficient technologies.

A.2.6. SSA research and reports

The potential for and challenges to integration of a climate change strategy and accelerated industrial plan in Ethiopia are described by Okereke *et al.* (2019). The need to focus on industrial policy is questioned by Rodrik (2016) given the poor prospects for industrialisation in Africa. Effects of international trade have been studied by Foster-McGregor *et al.* (2014, 2015). In their more recent productivity review for 19 SSA countries they provide results and evidence for positive effects of export in the manufacturing sector. Conditional effects of strong industrialisation and foreign investments in low income, middle income, and high income Eastern African countries are highlighted by Adom *et al.* (2016). They analyse the impacts of foreign direct flows and industrialisation in 13 Eastern African countries using a data panel covering the years 1980–2011. A study of energy subsidies and their reform in SSA countries by the International Monetary Fund (IMF, 2013) addresses the need for more targeted research and reliable data. The potential for national systems of innovation to accelerate green industrialisation in Ghana and Kenya are described in two UNIDO reports (UNIDO, 2012; Koria and Bartels, 2015). The need to focus on plant-specific factors and civil society pressures in addition to governmental policies in greening industry is documented in an investigation of the determinants of adoption of environmentally sound technologies by 98 plants in developing countries, including 19 leather tanneries in Kenya and Zimbabwe Luken *et al.* (2008).

References

Adom, P.K., Amuakwa-Mensah, F. (2016). What drives the energy saving role of FDI and industrialization in East Africa? *Renewable and Sustainable Energy Reviews*, 65:925–942.

Alabi, R.A., Gutowski, A., Hassan, N.M., Knedlik, T., Nour, S.S.O.M., Wohluth, K. (2018). *Science, Technology and Innovation Policies for Inclusive Growth in Africa: General Issues and Country Cases*. African Development Perspectives Yearbook (vol. 20). LIT Verlag GmbH & Co. KG WIEN. Zürich.

Altenburg, T., Assmann, C. (eds.) (2017). *Green Industrial Policy: Concept, Policies, Country Experiences*. UN Environment; German Development Institute/Deutsches Institut für Entwicklungspolitk (DIE). Retrieved from: www.greengrowthknowledge. org/sites/default/files/downloads/resource/Green%20Industrial%20Policy_ Concept%2C%20Policies%2C%20Country%20Experiences.pdf. Last accessed: 15. 08.2019.

AUC (2014). *Science, Technology and Innovation Strategy for Africa 2024*. STISA-20124. June. African Union Commission. Addis Ababa. Retrieved from: https://au.int/ sites/default/files/newsevents/workingdocuments/33178-wd-stisa-english_-_ final.pdf. Last accessed: 15.08.2019.

Foster-McGregor, N., Isaksson, A., Kaulich, F. (2014). Learning-by-exporting versus self-selection: New evidence for 19 Sub-Saharan African countries. *Economics Letters*, 125:212–214.

Foster-McGregor, N., Isaksson, A., Kaulich, F. (2015). Importing, exporting and the productivity of services firms in Sub-Saharan Africa. *Journal of International Trade and Economic Development*, 24:499–522.

IEA (2014). *World Energy Outlook 2014*. International Energy Agency. Paris. Retrieved from: www.iea.org/publications/freepublications/publication/WEO2014.pdf. Last accessed: 15.08.2019.

IISD/UNEP (2014). *Trade and Green Economy: A Handbook*. Third edition. International Institute for Sustainable Development and United Nations Environment Programme. Geneva. Retrieved from: www.iisd.org/sites/default/files/publications/ trade-green-economy-handbook-third-edition-en.pdf. Last accessed: 15.08.2019.

IMF (2013). *Energy Subsidy Reform in Sub-Saharan Africa: Experiences and Lessons*. Africa Department, International Monetary Fund. Washington, DC. Retrieved from: www.imf.org/external/pubs/ft/dp/2013/afr1302.pdf. Last accessed: 15.08.2019.

Kemp, R., Never, B. (2017). Green transition, industrial policy, and economic development. *Oxford Economic Review*, 23:1:66–84.

Koria, R., Bartels, F. (2015). *The Kenya National System of Innovation: Measurement, Analysis and Policy Recommendations*. 10.13140/RG.2.1.2226.8962. Retrieved from: www.researchgate.net/publication/273761627_The_Kenya_Nati_onal_System_ of_Innovati_on_Measurement_Analysis_Policy_Recommendati_ons_Disclaimer. Last accessed: 19.08.2019.

Luken, R., Van Rompaey, F., Zigova, K. (2008). The determinants of EST adoption by manufacturing plants in developing countries. *Ecological Economics*, 66:141–150.

Okereke, C., Coke, A., Geebreyesus, M., Ginbo, T., Wakeford, J.J., Mulugetta, Y. (2019). Governing green industrialisation in Africa: Assessing key parameters for a sustainable socio-technical transition in the context of Ethiopia. *World Development*, 115:279–290.

Rodrik, D. (2016). An African growth miracle? *Journal of African Economies*, 1–18.

UNEP (2016). *Green Economy and Trade Opportunities: Country Projects Synthesis Report.* United Nations Environment Programme. Geneva. Retrieved from: http://wedocs. unep.org/bitstream/handle/20.500.11822/22757/GE-Top_Country_projects_ synthesis.pdf?sequence=1&isAllowed=y. Last accessed: 15.08.2019.

UNIDO (2012). *Evidence-Based Policy Making: The Ghana National System of Innovation: Measurements, Analysis & Policy Recommendations.* December. United Nations Industrial Development Organization. Vienna. Retrieved from: www.unido.org/ sites/default/files/2014-09/GNSI_Report_2012_0.pdf. Last accessed: 15.08.2019.

Index

Note: Page numbers in *italics* indicate a figure and page numbers in **bold** indicate a table on the corresponding page.

absolute decoupling 11
administrative sanctions 20
African 10 Year Framework Programme on Sustainable Consumption and Production 38
African Development Bank (AfDB) 5, 48
African Ministerial Council on Environment 38
Africa Roundtable for Sustainable Consumption and Production 38
Agency for Workplace Innovation 10
agro- and wood-processing residue 53–54
AKOBEN programme 25, 146, 153
aluminium recycling 102
ambient quality standards 19
Asian Productivity Organization 27
Asia-Pacific Economic Cooperation (APEC) 86

Bamako Convention 67
Basel Convention 66–67, 68, 69, 93
better process control 26
Blue Angel 23

capacity building 47
'cap-and-trade' systems 21
Cape Verde 94
Center for Global Development 114, 126
certificate trading schemes 30
certification programmes 46
China: Cleaner Production Law 68; Cleaner Production Promotion Law 32; environmental goods and services 89; renewable energy projects 56; special economic zones 97–98
civil sanctions 20
cleaner production (CP): classification of 26–27; goals of 21–22; parallel approaches 27–29; programme to establish NCPCs 87–88
Cleaner Production Centre of Tanzania 38
closed-cycle manufacturing 8
CO_2-Adjusted Competitive Industrial Performance (CO_2-Adjusted CIP) 164
CO_2 emission intensity and decoupling **125**, 126
command-and-control regulation: ambient quality standards 19; effluent and emissions reports 19–20; effluent and emission standards **18**; hazardous waste management 65–67; industrial chemicals management 58–61; pollution control 17–20
compliance monitoring 19–20
composite indexes: global sustainable development indexes 161–165; industry-related SDG9 performance and progress indexes 165–169; overview 160–161
concentration standards 17
consumer advice services 31
cooperation instruments 30
corporate awards and reporting 25
corporate social responsibility (CSR) 22–23

covenants 23, 33–34
criminal sanctions 20

decoupling 5–6, 11, *11*, 45, 122–124, **125**, 126–127, 145–146
demand side management 47
demand-side strategy 7–8
dismantling 7, 102–105

eco-design: definition of 98; overview 98–99; policies and programmes 99–100; role in greening industry 13; SSA research and reports 100–101
eco-efficiency 28
eco-industrial parks (EIPs): overview 94–95; policies and programmes 95–97; role in greening industry 13; in SSA countries 97; SSA research and reports 97–98
eco-labels 23–24, 31, 34
economic instruments 29
economic policies 171
education/training programmes 30
effluent and emissions licenses/permits 19
effluent and emissions reports 19–20
effluent and emission standards **18**, 18–19
electronic waste (e-waste) 102–103, 104
end-of-life vehicles (ELVs) 102
energy intensity and decoupling 124, **125**
energy management/energy efficiency: capacity building 47; certification and labelling of performance 46; cleaner production and 29; covenants 23, 34; demand side management 47; energy demand 41–42; energy service companies 47–48; goals of 13; green industrialisation research 154; green jobs 9; industrial energy management standards 45–46; industrial equipment standards 46; information programmes 47; labelling 34; policies and programmes 42–48; potential 42; SSA research and reports 35, 48–52; supply-side/demand-side strategies for 7–8; system assessment standards 46; Top Runner programme 32; utility programmes 47; voluntary instruments 33

energy management/renewable energy: agro- and wood-processing residue 53–54; assessment 41; expansion of 6; geothermal 54; goals of 16, 45; green industrialisation research 154; green jobs 9–10; hydropower 54; jobs in 57; policies and programmes 54–56; role in decoupling 11–13; solar heating/cooling applications 53; SSA research and reports 49–52, 56–57; support policies **55**
energy service companies 47–48
energy subsidies 174
enforcement 20
enforcement sanctions 20
environmental control/enforcement 29
environmental fees 21
environmental financing 30
Environmental Goods Agreement 87
environmental goods and services: access to capital 91–92; definitions of 84–87; developing local 89–90; export support 92–93; government programmes 83–93; green industrialisation research 155–156; import support 90–91; industry support institutions 87–89; 'levelling the playing field' for 81–83; market size and growth for **81**; national strategy for developing 83; overview 79–81; policies and programmes 81–93; role in greening industry 13; skills base development 90; in SSA countries 93–94
Environmental Impact Assessment (EIA) 66
environmental liability 29
environmental management system (EMS) 22
environmental quality targets/monitoring 31
environmental taxes 30
equipment modification 27
Eskom 94
Ethiopia: Climate Resilient Green Economy 42–44, 50–51; integration of climate change strategy and accelerated industrial plan 174; National Cleaner Production Centres 94; special economic zones 97

European Commission 98, 100, 103–104
European Pollutant Release and Transfer Register 24
European Union (EU): Dangerous Substances Directive 59; European Pollutant Release and Transfer Register 24; Green Public Procurement programme 62; policies and programmes to promote eco-design 99–100; recycling of end-of-life vehicles 102; resource efficiency action plans 138; Seveso Directive 60–61; voluntary business-government agreements 23; waste electrical and electronic equipment Directive 103–104
Export Processing Zones (EPZs) 96

fees 30
fines 21
foreign direct flows 174
foreign direct investment (FDI) 171

general licenses 19
geothermal 54
Ghana: AKOBEN programme 25, 146, 153; effluent and emission standards **18**, 18–19; Environmental Performance Rating and Public Disclosure programme 25; e-waste management 104; findings of assessment 143–145; green industrialisation 174; green industry and trade assessment 143–147; National Cleaner Production Centres 94; recommendations of assessment 145–147; Resource Efficient Green Industry initiative 145–146; solar energy case study 172
global sustainable development indexes 161–165
good housekeeping 8, 26
grants 21
green economy 4–6
green enterprises 6
green growth 4–6
green industrialisation: definitions of 6–8, 11–13; dimensions of 11–13; Ghana 174; Kenya 174; policy and strategy options for accelerating *168*

green industrialisation research: energy management 154; environmental goods and services 155–156; green industry assessments 157–158; hazardous waste management 155; overview 151–152; pollution control 152–153; resource efficient and cleaner production 153–154; Sustainable Development Goals 156–157
Green Industrial Performance (GIP) Index 164
green industrial policies: definitions of 8–9, 171; *Practitioner's Guide to Strategic Green Industrial Policy* 132–139
green industry assessments: Ghana 143–147; green industrialisation research 157–158; Nigeria 139–143; *Practitioner's Guide to Strategic Green Industrial Policy* 132–139; Senegal 147–149
green industry indicators: accuracy of data 122; CO_2 emission intensity and decoupling **125**, 126; coherence of data 123; completeness of data 116–121; data quality 116–123; energy intensity and decoupling 124, **125**, 126; feasibility of meeting targets 123–126; literature review of data quality 114–115; manufacturing employment 124; recommendations for improving data quality 126–128; relevance of data 121–122; timeliness of data 122
greening growth 9
greening industry 11, *12*, 13
greening industry policies/programmes: energy management/energy efficiency 13, 42–48; energy management/renewable energy 13, 54–56; hazardous waste management 13, 65–68; industrial chemicals management 13, 58–62; pollution control 13, 16–25; resource efficient and cleaner production 13, 29–35
greening services: eco-design 13, 98–101; eco-industrial parks 13, 94–98; environmental goods and services 13, 79–94, 155; materials recycling

13, 101–105; overview *12*, 12–13; regimes 13
green inputs 8
green jobs 4, 9–10, 57
green productivity 27–28
green public procurement 30, 32, 62
Green Seal 24

hazardous waste management: command-and-control regulation 58–61; facilities in SSA countries **70**; green industrialisation research 155; market-based instruments/economic incentives 67–68; overview 13, 64–65; policies and programmes 65–68; SSA research and reports 69–71; transparency and disclosure measures 68; voluntary actions 68; wastewater treatment plants 93–94
hydropower 54

Inclusive Sustainable Transformation (IST) index 161, **162–163**
individual licenses 19
Indonesia 25
Indonesian Environmental Impact Management Agency (BAPEDAL) 25
industrial chemicals management: chemical bans 32; command-and-control regulation 58–61; green industrialisation research 155; labelling 61; market-based instruments/economic incentives 62; overview 13, 58; policies and programmes 58–62; Seveso Directive 60–61; SSA research and reports 62–64; transparency and disclosure measures 61–62; voluntary actions 62
industrial ecology 8
industrial energy management standards 45–46
industrial equipment standards 46
industrial policies 171–172, 174
industry-related performance and progress indexes 165–169, **167**, *167*
informal sanctions 20
information centres 31
information instruments 31
information programmes 47

input material change 26
Inter-Agency and Expert Group on SDG Indicators 161
International Centre for Small Hydro Power 56
International Monetary Fund (IMF) 174
International Organization for Standardization (ISO): eco-design 98; ISO 14000 88, 99; ISO 14001 22, 147; ISO 14001:2015 22; ISO 14006 99; ISO 50000 88; ISO 50001 41, 48
international trade policies 174

Japan 32

Kenya: Centre for Energy Efficiency and Conservation 94; eco-design 101; energy efficiency financing projects 48–50; e-waste management 104; green economy strategy and implementation plan 51; green industrialisation 174; National Cleaner Production Centres 94

low-carbon development 52
low-carbon zones (LCZs) 96–97

Mambilla Beverages Company 56
manufacturing employment 124
manufacturing value added (MVA) 116–126
market-based instruments/economic incentives: hazardous waste management 67–68; industrial chemicals management 62; pollution control 20–21
market-based plant certification framework 46
mass-based standards 17–19
Material Safety Data Sheets (MSDSs) 61
materials recycling: overview 101–103; policies and programmes 103–104; role in greening industry 13; SSA research and reports 104–105
Mauritius 94
Montreal Protocol on Substances that Deplete the Ozone Layer 59
Mozambique 41, 94
municipal solid waste (MSW) 93

National Cleaner Production Centres (NCPCs) 33, 38–41, 87–88, 94, 157
National Environmental Quality Standards (NEQS) 18
Netherlands 34
Nigeria: creating business incentives 142; energy efficiency financing projects 49–50; financing greening of industries 141; green industry policy study 139–143; improved infrastructure 141; industrial energy efficiency 140–141; low productivity 140; manufacturing sector energy consumption 41–42; materials recycling 104; policy implementation and enforcement 142; policy integration 139–140; pollution control 26; renewable energy projects 56; resource efficient and cleaner production 143; special economic zones 97; systematic data collection 142–143

on-site recovery/reuse 27
Organisation for Economic Cooperation and Development (OECD) 4, 59, 153
organochlorine pesticides 59

Partnership for Action on Green Economy (PAGE) 132
plastics recycling 102
pollution control: categories of instruments 16–17; cleaner production 21–22; command-and-control regulation 17–20; compliance monitoring 19–20, 21; corporate awards and reporting 25; corporate social responsibility (CSR) 22–23; covenants 23; effluent and emissions licenses/permits 19; effluent and emission standards 17–19; enforcement 20; environmental fees 21; environmental management system 22; fines 21; grants 21; green industrialisation research 152–153; instruments for 16–25; market-based instruments/economic incentives 20–21; policy instruments 17, **17**, 20–25; pollution trading systems

21; product labelling 23–24; public disclosure programmes 24–25; role in greening industry 13, 16; SSA research and reports 25–26; standards 17–19; toxic release inventories 24
pollution prevention 28
pollution trading systems 21
polychlorinated biphenyls (PCBs) 59
Practitioner's Guide to Strategic Green Industrial Policy (SGIP): high level vision setting 135; implementation and monitoring 139; initial activities 132–135; overview 132; policy domains and instruments 137–138; policy pathway design 138; prioritising intervention areas 137; steps of planning process 132–139; stocktaking 136–137
product innovation 101
product labelling 23–24
product modification 27
Programme for Improving Energy Efficiency in Energy Intensive Industries 46
Programme of Action for a Green Economy (PAGE) 147
public disclosure programmes 24–25

regulatory instruments 29
relative decoupling 5–6, 11, 124, **125**, 126
remanufacturing 8, 104
research and development (R&D) 30, 33, 89–90
research and educational instruments 29
resource efficient and cleaner production (RECP): barriers 35–37, **36–37**; case studies of projects 39–40; cooperation instruments 30; drivers 35–37, **36–37**; eco-efficiency 28; economic instruments 29, 32–33; enablers 35–38, **36–37**; energy efficiency 29; green industrialisation research 153–154; green productivity 27–28; information instruments 31; National Cleaner Production Centres supporting 38–41; Nigerian green industry policy study 143; overview 26–27; parallel approaches 27–29; policies for promoting interventions

29–35; policy instruments relevant to driving 29–31; pollution prevention 28; regulatory instruments 29, 31–32; research and educational instruments 29; source reduction 28–29; SSA research and reports 35–38; toxics use reduction 29; transparency and disclosure measures 34–35; voluntary actions 33–34; waste minimisation 28
resource pricing policies 171, 172–173
Rotterdam Convention 61–62
Rwanda: green economy strategy and implementation plan 51; National Cleaner Production Centres 94; renewable energy projects 56

Senegal: conclusions of assessment 147–148; Environmental Code 148; Environmental Impact Assessments 148; financial incentives 148; green industrialisation 148; green industry assessments 147–149; National Cleaner Production Centres 94; recommendations of assessment 148–149
Seveso Directive 60–61
solar heating/cooling applications 53
source reduction 28–29
South Africa: energy efficiency financing projects 48–49; energy efficiency strategy 44–45; Eskom 94; green jobs 10; industrial chemicals management 62; manufacturing sector energy consumption 41; National Cleaner Production Centres 94; organic farming case study 172; Private Sector Energy Efficiency 94
special economic zones (SEZs) 97–98
SSA research and reports: energy management/energy efficiency 48–52; energy management /renewable energy 56–57; green industrial policies 174; hazardous waste management 69–71; industrial chemicals management 62–64; pollution control 25–26; resource efficient and cleaner production 35–38
standards 17–19, 21, 29, 59–60, 88–89, 100
steel recycling 102

Stockholm Convention on Persistent Organic Pollutants 59
Strategic Approach to International Chemicals Management (SAICM) 61, 63–64, 155
subsidies 30, 32–33, 48
Superior Energy Performance Partnership 46
supply-side strategy 7–8
sustainability reporting 31
Sustainable Development Goals (SDGs): impacted by industrial development **113**; Indicators and Monitoring Framework 161; industry-related indicators 156–157; industry-related performance and progress indexes 165–169, **167**, *167*; overview 112; targets and indicators related to industrialisation **166**
Sustainable Development Goals Center for Africa 115
Sustainable Development Solutions Network 115
Swedish Energy Agency 46
system assessment standards 46

Tanzania 38, 94, 101
technological standards 18
technology and innovation policies 171, 173–174
technology change 27
technology transfer 30, 33
Top Runner programme 32
toxic/pollutant release inventory programmes 24, 34
toxics use reduction 29
trade policies 171, 172
transparency and disclosure measures: hazardous waste management 68; industrial chemicals management 61–62; pollution control 24–25; resource efficient and cleaner production 34–35

Uganda 94, 101
United Nations: Conference on Environment and Development in Rio de Janeiro 38; energy efficiency financing projects 48; green growth 5; Sustainable Development Goals 112

United Nations Commission on Trade and Development (UNCTAD) 5, 96

United Nations Economic Commission for Africa (UNECA): green industrialisation 7; greening 5; industrial chemicals management 63; materials recycling 104–105; SDG targets 128

United Nations Economic Commission for Europe (UNECE) 61

United Nations Environment Programme (UNEP): cleaner production projects 38; environmental goods and services 87, 94; green economy 4; green manufacturing 7; industrial chemicals management 59–60; National Cleaner Production Centres 33; SWITCH Africa Green project 51

United Nations High Commissioner for Refugees 56

United Nations Industrial Development Organization (UNIDO): cleaner production projects 38; CO$_2$-Adjusted Competitive Industrial Performance (CO$_2$-Adjusted CIP) 164; CSR benefits 23; eco-industrial parks 96; environmental goods and services 87, 94; green industrialisation 6; Green Industry Platform 139; industrial statistics 115, 116; materials recycling 105; National Cleaner Production Centres 33; renewable energy projects 56

United Nations Inter-Agency and Expert Group on Sustainable Development Goal Indicators 115

United States: Bureau of Labor Statistics 9–10; Department of Energy 46; Environmental Protection Agency 19, 28, 153; Toxic Release Inventory 24

user charges 30

utility programmes 47

Vietnam 23

voluntary actions: hazardous waste management 68; industrial chemicals management 62; pollution control 21–24; resource efficient and cleaner production 33–34

waste electrical and electronic equipment (WEEE) 69, 102–103

waste minimisation 28

wastewater treatment plants 93–94

World Bank 4, 26, 48, 96–97, 105

World Trade Organization (WTO) 87

Zambia: National Cleaner Production Centres 94; special economic zones 97

Zimbabwe 94, 101

For Product Safety Concerns and Information please contact our
EU representative GPSR@taylorandfrancis.com Taylor & Francis
Verlag GmbH, Kaufingerstraße 24, 80331 München, Germany